"Hardly worth the paper it's printed on. *Real* mediums would also make stunning and enigmatic predictions. Like I have done."
—Nostradamus

"That rascal Nostradamus copied my technique, my predictions, my innovative use of enigmatic metaphors. It was me, *saya*, King of Kediri, who gave the world yellow dwarves, ships that navigate in the skies, and women who dress like men. Oh, by the way, this is a terrific book, less poetic than my work, and less filled with Javanese mysticism, but still of notable value."
—Joyoboyo

"Enlightening. A noble companion volume to my own books on spiritualism."
—Arthur Conan Doyle

"Not a single raven. Not even a man buried behind a wall. Nevertheless, one of the better books about extraordinary dead folks to come around in a while."
—Edgar Allan Poe

"Sochaczewski has been following me for more than forty years. I finally got to speak to him, and our conversations are recorded in this fine book. But now maybe he'll leave me alone—I'm so busy—there's a pile of strange beetles to identify, papers to write, and endless toil just trying to earn a few shillings to keep the family in porridge."
—Alfred Russel Wallace

"Too bad Sochaczewski never knew my wife George; she was a much better medium than the poseurs in this book. Otherwise, a brave attempt to understand the widening gyres."
—W.B. Yeats

"I predicted this book would happen."
—Edgar Cayce

"Well done, son."
—The late Samuel Wachtel, Paul's father

Also by Paul Spencer Sochaczewski

Exceptional Encounters

Share Your Journey: Mastering Personal Writing

The five-book *Curious Encounters of the Human Kind* series:
Myanmar (Burma)
Indonesia
Himalaya
Borneo
Southeast Asia

Redheads: A Comic Eco-Thriller Set in Borneo

Distant Greens: Golf, Life and Surprising Serendipity On and Off the Fairways

The Sultan and the Mermaid Queen

Co-Authored with Jeffrey McNeely

Soul of the Tiger: Searching for Nature's Answers in Southeast Asia

Eco-Bluff Your Way to Instant Environmental Credibility

DEAD, BUT STILL KICKING

DEAD, BUT STILL KICKING

Encounters with Mediums, Shamans, and Spirits

PAUL SPENCER SOCHACZEWSKI

EXPLORER'S EYE PRESS
GENEVA, SWITZERLAND

© Paul Spencer Sochaczewski 2019

All rights reserved. No part of this publication may be reproduced, distributed, or transmitted in any form or by any means, including photocopying, recording, digital scanning, or other electronic or mechanical methods, without the prior written permission of the publisher, except in the case of brief quotations embodied in critical reviews and certain other noncommercial uses permitted by copyright law.

Special thanks to the spirits of famous people who generously provided blurbs.

And much gratitude to Alfred Russel Wallace, whom several mediums have told me co-authored this book.

The photos on the cover feature individual humans/spirits/ghosts/gods who each feature in a chapter.

Top row, left to right:

Samuel Wachtel (né Sochaczewski), Paul Sochaczewski's father
Alfred Russel Wallace
Ali, Wallace's "faithful companion"

Bottom row, left to right:

A *pontianak*, perhaps Farida, the female vampire ghost
Prince Senopati, the founder of the Mataram Empire, with Kanjeng Ratu Kidul, the Mermaid Queen of the Southern Ocean
U Hla Tin Aung, one of the two protector *nat* spirits of the Zee-O Thit-La sacred forest in Myanmar

Author's portrait, page 257, by Dot Bourquin

ISBN: 978-2-940573-32-5 paperback
ISBN: 978-2-940573-33-2 ebook

Book design by Stacey Aaronson

Published by:
Explorer's Eye Press
Geneva, Switzerland

Printed in the United States of America and the United Kingdom

Dedicated to ancestors and descendants.

The Three Tenets of Spiritualism

1. Each of us is made up of a corporeal body as well as an unseen, ethereal, eternal entity called (take your pick) "soul," "spirit," or "energy."[1]

2. We can contact those spirits; they can contact us.

3. Such contact is not a sure thing.

TABLE OF CONTENTS

PROLOGUE

THE BIG QUESTION | 1
When we die, is it the end? Or the beginning of the next phase?

THE EXPERIENCES

MOSES SENDS ME ON A PEACEKEEPING MISSION | 7
Psychics predict the future. Can mediums look into the past to enlighten the present?

"BEINGS OF A LIKE MENTAL NATURE TO OURSELVES" | 31
The creator of the Theory of Natural Selection was also a confirmed spiritualist. I sought his advice.

THE SEARCH FOR ALI | 105
Can eager shamans solve the mystery of Wallace's "faithful companion?"

"ARE YOU STRONG ENOUGH TO GO THROUGH WITH THIS?" | 161
Conversations with a female vampire spirit in a city built on a ghost story.

AN INVITATION TO MEET THE MERMAID QUEEN | 189
Some relationships aren't meant to be analyzed too closely. "Accept it. Or not."

THE TREES SPEAK | 205
Vital energy meets conservation imperative—the eloquent spirits of nature plead for their lives.

EPILOGUE

WHAT IF? | 243
Do I believe in spirits? More important, do you?

ENDNOTES | 258
REFERENCES | 276

AUTHOR'S NOTE

Each chapter has two parts: The Setup, which describes the background of a particular encounter, and The Conversations with Spirits, which is an annotated transcript of conversations with dead folks, ghosts, mythical figures, and elementals. These attempts at communications continue and will be updated in future editions.

PROLOGUE

THE BIG QUESTION:
When we die, is it the end?
Or the beginning of the next phase?

"Can I work with you?"

I looked around the meeting room at the Spiritualist Association of Great Britain, near Victoria Station in London. Some fifteen people, the majority women of a certain age, were listening to a well-coiffed medium standing in the front of the room, waiting for her to offer insights from relatives who have "passed."

What did these folks hope to learn from their dead relatives?

Are these people merely seeking news from the otherworld? Or are they hoping for evidence that clarifies a more fundamental question? *What happens when I die?*[2]

It's a binary question. Annihilation or metamorphosis?

∽

I am an Agnostic Spiritualist. I appreciate science. I don't believe in organized religion. I think that when we die that's it. Life is a beer commercial—live life for all its gusto because you'll only go around one time. *Carpe diem* and all that.

And yet.

I am convinced that, to paraphrase Hamlet, there are things in our world that cannot be explained using Cartesian logic. Most of the readers of this book will have had a Western education and upbringing that stresses evidence-based science.

Yet when you ask people, "Do you believe in spirits?" they often prevaricate. "Not really, but I'm not sure. There are things that happen that we can't explain."

◈

My cynical friend Glenda claims that the belief in spirits is simply a creation of religious myth-makers to ensure adherence to a set of beliefs; it's the most important element of religion marketing. The majority of people in the world profess some kind of formal religion. But what is a religion, Glenda asks, but a set of rituals and rules that uses miracles and parables to accomplish two things. First, a religion establishes the existence of a Super-Entity, usually either a Hairy Thunderer or a Cosmic Muffin, which has oversight and free reign over everything. And second, to ensure fealty to this Super-Entity, religious leaders say that each of us has a soul of some kind. This soul, the priests suggest, can survive the death of the body and, provided we collect enough karma points, permit us to enter a form of happy afterlife. (Without the requisite credits we might descend into an eternal hell, or be forced to try again. And again. And again, until we get it right.) Salvation or damnation.

Regardless of whether we are religious (and the idea of eternal souls is an equal opportunity concept embraced also by countless atheists, agnostics, Pagans, Animists, and free-thinkers), many of us believe, at least partially, that ghosts, spirits, and djinns exist.

This belief requires an individual to buy into the following sequence of logical assumptions for illogical happenings:

1. We are more than our bodies. In addition to our physical bodies, each of us has an unseen, ethereal, eternal entity called a soul. Or spirit. Or energy.[3]
2. This soul/spirit/energy lives on after the body dies.

(The location is unclear. "Everywhere and anywhere" seems to be the best assumption.)

3. This soul/spirit/energy is generally benign. Except in horror films.
4. This soul/spirit/energy is willing to contact still-living descendants. Such contact is rarely in the form of a complete or coherent discussion.
5. Each of us theoretically has the power to contact this soul/spirit/energy. But just as most of us wouldn't attempt to fix a plumbing problem in the house, it's generally more effective to work via a skilled medium/channeler/psychic/shaman who can act as a go-between.
6. There is no guarantee that we can contact a specific soul/spirit/energy at any given time.

⁓

Is belief in a spiritual existence insight or delusion? Our ability to *reason*, our all-powerful brain that has been nurtured by a diet of algebra and the red pencil of stern Mrs. Olsen in fifth grade who scolded us when we misspelled a word, says there's no such thing as spirit. It's an illusion. You can't prove it, therefore it's myth.

Yet plenty of people, often intelligent, well-educated people, believe in spirit, just as they believe in love, intuition, and superstition.

Let's put it another way. An acceptance of the idea of spirits and mediums involves "letting go" of our materialistic worldview and admitting there are some elements of our existence that we don't understand and can't prove. It's like quantum mechanics, which arose from theories to explain observations that could not be reconciled with classical physics. Quantum mechanics suggests that consciousness (not matter) is the primary mover and creator of reality. You might be frightened and confused and want such stuff to remain in the genie's bottle. Or you might be thrilled by the unprovable idiosyncrasies of the universe and be willing to explore your psychological horizons.[4]

⁓

Belief in spirits is enhanced by what psychologists call a self-perpetuating loop. We invest energy in a belief, and through repetition and endorsement by others, the idea increases in value. Psychologists call this embedment: "The more we repeat some idea the stronger it becomes, and the harder for us to eliminate." We need to believe in our "story." Put another way, author Neil Gaiman said, "Things need not have happened to be true," an observation as relevant to politics as it is to the spirit world. We get entangled in wishful thinking—we want to desire something so we believe it to be true.[5]

At its essence, belief in spirits is more than simply trying to say hello to ancestors. It's also a confirmation of our own complex presence, a basic validation that some essence of us will survive physical death. *I have a value and existence beyond my body.* This belief enhances our desire to leave a legacy. How are we otherwise remembered by later generations for whom our lives become ever-distant folklore?[6]

⁓

This book is not a catalogue of things we can't explain. It's not a catalogue of how faiths construct our world. It's not an academic study. It's not a defense of Spiritualism, nor a critique of charlatan psychics. Just a few stories about my own experiences with dozens of mediums and shamans worldwide. Plus a few musings, and plenty of unanswered questions.

Do *you* believe in things that go bump in the night?

THE
EXPERIENCES

Moses Sends Me on a Peacekeeping Mission

Psychics predict the future. Can mediums look into the past to enlighten the present?

Is my fate determined by Moses telling me to achieve peace in the Middle East?

LES MARÉCOTTES, Switzerland
LONDON, United Kingdom
SULAWESI, Indonesia

During my thirties and forties I visited dozens of psychics and fortune tellers worldwide. It was a hobby, giving me a chance to meet interesting people in distant places. I was testing them all, taking notes on their predictions and guesses. Numerologists, psychics, tarot card readers, astrologers, palm readers. I was an equal-opportunity pigeon.

I had a substantial file of such reports. As my fiftieth birthday approached, I booked a mountain hotel in the Valais canton of Switzerland for a party. I invited my son David from Indonesia and my girlfriend (later my wife) Monique. I carefully packed the file, which I called my "prophecy portfolio" in the trunk of the car, along with wine for the party, changes of clothes, and a few books. We were going to go hiking for a couple of days, then go to the party, and then stay on for a few days to relax. I figured that would be an appropriate time to review my collection of predictions.

We returned from the hike and found that the car had been broken into and all our luggage had been stolen. Such things shouldn't happen in boring, law-abiding Switzerland. We made a report to the police, went out and bought some clean clothes and a few more cartons of wine, and the party was a big success.

But of course, my file had disappeared. I took it as a sign. I wasn't meant to dabble in speculation about my future.

But that still left plenty of opportunity to look to the past for insight into the present.

THE SETUP

One of my favorite books, a cult classic, is *A Fortune-Teller Told Me*, by Tiziano Terzani. Terzani was the far-eastern correspondent of the German news magazine *Der Spiegel*. As he recalled in his book, in the Spring of 1976 an old Chinese fortune teller in Hong Kong told him: "Beware! You run a grave risk of dying in 1993. You mustn't fly that year. Don't fly, not even once." Surely one of the great opening lines.

And, like good writers, Terzani turned that chance encounter and seemingly random warning into a quest. A hero's journey if you will. He had seventeen years to contemplate the warning, which sat in his consciousness like malaria sticks in the bloodstream. Terzani, an Italian who had lived for more than twenty years in Singapore, Hong Kong, Peking, Tokyo, and finally Bangkok, decided that the best way of confronting the prophecy was the Asian one: not to fight against it, but to submit.

So Terzani, to the amusement of his colleagues and the consternation of his editors, declared that 1993 would be a "no-fly" year.[7] He promised to continue his reporting duties, but would move around Asia by car, train, and ship. His book is the result of that year with his feet stuck on terra firma, but his head high in the clouds of the firmament of "What If?"

Some readers are fascinated by his personal journey. His growth. "I was marked for death," he wrote, "but was reborn."

Other readers are engrossed that he used the year to seek out fortune tellers, shamans, and soothsayers wherever he went. Spoiler: none of the prophets repeated the dire warning of the Hong Kong fortune teller who started all the drama.

Virtually all readers wait anxiously for the money shot, the incident that "proved" the initial warning was valid. The climax comes early, on page ten. Joachim Holzgen, Terzani's replacement, was one of fifteen journalists traveling on a UN helicopter that crashed in Cambodia. It was Holzgen's first trip to Indochina; he suffered a broken leg and a compressed spinal cord. Terzani wrote: "The helicopter that crashed was one I should have been on. Then was it my fault it had crashed?"

Terzani made that incident the main theme of the book:

> The story of the helicopter kept whirling around in my head. I could not see it as the realization of the prophecy, nor as a simple coincidence either. I went on repeating to

myself that in the light of reason every prediction is half-true and half-false, that the helicopter might or might not have crashed; but I found it difficult to set my mind at rest and accept that the event had been a simple matter of statistical probability. Up till that moment, the whole business of the fortune teller and his prophecy had been partly a game, and the resolution not to fly a sort of bet between me and me to put myself to the test . . . Was this proof that the fortune teller had been right? What had he "seen"? In my heart of hearts I most assuredly did not want it to be thus. *I liked to think of the occult as a possibility, not a certainty.* I wanted to hang on to my doubt, not to become a believer. All my life I have avoided faiths, and I certainly did not want to talk myself into adopting this one. In accepting the fortune teller's prophecy and deciding not to fly I had wanted to add a bit of poetry to my life, not another reason for despair. *Because if this episode proved that everything was written, then life had no meaning any more.* [italics added]

～

Now, this book you're reading isn't about fortune tellers. Telling one's fortune is an act of prophecy, of looking into the future. The mediums I am dealing with are first cousins of soothsayers. But unlike soothsayers, my medium friends look sideways, into another dimension. Nevertheless, I'm delving into the waters of similar conundrums. Are there things in this world we can't understand? Which of the many "wise men and wise women" should we trust? And, most tantalizingly, *is there any proof?* This last is essential, especially to a Western-educated observer.

We are brought up with an overdeveloped left brain that emphasizes logic, facts, information, double-blind experiments, and academic citations. The "watching mind" keeps us Earthbound. That's fine, but we sometimes discount the need for the wisdom of the right brain (which might better be called the heart), which is the world of emotion, intuition, story, questioning, senses, quests, inspiration, creativity, and instinct.

We need both—logic *and* emotion. Asian philosophy teaches us that the balance of the world, and hence its very existence, hinges on a duality. Yin and yang. Female and male. The Hindu god Shiva teaches us that in order to have creation we must first have destruction. Certain actions in this life have an impact on existence in the next life. Night and day. Sun and moon. Good and evil. Or, to put this into writing terms, conflict, the essence of story, is generated by a continual binary dynamic. "Yes, I will climb that mountain," you say. "No, you won't," replies the mountain, which fights back with snow storms, high altitude, and treacherous terrain. "Yes, I will go to France to defeat the Germans and save democracy," says the young British infantryman. "No, you won't," says the German bomber pilot flying over Normandy. "Yes, I will go to Hollywood and become a respected and successful actor," says the young woman from Ohio. "Maybe, but only if you sleep with me first," says the film producer. *Yes. No.* That dynamic is the locomotive of life.

In communications, whether personal or professional, we need left-brain attributes that appear as good grammar, accurate spelling, fact checking, and solid interview techniques. We like, indeed we need, facts.

But in communications, as in life, we must not ignore the heart. Eye-to-eye contact. Touch and smell and posture. Pheromones. When we speak with a good friend we tell stories, invoking the five elements of a good scene—characters, setting, dialogue, conflict, and movement—a good story leads to another good story. That's the main job a writer has—to get the reader to turn the page, to ask "what happens next?"

Is this relevant to my search for spirits?

I've tried to understand how these conversations with spirits occur. With each medium I ask similar questions. *Where did you get this gift? Does everyone have this ability? How do you know who's going to "pick up the phone" when you call?*

Mediums speaking different languages, from different cultures, with different social and religious upbringings, have similar answers to these questions.

Many mediums realized that they had a gift as youngsters. (One medium told me that when she was eight, she could tell the sex of a neighbor's unborn child.) Often someone else in the family had a similar ability.

Mediums tell me everyone has psychic powers. But often society does not give people permission to explore these powers.[8] And, which I find more interesting, is that most people do not give themselves permission to walk down this path. That's certainly my case. People tell me I have some kind of ability, a special energy. But I don't quite accept it. I don't pursue it. I let other people do the heavy psychic lifting.

Virtually all mediums have some sort of spirit guide or guardian that protects the medium, offers subtle advice, and acts as a gatekeeper with the spirits. Each medium has her own version of Obi-Wan Kenobi.

And it's the spirit that chooses whether to join in a conversation. As one British medium told me, she has to enter the psychic activity in a spirit of truth, love, and light. While the spirit guide or gatekeeper will determine whether a particular conversation is appropriate, it's the spirit itself that will decide whether to engage with the medium and the seeker (or "sitter" in psychic parlance). And the spirit needs feedback. Which is why many of the mediums I've consulted will tell the sitter to give feedback. "Tell me yes, or no, or I don't know." The medium will say this is a necessary action to keep the spirit involved. The cynic will say that this is a tactic to help the medium formulate answers that provide an "aha" moment.

And for some people that's really what it's about—the moment when the sitter feels she has made a connection. Most people who engage with spirits seek what might be called an "Oh my god, that's Daddy!" moment.[9] They deliberately go into an event desiring to speak with a loved one who has "passed." They are like poor miners in the California Gold

Rush seeking a few shiny eureka moments, a "hit" in psychic parlance that shifts the sitter's experience from doubt to faith.

And some mediums (or charlatans, depending on your point of view) might use a technique I call "chumming" or "fishing." They'll throw out messages they say they are receiving in the hope that the sitter bites on one of them.

These tend to be generic statements that are likely to apply to a majority of people. The medium might say, "I sense a serious illness. Heart disease, or stroke. Maybe cancer. Or diabetes?" The skeptic might say, "That's a no-brainer, everyone has someone in the family who suffers from one of these diseases." Or "I sense a death. Have you experienced a loss?" Or "I see a much-loved family pet, maybe a dog or a cat?" These statements are virtually universal in their appeal, and the sensitive (or gullible) sitter will grasp on to them as proof that "Yes! Grandma had a stroke! And she had a pet dog named Scruffy! Scruffy got hit by a truck. Poor Scruffy. Grandma's passed on, but she's not really dead. Praise be!"[10]

THE CONVERSATION
WITH SPIRITS

Part I – The Mid-Week Mediums

I go to the Spiritualists Association of Great Britain (SAGB). It was founded in 1872; Arthur Conan Doyle was among the group's active members.

SAGB offers daily one-hour group events, each run by one of the eleven mediums who are part of their active roster.

I expect (perhaps hope) that their offices would be in an old, crumbling Victorian house full of ghostly character and dusty furniture. But their headquarters are in an ugly 1960s-era office block near London's Victoria station, on the same floor as the offices of the International Organization for Migration.

I attend two of the public gatherings, paying the £6 entry fee.

The first reading is by Pauline Mason. The woman seated next to me, a conservatively dressed gray-haired lady who describes herself as a regular, explains that Pauline is "very good."

Some excerpts from Pauline's interactions with various "seekers":

With Seeker I.

Pauline stands at the front of the room. She appears to concentrate, as if intent on helping the mostly female seekers who sit anxiously, awaiting their turn. She turns to one seeker.

"*I get a month of birthday or anniversary, around May 20.*"

Seeker I replies, in a tentative voice: "No."

"*Don't say 'no.' Say 'I don't know.'*"

Seeker I nods.

"*Links to southeast London.*"

"No."

"*Three story house.*"

"Yes."

"*Thank you.*"

"*Sometimes you don't trust yourself.*"

I have to stop myself from rolling my eyes. I want to shout, "Come on, Pauline, who hasn't had moments of self-doubt?"

❧

With Seeker II.

"*Tap shoes,*" Pauline says.

"I loved tap dancing." Wonderful, this is a true aha moment. A juicy factoid that Pauline has no way of knowing. Moments like this form the holy grail of spiritual contact. We want exciting details that the medium couldn't possibly know.

"*Back problems.*"

Who hasn't had back problems, or known someone who has had such ailments?

"*I see a man standing behind you. Father? Husband?*"

"Yes." Seeker II is getting excited. Clearly she is hoping to contact her departed husband.

"Tactile man, hugs."

"Yes."

"A trumpet. Anniversary of death coming up?"

"Yes."

"Long washing line and it all collapsed."

❧

With Seeker III.

"Rosary, any Catholics in your family?"

"Plenty."

"Old watch in box."

"I don't know."

"Elizabeth."

"Oh god, yes. My grandmother."

"Unusual piece of jewelry."

"Yes. A ring."

For me this is a classic "fishing" pronouncement. Every woman has an unusual or important piece of jewelry that has some emotional importance. The sitter wants to encourage the medium, she wants her to be right and continue. It's a form of psychic foreplay. The sitter is desperate for that aha moment that she can tell her friends about later over a nice glass of wine.

Then Pauline looks at me.

"Can I work with you?"

I stay neutral, curious, an observer more than a participant. "Of course."

"When I saw you at the reception desk I thought, 'Here's an interesting man.'"

Flattery! It works. I'm immediately convinced Pauline is a woman of style and good judgment.

"You have important work. Do you have people working with you or under you?"

More flattery, she accords me a certain professional status. But her question is clever because she covers all possible answers—even the lowliest laborer works *with* someone.

"You have great success."

What a wonderful woman. Don't stop.

But she changes direction.

"Jaguar."

"Car or animal?"

"Car."

Damn. If she had said animal there is a vague connection to my conservation work at WWF. But nada for car, except for the desire I had when I was younger to actually own an XKE. Does this count as an aha moment?

"Mother—short."

Well, Pauline saw me when I walked in, and probably noticed I'm not tall. And all old ladies get diminutive.

"She ran a good home."

This is interesting. My mother probably *thought* she ran a good home, so maybe Pauline is accurately conveying a conversation with my mother's spirit. My reality is different—I was never too impressed by my mother's domestic cleanliness, cooking, or choice of home decorations. I was embarrassed by her love of figurines and her inclination to cover every surface with plastic so the sofa and carpet wouldn't get dirty.

"Big family, about 12."

An emphatic "No." I rub it in: "I was an only child."

"London Tube."

"Like everybody, I suppose." Come on, Pauline. Everybody in this room has daily contact with the London Tube.

"Big ships. Coastline."

"Not really." I want to tell her that everybody has some contact with a coastline. True, I almost drowned in the South China Sea when I was in the Peace Corps in Borneo. But it feels like she's chumming, throwing out ideas in the hope that one of them will be right.

> "Maybe you visited Cornwall or Devon."

Several times, for pleasant, uneventful holidays that had nothing to do with any ancestors.

> "Taking more care of yourself, health."

I suppose this is true. But so what? I'm seventy; of course I'm concerned about my health. And what connection does this have with ancestors?

> "Father or uncle had an old black car."

Nope.

> "Black Citroen, big old car with sideboards and big headlights. Links with France."

"My wife is French. I live in Switzerland. I go shopping and play golf in neighboring France." Later I ask my wife if she had relatives who owned a big black Citroen. *Non.*

The second SAGB reading is by Terri Stromeyer. She is an elegant woman—dressed in stylish black, little jewelry, well-cared-for black hair, Indian-patterned scarf, bright red nail polish, fun and attentive. I sit next to a mature woman who confides that she comes regularly to these gatherings and that Terri is "one of the best."[11]

> Terri stands at the front of the room, composed, relaxed but intense, like a skilled presenter about to make a TED talk, and looks at the ten participants in this midweek, mid-afternoon session. In no particular order she looks at

someone and offers observations like these, with responses from seekers ranging from an emphatic "No" to a Molly Bloom–like "Oh my god, yes!"

> "There's a smell of face powder."

> "A pub, people smoking."

> "I see a robin."

> "Embroidery."

> "Long illness."

> "Grandmother lost weight and had false teeth that didn't fit, gummy, not attractive look, difficulty talking and eating."

> "Fox fur, love of clothes."

> "Made bridal clothes, didn't need a pattern."

> "Butterflies in buddleia, hydrangeas and climbing roses."

> "Old Singer foot-powered sewing machine."

> "Yes, life is so chaotic."

Once in a while she gets a dramatic hit.

> "Lived near RAF camp. Romantic lunch with American soldier."

The seeker replies: "Yes, it was just after the war. My grandmother had a lovely relationship."

Terri then looks at me. She stares, pauses a moment.

> "I see a father spirit. Would you say he was a violent man?"

"No. Just the opposite," I say clearly. "My father was strong, but he was a peacemaker."

She self-corrects.

> "Oh, now I see. The man I'm seeing is in back of you, and he's actually related to the man seated just behind you."

I turn to look at a large man, short hair, rugby physique, tattoos.

> "Your father was brutal, a drinker, violent. His behavior, he says, was tough love, for your own good. You lost respect for him."

The air has gone out of the room. Up to now all of her observations have been powderpuff-like in their innocence. But now Terri is raising the specter of child abuse. Raising the stakes.

"Yes, that's correct," the man behind me says.

> "He broke the family and your mother suffered, with dignity, but she was in pain. There was always some drama happening at your house.

"Yes." It's unsettling when a large, physically imposing man speaks softly, like a child.

> "He was a serial, conniving liar. He believed his lies."

"Yes." Sadness in his voice.

This is extraordinary. Virtually all the mediums I have spoken with self-censor. They consciously try to avoid overly ugly or controversial language and thoughts. But Terri is brutal in her reading with the man behind me. I admire her for that. A gentler medium might have tempered her comments with statements like, "I sense that there was some conflict with your father," or "Are you carrying resentment against your father?" and moved on from there, depending on the sitter's reaction. Terri goes for the jugular.

> *"You had a brutal upbringing, but loving grandmothers."*
>
> *"You hated school, bunked off, always in trouble, you smashed a window with a catapult, took the tops off milk bottles."*
>
> *"Caravan holidays."*

"Yes."

> *"Now your father is sorry. Wishes you well. Loves you."*

There it is, the happy ending that most mediums like to end with. He was a bastard but now that he's passed into another dimension, he's really sorry for all the bad things he did and sends his love.

The man in back of me is crying.

Terri never gets around to connecting with my dead relatives.

Part II – Moses Sends Me on a Peacekeeping Mission

My friend Yan Mokoginta invites me for dinner at his brother's house. The family has large landholdings in this part of northern Sulawesi, Indonesia, but the house is simple, middle class. Tile floor, whitewashed walls. Plastic flowers. Brown upholstered furniture. Straight curtains over the doorways—red and gray leaf pattern. Two paintings hang on a far wall, dull-colored fish and reindeer.

We are four—I'm with Yan, Yan's brother Usman Mokoginta, and a family friend named Sukardi.

Over dinner, casually, Usman he tells me he sees two other men in the room.

> *"There's a big man with a long white beard and long white hair,"* Usman says. He sounds relaxed, as if big men with long white beards come to dinner every night. *"He wears a white wool cap, jacket, and tie."*

I don't know who he's referring to.

> *"I see another man, with a black jacket and tie, a big man, bald."*

Usman asks if this could be my father.

"No," I answer. "My father was short and had all his hair."

> *"Then he must be a* jaga*,"* he decides. Guardian.

I have been to see numerous fortune tellers, mystics, prophets, and holy men. Usually I feel neutral in their presence. I am curious but not a believer. I wait to hear what they have to say. I am cynical; I am strong.

Although Usman starts out unconvincingly, I am strangely apprehensive. My posture is twisted. I try to center myself. My body remains off balance. I taste my lunch. I sense a powerful energy. Not dangerous or evil, but unsettling. This surprises me because I am normally not susceptible to such things.

I sit with my back to the doorway. I turn around just in time to see a man poke his head in the front door, then quickly withdraw it. A moment later he enters the room and we shake hands. His name is Mansur, and he sports a generous moustache, wavy black hair, and a mischievous smile. I am startled, because he resembles a man I never met. He looks like my grandfather, whom I know only from a single 1910 photo in which he stands stiff, alongside his wife and two children, one of whom is my father. Both Mansur and my grandfather appear stout, proud, with neat moustaches. To me, both men resemble Luciano Pavarotti.

After eating we go into a smaller room, a bedroom. The commentary from a tennis match being played in distant Jakarta, several thousand kilometers and a time zone away, is on the television in another room and the sound seeps through the thin walls. Carl-Uwe Steeb is beating Michael Chang.

The room is hot and crowded. We sit on the floor. My back hurts, and I lean against a bedpost.

Mansur—the man who reminds me of my never-met grandfather—sits cross-legged. He bends forward, puts his right hand to his forehead, then thrusts out his hand. At that moment Sukardi, who is the medium, suddenly shivers, pounds his chest, hits his forehead with a fist, shakes his fist, and makes an abrupt rowing motion. He hunches his shoulders and resembles a bear. His hands shake. He points to a spot next to me.

"Your father. He's there. Small body."

I stare at Sukardi's eyes. They protrude like those of an ornamental goldfish, like those of the actor Marty Feldman.

> *"Your father is very clever, likes to write,"* Yan says, trying to translate. Yan has trouble following, since Sukardi speaks partly in Bahasa Mongondow, a rarely heard archaic local tongue.

Sukardi hunches again, a stylized movement that reminds me of Javanese *wayang wong*, where men dance like wooden puppets. He reaches to shake each of our hands.

> *"You've made contact with your father three times,"*
> he says.

This is true if I consider that I had visited three other mediums who claim to have contacted him. But otherwise Sukardi is a bit of a psychic washout. Nevertheless, I play along, wondering, What is the correct question to ask a dead relative?

> *"Your father is here. He wants to talk with you."*

Instead of asking what the weather's like in heaven, or if there are pretty angels there, or how the food is, I ask my father, rather feebly in retrospect, if he is all right.

Sukardi speaks with a gruff, theatrical voice. Mixed in with the words are many guttural, animal-like sounds.

> *"He's a writer, like you."*

No, I think. You're wrong. He's wasn't a writer. Sukardi is fishing, I think. No doubt he is guessing based on the likelihood that Yan told him I'm a writer.

> *"You are like him."*

It's a stretch, but yes, in some ways we're similar. My father was a dreamer. Like me.

I ask about a man called David, without explaining that he is my son.

> *"He is smart. Do whatever you feel is right. Your father will help."*

"What will happen to my son?"

> *"He will be like you."*

I am not sure this is a good thing.

Sukardi has been giving me vague answers, and I am full yet unsatisfied, the Chinese Dinner Syndrome in a spiritual context.

I reflect on the strange circumstances that brought me here. I had met Yan Mokoginta in Jakarta more than a year earlier, through Russ Betts, head of WWF in Indonesia. I was interested in Yan's work in developing the Wallace University, a project named in honor of Alfred Russel Wallace, whom I have been following for decades. Since then we had lost contact. Then, I ran into Yan Mokoginta at the Ujung Pandang (now Makassar) airport. The circumstances were serendipitous. I had planned to fly on a Sunday from Bali, where I was spending my sabbatical year, to Ujung Pandang, then catch another flight to Manado and then take a local bus down to Bogani Nani Wartabone National Park. The trip was part of my research for the book I was writing about Alfred Russel Wallace. A friend convinced me to leave on the Monday instead. By coincidence, Yan was on a Monday flight from Jakarta to Ujung Pandang, and then he planned to connect to the same flight to Manado I was on. His destination? Bogani Nani Wartabone National Park. He was traveling with Gunawan Satari, the number two man in the Ministry of Research and Technology, and officials of the Indonesian Red Cross, the British Council, and the Wallacea Development Institute. They were preparing a workshop on biodiversity in the Wallace region. They invited me to join them for the recce and to come back for the workshop several weeks later. Coincidence? Destiny?

> "Your son is in Java," Sukardi says, taking a guess.

"Yes."

> "Jakarta."

Another easy guess, but wrong. He is in Bogor, 45 minutes from Jakarta.

And then Sukardi tells me something personal that shakes my smug Western cool. He tells me a well-concealed family secret.

I sit stunned. This man has no way of knowing what he just told me. He has no business in knowing that. It's as if he's violated my privacy. I stare at the man with bulbous eyes, legs folded, shoulders hunched like a Neanderthal, speaking an ancient language. He's been giving me softball answers and then comes out and tells me something I have told few people. Is he reading my mind or does he have deeper powers? Sukardi grunts. My spine feels like a pretzel.

I finally give in and ask a typical psychic-groupie question. "What about *jodoh*?" I ask. "What is my fate?

> "You have two destinies. Romance and work. You have success in both, but need great patience."

More softball answers. "My mother?"

"*Sick.*"

He makes asthma sounds, massages his leg.

I explain she's dead.

Sukardi extends his hand and, acting as medium, conveys my parents' love to me. He is shaking. Why do Indonesian mediums appear so twisted and tormented in comparison to Western mediums?

"*Your parents protect you,*" he says.

Part of my brain is cynical and realizes that he is using the same "peace and love" tactic of the mediums I saw in London. *Your father loves you and protects you.* He's giving me the same feel-good cliché that most psychic groupies want to hear.

Sukardi closes his eyes and shudders. His body relaxes and he "awakes" from the trance. He does not remember the previous half hour and asks what happened.

Later, I ask Mansur how he got his gift. He explains he has only had it for two years, since he was forty. He had a dream in which he was fighting against many people, when the "force" came to him and he was able to vanquish his enemies. Now, whenever he is in trouble, he listens to a voice that tells him what to do.

Before we leave, Yan disappears with his brother into another room. I assume they are talking about family matters.

Back in the car, however, Yan tells me what his brother said.

> "Remember the man my brother saw protecting you at the beginning of the evening? The big man in white?"

I remember.

> "That was Moses. Moses protects you."

I don't know what to make of that. I don't want to hurt Yan's feelings, but I also have trouble taking this too seriously. I am well over the brush with discomfort I had half an hour earlier and back to my normal skeptical self. Again, someone (or something) gives me the wisdom to shut up.

> "My brother also saw Moses protecting me," Yan says. "We both have a task. You are Jewish. I am Muslim."

"And what is the task?" I ask.

> "Peace in the Middle East."

"Yan, I can't get away. I have a book to write," I protest, trying to lighten the mood.

> "Not now. You don't have to go now. The time will come," Yan says. "But that was Moses."[12]

"BEINGS OF A LIKE MENTAL NATURE TO OURSELVES"

The creator of the Theory of Natural Selection was also a confirmed spiritualist. I sought his advice.

Alfred Russel Wallace with his deceased mother, a photograph taken in 1874 by spirit photographer Frederick Hudson. Wallace declared it genuine, noting "even if [Hudson] had by some means obtained possession of all the photographs ever taken of my mother, they would not have been of the slightest use to him in the manufacture of these pictures." Contemporary critics considered the photo a hoax created by a double exposure.

LONDON, United Kingdom
ATTAMBUA, West Nusa Tenggara, Indonesia
GENEVA, Switzerland

I want to "speak" with Alfred Russel Wallace.
I have been following Wallace's trail for some fifty years—far up the Rio Negro in Brazil to the Colombia–Venezuela border, and to dozens of obscure and seldom-visited

islands in the territories that are now Singapore, Malaysia, and Indonesia. I've written about that ongoing quest in numerous articles and books, including *An Inordinate Fondness for Beetles*,[13] but many questions remain. I want to contact Wallace to understand his motivation for traveling far and hard, the nature of his "delicate arrangement" with Darwin (did he feel Darwin stole Wallace's Theory of Natural Selection?), and his relationship with his "faithful companion" Ali. Who knows, maybe Wallace's spirit might even give me Ali's full name so I can finally trace Ali's descendants. That particular quest is documented in the following chapter: "The Search for Ali."

Above all, I want to speak with Wallace about his belief in a "superior intelligence" that was responsible for the existence of *Homo sapiens*, and his lifelong argument with Darwin about this proposition. And, given his belief in spirits, I thought it would be fun to ask Wallace about his own experiences as a ghost.

Worthy objectives. But I need a talented medium to make it happen.

The Setup

Call it a Bromance.

My interest in Alfred Russel Wallace began in 1969, while I lived in Sarawak, a Malaysian state on the island of Borneo. The longer I lived in Southeast Asia, the more my interest in conservation, biology, local cultures, and history expanded. Coincidentally, I found that I was living in places that Wallace had visited. It was as if our lives were intersecting by happy accident.

How could I not like this guy? In 1848, at the age of 25, he and his friend Henry Walter Bates said, "Hey, let's go to the Amazon." Never mind that neither had ever left England, neither spoke Portuguese, they had no important contacts, and they were basically broke. Wallace spent four years on the Amazon and Rio Negro rivers, after which the ship carrying him and much of his collection (thousands of new species of birds, mammals, insects, and butterflies), along with most of his notebooks, caught fire and sank in the Atlantic Ocean. He barely survived ten days in a lifeboat and swore never to go to sea again.

But he did, heading to Southeast Asia in 1854. During his eight years in that region, Wallace traveled some 22,000 kilometers, moved his jungle camp more than a hundred times while visiting dozens of isolated tropical islands, collected 125,660 specimens, including 212 new species of birds, 900 new species of beetles, and, most astonishingly for me, 200 new species of ants.[14] He studied indigenous tribes and often found their simple life was more civilized than that of his compatriots back in England. He was self-supporting, earning a very modest living by sending "natural productions" back to his beetle-agent Samuel Stevens in England. He lived hard, slept rough, and had zero institutional support—no floating base camp like Darwin had aboard the *Beagle*, no official government mandate, no diplomatic cover, no rich daddy at home to help out during lean times. He survived by his wits (and, although he was shy and opinionated, his ability to schmooze). Wallace developed the Theory of Evolution by Natural Selection, and then allowed Charles Darwin to take the credit.[15]

Like all interesting people, Wallace was a bundle of contradictions—both a soft-hearted conservationist and a hard-nosed hunter who shot seventeen orangutans.[16] He saw dignity in the indigenous people he met, but he neither refrained from calling them "savages" nor called for an end to colonialism. His collections of birds of paradise fed an increased demand for the birds' feathers in Europe, which caused various species of those birds to become threatened in the wild.

But perhaps his most intriguing contradiction, at least to many of his contemporaries, was that he was both an acclaimed scientist *and* a committed Spiritualist.[17, 18]

⁓

While growing up in England, Wallace developed an interest in the supernatural. He learned mesmerism, and in 1844, four years before leaving for the Amazon and ten years before leaving for Asia, he discovered he had the power to hypnotize. During his travels he spent years with tribal societies, people whose lives are influenced by bird omens, animal totems, and conversations with dead ancestors. It is likely that these fireside conversations opened his eyes to the fact that the people of the Amazon and Southeast Asia had a different worldview to that of Wallace and his UK-based friends.

Surprisingly, he only wrote about one "bump-in-the-night incident in *The Malay Archipelago*, his classic 1869 travel journal that has never been out of print. Perhaps he felt that an overemphasis on mystical happenings would detract from the serious nature of his book.

> A Bornean Malay who had been for many years resident here said to Manuel [an assistant], 'One thing is strange in this country—the scarcity of ghosts.' 'How so?' asked Manuel. 'Why, you know,' said the Malay, 'that in our countries to the westward, if a man dies or is killed, we dare not pass near the place at night, for all sorts of noises are heard, which show that ghosts are about. But here there are numbers of men killed, and their bodies lie unburied in the fields and by the roadside, and yet you can walk by them at night and never hear or see any thing at all' . . . And so it

was settled that ghosts were very scarce, if not altogether unknown in Lombock [Lombok, just east of Bali]. I would observe, however, that as the evidence is purely negative, we should be wanting in scientific caution if we accepted this fact as sufficiently well established.[19]

This single passage is the only mention of the spirit world in *The Malay Archipelago*. I've often thought it odd that Wallace didn't mention other strange happenings. I say this for two reasons. The first is that throughout the Malay Archipelago people need very little encouragement to start telling ghost stories—sitting around the campfire Wallace must have frequently heard strange tales. The second is that in later life he was not at all shy about experimenting with, and writing about, Spiritualism, seances, and other psychic phenomena.

Once Wallace returned to England, his interest in the spiritual world blossomed. In 1865, just three years after returning from Asia, he adopted Spiritualism. This was a brave move for a scientist, and some people thought that by embracing the world of spirits and seances, he was jeopardizing his hard-won position as a respected scientist and harming his chances of being accepted into the conservative scientific community of Victorian Britain. A year later, in 1866, Wallace wrote "The Scientific Aspect of the Supernatural,"[20] in 1875 published *On Miracles and Modern Spiritualism*, and in 1896 *Miracles and Modern Spiritualism*.[21]

Wallace's writings serve as a precursor to the Three Tenets of Spiritualism.

He directly endorsed the idea that people have both a physical *and* a spiritual existence.

> *Man is a duality*, consisting of an organized spiritual form, evolved coincidently with and permeating the physical body, and having corresponding organs and development . . . Death is the separation of this duality, and effects no change in the spirit, morally or intellectually. [italics added][22]

And he proposed that the actions we take while alive affect our spiritual personality.

> The present life will assume a new value and interest when men are brought up not merely in the vacillating and questionable belief, but in the settled, indubitable *conviction, that our existence in this world is really but one of the stages in an endless career,* and that the thoughts we think and *the deeds we do here will certainly affect our condition and the very form and organic expression of our personality hereafter.* [italics added][23]

Wallace was convinced that such spirits can be contacted.

> Spirits can communicate through properly endowed mediums.[24]

And noted that such contact can ease the pain of death to the survivors.

> What more natural than that [the spirits] should wish, whenever possible, to give some message to their friends, if only to assure them that death is not the end, that they still live, and are not unhappy. Many facts seem to show us that the beautiful idea of guardian spirits is not a mere dream, but a frequent, perhaps universal reality.[25]

He elegantly described the existence of spirits as:

> The agency of *beings of a like mental nature to ourselves*—who are, in fact, ourselves—but one step advanced on the long journey through eternity. [italics added][26]

Just as many people disagreed with Wallace's views on evolution, many people similarly discounted and mocked his promotion of Spiritualism.

Wallace's books and papers about Spiritualism (including three chapters of his autobiography) include extensive correspondence with skeptics. Wallace was continually inviting doubters to attend seances, scolding them if they only came once, and forcefully disagreeing with them if they didn't believe in the demonstrations of psychic writing, table rapping, table levitation, apparitions, bell ringing, an accordion playing without human contact, and other psychic phenomena that he felt could only have been achieved through the agency of ethereal spirits.[27]

He was undeterred by the skepticism of some of his contemporaries.

> I thus learnt my first great lesson in the inquiry into these obscure fields of knowledge, *never to accept the disbelief of great men* or their accusations of imposture or of imbecility, as of any weight when opposed to the repeated observation of facts by other men, admittedly sane and honest. *The whole history of science shows us that whenever the educated and scientific men of any age have denied the facts of other investigators on a priori grounds of absurdity or impossibility, the deniers have always been wrong.* [italics added][28, 29]

As a scientist, Wallace looked for proof of phenomena that could not be confirmed by normal scientific inquiry and therefore could only have been accomplished through the assistance of spirits. He used a reverse argument to convince doubters, aggressively writing to one skeptic whose own observations convinced him that a particular medium was a fraud.

> All these facts and many others of like nature have been published . . . every investigator knows that your failure to obtain phenomena under the test, was no proof of any dishonesty in the medium, or of impossibility of obtaining the

phenomena under such conditions. Such tests often require to be tried many times before success is attained. To me, and I believe to most inquirers, it will appear in the highest degree *unscientific* to reject phenomena that could not possibly be due to imposture, and to ignore the hundreds of corroborative tests by other equally competent observers, and then, after this, to call such observers (by implication) fools or lunatics![30]

Using similar logic, Wallace was impressed by a photograph of him with his deceased mother (see photo caption at the beginning of this chapter). He wrote:

I sat three times, always choosing my own position. Each time a second figure appeared in the negative with me. The first was a male figure with a short sword, the second a full-length figure, standing apparently a few feet on one side and rather behind me, looking down at me and holding a bunch of flowers. At the third sitting, after placing myself, and after the prepared plate was in the camera, I asked that the figure would come close to me. The third plate exhibited a female figure standing *close* in front of me, so that the drapery covers the lower part of my body. I saw all the plates developed, and in each case the additional figure started out the moment the developing fluid was poured on, while my portrait did not become visible till, perhaps, twenty seconds later. I recognized none of these figures in the negatives; but the moment I got the proofs, the first glance showed me that the third plate contained an unmistakable portrait of my mother—like her both in features and expression; not such a likeness as a portrait taken during life, but a somewhat pensive, idealized likeness—*yet still, to me, an unmistakable likeness.*[31]

Sir Arthur Conan Doyle, an ardent Spiritualist and admirer of Wallace,[32, 33] said that "the second portrait, though indistinct, was also recognized by Dr. Wallace[34] as a picture of his mother. The first 'extra' of a man was unrecognized."

Other observers claimed that Hudson was a fraud and

used a sophisticated double-exposure technique to create the ghost-like image.[35]

~

Wallace went to great lengths to document and defend his spiritual journey.

> The majority of people today have been brought up in the belief that miracles, ghosts, and the whole series of strange phenomena here described cannot exist; that they are contrary to the laws of nature; that they are the superstitions of a bygone age; and that therefore they are necessarily either impostures or delusions. There is no place in the fabric of their thought into which such facts can be fitted. When I first began this inquiry it was the same with myself. The facts did not fit into my then existing fabric of thought. All my preconceptions, all my knowledge, all my belief in the supremacy of science and of natural law were against the possibility of such phenomena. Every other possible solution was tried and rejected. Unknown laws of nature were found to be of no avail when there was always an unknown intelligence behind the phenomena—an intelligence that showed a human character and individuality, and an individuality which almost invariably claimed to be that of some person who had lived on earth, and who, in many cases, was able to prove his or her identity. Thus, little by little, a place was made in my fabric of thought, first for all such well-attested facts, and then, but more slowly, for the spiritualistic interpretation of them.[36]

Wallace was adamant that spiritual phenomena are "natural."

> I argued for all the phenomena, however extraordinary, being really "natural" and involving no alteration whatever in the ordinary laws of nature.[37]

And he suggested that spirits, like nature, reflected a form of "survival of the fittest."

The organic world has been carried on to a high state of development, and has been ever kept in harmony with the forces of external nature, by the grand law of "survival of the fittest" acting upon ever varying organizations. In the spiritual world, the law of the "progression of the fittest" takes its place, and carries on in unbroken continuity that development of the human mind which has been commenced here.[38]

Ah, the "survival of the fittest." There is a contentious and ongoing debate about whether Charles Darwin is guilty of plagiarism by stealing Wallace's Theory of Evolution by Natural Selection.[39] The evidence against Darwin is moderately strong, although hotly debated. True or false, Wallace never complained that he was done wrong. Just the opposite, he gave the older and better-placed Darwin ample praise for his classic *The Origin of Species*, and was seemingly content to allow Darwin the challenge of promoting the controversial theory to an often critical audience. If I could only have a decent conversation with Wallace, I would like to know his take on the question of priority and whether he bears a grudge against Darwin.

There was, however, one theory on which Wallace and Darwin disagreed strongly—whether natural selection applied to people.

Put simply, Darwin felt that natural selection accounted for the existence of all life on Earth, up to, and *including*, *Homo sapiens*.

Wallace disagreed, arguing that natural selection accounted for all life up to, but *not including*, *Homo sapiens*. The two men never resolved this major difference of opinion.[40]

Wallace summed up Darwin's position:

[Darwin concluded that] Man's whole nature — physical, mental, intellectual, and moral — was developed from the lower animals by means of the same laws of variation and survival; and, as a consequence of this belief . . . there was no difference in *kind* between man's nature and animal nature, but only one of degree.[41]

And Wallace was equally clear in promoting his own theory invoking the intervention of a "different agency."

[I believe] that there is a difference in kind, intellectually, and morally, between man and other animals; and that while [man's] body was undoubtedly developed by the continuous modification of some ancestral animal form, some different agency, analogous to that which first produced organic *life*, and then originated consciousness, came into play in order to develop the higher intellectual and spiritual nature of man.[42]

∽

On what evidence did Wallace base his argument that a "different agency" was responsible for *Homo sapiens*?

According to Wallace, man has countless abilities and skills that go beyond mere evolutionary survival.

Wallace considered the specific evolutionary anomalies of the human body, and drew attention to our naked skin, the sophisticated physiology of the human hand and foot, as well as the size and abilities of the human brain. He included speech on his list, as well as our highly developed intellect.

For all these characteristics Wallace gave credit to supernatural powers.

Wallace deliberately never mentioned god to explain why *Homo sapiens* are human—indeed he was adamantly areligious and had little patience for organized faiths.[43] Nevertheless he employed a series of euphemisms that sound suspiciously god-like, at least in the context of the three stern desert religions: "Overruling Intelligence," "some other power," "some intelligent power," "a superior intelligence," "a controlling intelligence," "higher intelligences," "different individual intelligence," and "one Supreme Intelligence."[44]

The conundrum is that Wallace was, and actively positioned himself as, a scientist, not a theologian or philosopher. He strove for scientific proof of various phenomena, not only his "higher intelligences" concept but also such slippery ideas as Spiritualism and the ability to communicate with the dead.

He recognized that sometimes truths, as he saw them, might be difficult to prove, but they nevertheless exist.

> It is more probable, that the true law lies too deep for us to discover it; but there seems to me, to be ample indications that such a law does exist.[45]

This aspect of Wallace's thinking fits neatly with his belief in Spiritualism. I want to quiz him about this, and learn what his life is like as a spirit.

Wallace's belief in Spiritualism gave me hope that I might contact him if I could find a suitably talented medium.

My first thought was to seek a medium around Poole, in Dorset, where Wallace is buried.

Being near Wallace's decaying body is, of course, a senseless notion if you adhere to the first Tenet of Spiritualism—the spirit has no fixed abode and is "everywhere." Sort of like the internet.

Nevertheless, I Googled "mediums poole dorset uk" and got a dozen leads. There are commonalities among the people listed:

- Most of the mediums are women, mostly middle-aged, and from their photos seem like pleasant people who wouldn't draw a second glance if you saw them at your neighborhood Starbucks.
- Some have big hair.
- They have families, and often have other occupations.
- All have personal mission statements—how they got the gift, their desire to help others.
- They employ a variety of techniques and concepts—psychic readings, clairvoyance, clairaudience, past-life regression, spiritual counseling, aromatherapy, tarot, aura, reiki, inner light, crystal, pendulums, angels, drumming.
- They emphasize beneficial outcomes, particularly bereavement support, healing, and self-empowerment.
- They never promise specific results, but happily post comments from pleased clients.
- And most of the mediums in Dorset, and throughout the United Kingdom and United States for that matter, give regular clairvoyant and psychic demonstrations for Spiritual church groups and parties.[46]

I wrote to two of the Dorset-based mediums, briefly outlining my quest. Neither responded. I did, however, have better luck with mediums in London, Indonesia, and Switzerland.

The Conversation *with* Spirits

Part I – Wallace Visits the Dormitory

In London I sign up for a one-day workshop involving shamanism and voice. I want to try to give my logical left brain a rest, and hope for lots of drumming, perhaps even a trance or two. Instead I learn of a medium who might be able to help me contact Alfred Russel Wallace.

Over lunch I speak with Susan. She's a psychic healer. I mention my interest in speaking with Wallace and she says, "You've got to meet my friend Rita."

Well, that's how the world works. Rita Congera is a part-time medium (her day job is senior communications officer for a large financial institution). She doesn't advertise and only works by referral. We speak on the phone and I give her some background about my connection with Wallace. I don't want to tell her too much, but she says she needs something to work with. She asks if I am in touch with spirits. "No," I reply, "but I'm interested." Rita says that I have more sensitivity to such things than I think. "My father was intrigued by Edgar Cayce," I tell her, referring to a prominent (and perhaps fraudulent) American psychic. She hasn't heard the name.

I meet Rita at the Prêt à Manger opposite the Russel Square tube station in London, and take her to my wife's nearby dorm room.

> Her first comment is, *"Somebody's died here. Maybe not in this room, but perhaps on this floor."*

What an interesting way to begin a conversation with people you've just met.

> *"Do you smell something like lemon?"*

I do, my wife Monique doesn't. The soap used by cleaners, we agree.

Rita wants to "cleanse" the room of external, possibly impure energy. Most Western psychics similarly feel that every space (and every psychic accessory, like a pendulum or crystal ball) gathers psychic dust (my phrase) that can influence a reading. I stop her when she gets out the incense. "It's a no-smoking facility. Sorry."

> *"No problem."*

She shoos us out into the hallway while she purifies the space.

Rita starts like the mediums at the Spiritual Association of Great Britain. Monique and I sit on the edge of the bed; Rita sits in the desk chair and speaks to Monique. In a normal voice, she mentions a man named John or Jonathan, a farmer, who smokes a pipe. Rita is "away," apparently talking with her spirit guide, but she is present. She is double-tasking, like talking while driving.

The names John and Jonathan mean nothing to Monique, nor can she remember a farmer in the family.

> "There's a legal document, it's important to read every word and understand it fully."

Monique's family is dealing with a complicated real estate sale that is part of an inheritance.

> "Be careful of diet. Problems with digestion, maybe an ulcer or allergy."

Correct, Monique has some food allergies. So do millions of other people. Cynics might say this is the kind of fishing statement that is true for most people. Susceptible people, however, will accept it as an insight—"Yes! I can't digest gluten!"

> "He's protecting you. Proud of you."

But all of this is inconclusive and unconvincing. After Rita offers some more details, Monique half-heartedly speculates that, although he had a different name, the person might be her grandfather.

Then Rita speaks to me.

> "Your wife is very intelligent and she too has ability to publish a work of great integrity."

Well, Monique's working on a PhD. But then Rita knows that. And I find it strange that she speaks about Monique in the third person, instead of addressing her directly.

> "So many theories left to explore and that is a key

> part of the human mind—challenge and ask questions to share what we learn with others."

Nice truism. Unclear whether Rita is referring to Monique or has already started to channel Wallace.

Rita then turns to me.

> "There is a man in a checked shirt. He protects you."

My, all of these spirits must be very busy protecting all of their descendants.

The man she describes could be my Uncle Joe, but I have to stretch my imagination to make her few clues fit. Her comments don't resonate. (Rita later tells me to "challenge everything, but don't overanalyze." Useful advice from a medium.)

But I hadn't invited Rita to come across London to get platitudes about how our unrecognized ancestors are protecting us. I am restless. It is time for the main event—trying to contact Wallace.

> "I see bookshelves. A room filled with books. Overflowing with books on tables, on the floor."

Not convincing, and confusing. Is Rita describing Wallace's study or mine? Wallace was a writer and collector; no doubt his study was a jumble of books, papers, and curious objects. I'm a writer as well, she knows that. And writers, by definition, collect books. In my (neat and orderly) study in Switzerland I have some twenty meters of bookshelves, with a similar quantity stored in the garage and basement—books about South America, Micronesia, Africa, eco-botany, brain physiology—all stored away due to lack of shelf space.[47]

Come on, Rita, let's get back to Wallace.

"Do you have a photo of Wallace?"

I open my book and show her what he looked like.

"And anything you carried with you on your travels?"

I let her handle a small Ganesha amulet that has been on my backpack for many decades. This Ganesha has seen what I've seen, lived what I've lived.

"I see you in the jungle, with your footprints covering Wallace's footprints."

Too obvious, a cliché. Yes, I was following his footsteps through Southeast Asia.

"A tall tree. Is this a tree he would have written about?"

Wallace saw a zillion trees. And in many of them lived the birds of paradise, the orangutans, the butterflies and beetles that he collected.

"There's a connection between you two, he's aware of that."

OK, now we're getting started. Wallace is aware of my interest in his life!

"He saw so many things in different ways."

Yes.

> "He has a strong spiritual side."

I had mentioned that earlier, so no points.

> "He combined science and humanism, so many money problems, because of lack of money he couldn't achieve all his plans. He was poor but had experiences."

Now this is interesting. She's correct that Wallace was never financially secure. Let's give Rita the benefit of the doubt and say that she hadn't gone to Wikipedia to look up anything about Wallace's life.

> "He's speaking calmly, not arrogant, humble, pockets are empty, he struggled."

True. That could have been easily ascertained by a quick Google check. I doubt Rita had done the research, but had I inadvertently tipped her off?

> "Not all of his paths made public, information has been lost."

Like all mediums, Rita speaks in fragmented phrases that can be interpreted in various ways. When transcribing our conversation I hesitate to put her comments into logical grammatical structure for fear of introducing my own bias.

Then Rita goes into a trance. Her posture changes to become more upright, and her voice changes tone, becoming slower, more studied. She is in a place we might call "elsewhere." Her comments become even more abstruse—sometimes she continues to speak as if filtering them through her own voice or that of her spirit guide, yet frequently (and somewhat frighteningly) she seems to be channeling Wallace directly, without the filter of an intermediary—her voice takes on a masculine tone and her comments reflect a vaguely Victorian structure. And, as with all mediums I've consulted, her observations often come out in sound bites, rarely complete or coherent sentences. Sometimes it's as if James Joyce or Tom Wolfe is on the other end of the line.

> "Lots of beetles."

Too obvious, that's the title of my book—*An Inordinate Fondness for Beetles*—sitting right there on the desk.

> *"Things are here for a purpose, not for us but for a divine purpose, he sought a higher level, indefinable state, a higher state, and would have been unable to tell about these at the time for fear of retribution."*

How exciting. A long, wandering, complete sentence. Here she's paraphrasing him again, but the content is fascinating and relates to Wallace's belief that some "superior intelligence" has been at work in creating *Homo sapiens*. (See The Setup section of this chapter.)

I ask about his relationship with Darwin.

> *"Wallace extended his hand to Darwin but not reciprocated."*

She's paraphrasing again. More importantly, what does this mean?

> *"He saw things that Darwin didn't see. Each person brought something new—but like life, some theories can grow and evolve and some don't change, like gravity. There are things we cannot measure in our bodies, just as he learned from Darwin's teaching, as others learn from him."*

Ambiguous, but fascinating. What startles me is that this sounds like Wallace's voice, his speech pattern, his beliefs.

> *"His theory could only go so far and couldn't capture all lessons of evolution, aware that science couldn't account for all his questions—mind and soul in each of us cannot be measured by science."*

I am thrilled. I am uneasy. I am impressed. I don't know what to think. This is Wallace at his essence. Unless Rita is reading my mind, giving me what I want to hear? And that in itself is intriguing—the idea that psychics are adept at telepathy and interpreting another person's thoughts and emotions. But still, the voice seems to be that of Wallace.

I ask again about Wallace's relationship with Darwin, whether he held any animosity toward him.

> *"Curious relationship with Darwin, each had his own task to do and his own depth of understanding, connected in spirit world but aware of competition."*

I'm intrigued by this continued shift into full sentences. Again, she's mixing paraphrase with what sounds like direct statement. I wonder whether Rita has read about the Wallace-Darwin controversy concerning which man should get credit for developing the Theory of Natural Selection. It's something I have written about extensively—one could make a strong case that Darwin, with the help of his friends, deliberately stole priority for the theory from Wallace. Or perhaps I had inadvertently mentioned it earlier. Had I said something like, "Wallace developed the Theory of Natural Selection and got ripped off by Darwin" and Rita adapted and adopted that concept during the reading?

But Rita/Wallace isn't finished talking about the theory. It is almost as if I am the first person to ask about this for quite a while, and Wallace is anxious to get it all out. *Finally, an interlocuter!* Wallace has found a pal, or at least someone willing to listen to his stories. The result is a rambling monologue that nonetheless is a delight to listen to.

> *"There is a bigger lesson in the theory, Darwin's theory did not look at evolution of mind, and the spiritual soul, and one can search in libraries for these answers but the more you look the more they are like riddles, you must read me and confuse yourself further or find that head space. Your mind is like a complex jigsaw and you spend so long looking for missing pieces. Answers will be found when you let go of things you know you must let go of. Teachings will help countless others, and each pupil will take what he needs, some questions you can never find answers to and don't spend your life trying to find those pieces because you have many roads to walk and I will watch."*

At this point I'm flabbergasted.[48] First, Wallace talks about the intellectual disagreement between himself and Darwin. And then he switches to the "you" form. Is he using the modern construct "you" to refer to "all of us"? Or is he speaking specifically to me? Based on the last line "I will watch," I choose to think he's talking to me. My ego is flying. *Wallace is looking after me!*

Before we started, Rita told me that there might come a point where she would be in a trance and start to tire. When that happened, she asked me to speak up and ask Wallace (or her spirit guide) to release her. After twenty minutes she's starting to slow down, and I realize I had better speed things up. I change the topic to Ali. "What was Wallace's relationship with Ali?"

> *"Ali was a friend."*

"Beings of a Like Mental Nature to Ourselves" | 53

Come on Wallace, give me more.

> "When we leave here it's not a big party in God's house."

What does that mean? And why is Wallace using a religious concept?

> "Ali was lost, his path went in a different direction."

That's pretty vague. This is getting frustrating. I want to shout: *Speak clearly, Wallace! Stop these evasive platitudes!*

> "Look at changing the question—do your own research."

"Wallace, I don't understand. I'm asking about your relationship with Ali. I want to speak with Ali, find his descendants." This seems to wake Wallace up. And he gets angry.

> "*You have asked this question* [see following chapter, "The Search for Ali"] *for many years. Some things are meant to be out of the light. This was a strong, personal bond, someone I was very strongly close to. Feel very sad.*"

What do you mean "out of the light"? This is beginning to sound like a cover-up. Something sordid? What's going on?

> "*I know we are in different places for his place is not with me but I know his soul is with God.*"

Now I'm totally freaked out (terrible phrase, I know, but that's the only way I can describe my feelings). Wallace alludes to a secret that he doesn't want to talk about. And

Wallace, who never professed to having a religion, again makes a reference to God. Curiouser and curiouser.

Of course, I'm guilty of reading things into the conversation that might not be Wallace's intention. I'm guilty of analyzing each ungrammatical phrase for meaning and literal "truth." I'm guilty of putting my own spin on this. I'm guilty of believing I'm actually talking with Wallace's spirit.

Rita is getting tired. It might be time for Wallace to let her go.

But Wallace seems to be enjoying this. He goes off on a tangent and starts talking botany.

> *"Science of flowers fascinates me, nothing more beautiful than bees pollinating freshly opened flowers and what happens subsequently—honey, nectar of flower. Yellow flower."*[49]

Wallace is enjoying this! He doesn't want to leave. He gives me another ego boost.

> *"Keep asking your questions, Paul, and sometimes check if they are the right questions."*

Life advice from Wallace! But then he brings me down to earth.

> *"There comes a time to stop asking questions."*

Is he speaking in general terms? Or commenting specifically about my questions relating to his relationship with Ali? Questions about what?

> *"When you do ask questions, try to make them the right questions."*

Time to finish up. "Thank you Wallace. You can release the medium."

"*Thank you. I am honored.*"

Wallace is honored? To talk with me? That I've followed him for most of my adult life? That my writings have helped stimulate a resurgence of interest in Wallace and his achievements? That I've given him a few minutes of respite from his daily routine in the otherworld? I wonder what else he might have been doing if he wasn't speaking with me? Learning classical Greek? Watching reruns of *Doctor Who*?

I again suggest we should wrap things up. I'm getting concerned about Rita, who is visibly fatigued.

But Wallace doesn't want to leave. I'm reminded of the famous "Buona Sera" scene in *The Barber of Seville* when the unwelcome Don Basilio repeatedly says he's leaving, but never actually goes out the door.[50] He sings over and over, "I'm leaving now," and the others, increasingly frustrated, repeatedly reply, "But you don't go."

> "*Adventure, so many layers and levels, one can get lost in intricacies, don't punish yourself that you want to pursue all of them.*"

I'm reminded of my imaginary conversation with Wallace in the final chapter of *An Inordinate Fondness for Beetles*. Some of my finest writing, I say humbly. "Wallace, you need to release this medium."

> "*I am with you, it pleases me that you learn what I learned, but that is the joy of life.*"

He doesn't want to leave, but Rita is exhausted. I have to get tough. "Wallace, time to let the medium go."

> *"No two paths are the same."*

And he's gone. Rita shakes. Her body vibrates, as if awakening from a nap. She has no idea what transpired and I give her some highlights. She is surprised by both the content and length of the experience.

> *"For me to go into a trance there has to be some resonance, some empathy, otherwise my spirit guides wouldn't allow it,"* she says.

I phone Rita the next day.

> *"After I left you last night, I listened to the recording of the session,"* she says. *"I had goosebumps. I've never had an experience like that."*

"Why was it so strong?"

> *"You and Wallace had a connection."*

Part II – The Family of Shamans in Timor

I believe in enhanced serendipity. I find that when I precipitate an action, unexpected doors often open.

I am in Kupang, the capital of the Indonesian province of East Nusa Tenggara. This is the far east of Indonesia, much closer to Australia than to the nation's capital of Jakarta, three time zones distant. It is a region seldom visited by sophisticated residents of Sumatra, Java, and Borneo, whose attention is more likely to turn to the bright lights of Singapore than to the less-developed periphery of their country. Nevertheless, Kupang is a city of 350,000, a bit sleepy but blessed by simple and good seafood restaurants and several comfortable hotels.

Captain Bligh spent 47 days here after that emasculating mutiny on the *Bounty* incident in 1789. More to the point, Alfred Russel Wallace visited Kupang, and Timor, the island on which it sits, several times, finding it without much biological interest.

I am checking in to one of those good hotels at the same time as another man, who is wearing the white shirt, sober tie, and dark trousers of an airline pilot. We start chatting.

It doesn't take long for the conversation to turn to spirits. Oh, what a predictable bore I am. My new friend's name is Haryadi Meddiyanto, but he asks to be called Edith; he was apparently unaware that this is a woman's name (my mother's, in fact) in the West. We have dinner together and I ask if he knows a good medium. "Sure." He calls his friend Boy, who lives in Attambua, a small town near the border with Timor Leste. Yes, Boy thinks he can help me. The name Attambua, he says, means "place of mediums." I book the one-hour flight for the following day.

Boy meets me at the Attambua airport, wearing his starched white civil aviation shirt. He's an information officer at the airport, but it's an easy job since few visitors seek information. We have a cup of tea and plan my program for the 24 hours I will spend in the region.

"*Let's go,*" he says.

"But don't you have to work?"

"*I called my boss and told him I had an important visitor.*"

We hire a taxi. Our first stop is the village of Bolan, two hours to the south, where I have the name of a woman who knows about a local healer, Laubertus Mahak Muti, 82. A nice old man, thin to the point of emaciation, partially deaf, wearing a worn T-shirt and a faded blue and white sarong. He's primarily a healer but can predict when someone is going to die. We have a cup of tea, give him a donation, and thank him for his time.

Interesting stuff, but of no use in my specific quest.

That evening I meet Boy's family and we discuss my interest in speaking with Alfred Russel Wallace.

"*I'll arrange it,*" he says. "*I'll pick you up tomorrow morning.*"

Boy comes from a family of shamans.

"*It's a family gift. It just comes, not from meditation.*"

Earlier, Boy explained that during a flood, his grandfather prayed and the waters went around the village, saving dozens of homes. He could speak with nature spirits, converse with animals. His grandmother used Christian prayer to heal and exorcise evil spirits. Boy treated a man with nails in his stomach, a popular black magic infliction that one hears about throughout Indonesia. The X-ray showed seven nails, but doctors couldn't operate because the five-centimeter-long nails were moving. Boy said a prayer and the man, now a policeman near Surabaya on the island of Java, vomited the nails.

Doesn't Boy get frightened?

"*Not really,*" he says. "*Most people are afraid of talking with dead spirits, but we're used to it.*"

Boy and his family are Christian. I've had similar conversations with mediums who identify as Animist, Moslem, Jewish, Wiccan, Hindu, Buddhist, and Spiritualist—people with various, sometimes strong, religious beliefs. At times, when I speak with people who don't believe in spirits, there are fireworks. Many of those individuals, particularly evangelical Christians, shudder and scold me when I tell them about my interest in mediums and spirits. "That's the Devil's work. Blasphemy," they say. I ask them what they believe in. "God, Jesus, and the Bible," they reply. So, I point out that what they believe is a just a series of myths and parables based on alleged miracles and impossible-to-explain phenomena. Angels and demons. Resurrection. "What's the difference between my interest in mediums and your belief in parting the Red Sea, curing blind Bartimaeus, raising Lazarus from the dead, and turning water into wine? Noah's ark? A virgin birth? I could go on." At this point my interlocutor starts to get either angry or nervous. "Those things are written in the Bible," he might say. "They really happened." And the conversation either breaks down in a standoff or one of us gets sufficiently annoyed to walk away.

As with mediums in other parts of the world, Boy's family and friends wouldn't draw a second glance in the supermarket. Boy studied in the Philippines and brought back an impressive fluency in English and an adopted, distinctively Filipino, prenom. He introduces me to his mother Maria Erni, who works for the government; aunt Silviana Evelin, a businesswoman; and sister Monique, a law student. Silviana knows "if something bad is going to happen" to a person she has just met, but if she tells the person about her premonition the event won't occur. She knows what people will say, who they will marry, when they will divorce. "It's a gift," she says, but also a huge burden. "I'm trying to learn how to 'not see.'" Boy says that on several occasions Silviana was late to catch a plane but she caused the flight to be delayed—mechanical problem, heavy rain, sick pilot—long enough for her to make the flight. She is a sensitive woman, cries easily, and has a major regret that still haunts her. No need to expose it here.

In Ternate, when I was channeling Ali (see following chapter "The Search for Ali") I was impressed to have the Three *Dukuns* working on the case. In Kupang even more people attempt to contact Wallace. Seated on the floor are Silviana, in a red T-shirt; Ewi Gulo, a motorcycle taxi driver—a large man wearing a black Bayern Munich shirt; and Ernestus Bere, a family friend—a short man wearing a white shirt, fake Oakley sunglasses, and holding a Catholic rosary. Seated nearby are Boy and his mother Maria. It is a Five *Dukun* moment.

Ewi is the supervisor, who helps Ernestus into (and out of) a trance. Silviana is a quiet and intense presence, silently adding energy to the group.

Five *Dukuns*. Everyone is talking. I'm trying to listen, take notes on the snatches of Indonesian that I catch, but it's mixed with local dialect and I'm paying most attention to Boy, who is part of the trance group, but also translating for me. It's like a psychic version of a Rossini comic quintet, delicious to listen to, impossible to unravel.

From the beginning it's clear that this challenge might be a bit too much for the group, since they are dealing with a spirit that is geographically distant and speaks English, a foreign language.

All is quiet for a moment. I ask Boy what's going on.

"*They're calling 'Mister Thomas.'*"

"And who might be this 'Mister Thomas?'"

"*I think he's a kind of a spiritual anthropologist,*" Boy says. "*It's not clear, but he's English, I think. They are asking him to help them contact Wallace.*"

Mister Thomas, in spite of perhaps being English, doesn't seem to be able to help (I never did understand who he was), but another spirit enters the conversation, acting as a sort of telephone switchboard operator in the 1940s.

"*You want to contact Mister Wallace?*" the anonymous spirit asks.

So now we have five *dukuns*, a spiritual anthropologist named Mister Thomas, and an additional, unnamed but helpful telephone operator spirit. Seven people/spirits all trying to connect with Wallace. I'm reminded of the Marx

Brothers scene in *Monkey Business* where an overload of people crams into a tiny ship's cabin.

> As politely as addressing a visitor at his home, Boy says, *"Hello, are you Mister Alfred Russel Wallace?"*

Quiet.

> *"Are you there?"*

I'm reminded of the telephone "party line" we had when I was a child in which several households shared the same phone number. It wasn't uncommon to be speaking with someone on a clickety-clack connection, when a neighbor would come on the line. The conversation would go something like this:

"Hello, I'm on the phone."
"Sorry, but who are you?"
"This is Paul."
"Paul who?"
"Is this Harry?"
"Can't hear you."
"Paul, from the green house with the yellow shutters."
"Oh, hi."
"Who do you want to speak with?"
"No problem, I'm already speaking to him."
"Oh, sorry, I thought the call was for me."
"Will you be long?"
"As long as it takes."
"It's okay."
"Yeah, thanks. See you at baseball practice tomorrow."

Boy is the politest medium I've met. As the only English speaker among the Five *Dukuns*, he's the designated intermediary:

> "I'm sorry to bother you, sir, but Mister Paul is a writer from Switzerland and wants to know you more."

I look at the participants in this little drama. They are intent, concentrating. I am once again grateful that they have given their time and energy to help me on my quest. The room is quiet.

> "Hello, Mister Wallace, are you there?"

Rustling. Ernestus shuffles and twists. Grunting sounds.

> Silviana says, "*He's already here, entering medium.*"

Boy speaks slowly, as if talking with a child.

> "*We are in Indonesia, the island of Timor. The year is 2018,*" he says, hoping Wallace is listening.

Ernestus is grimacing.

> "Hello, Mister Wallace," Boy says. "I know you were in Kupang and Dili. We are in between those towns, in Attambua. Maybe you came here."

Ernestus is pointing to his mouth.

> "Wallace is surprised that he can come," Boy says.

I figure I had better join the conversation. "Hello Wallace, this is Paul. I've been following you and I'm happy to meet you."

What a truly idiotic thing to say. But what else could I have said?

> Boy says: *"He doesn't want to speak. We must do it at night, cannot do it during the day. The spirit time and our time are different."*

Ah, once again, as I see with Amalia in Ternate (following chapter, "The Search for Ali"), the spirits keep office hours.

> Ewi says, *"I see him a little bald. Thin and tall."*

Yes, Wallace was thin and tall.[51] No, he wasn't bald, Wallace died with a full head of hair. Do I count this as a semi aha moment?

> *"He died wearing a jacket."*

No idea if that's correct. But this group seems especially focused on Wallace's death.

Boy says he sees Wallace standing in a doorway.

> *"He wants to speak, but can't. Hands folded in front. He is confused, friendly, and surprised—he doesn't know why he's here."*

Ernesto weaves and bobs, holds his head. Tries to speak but is mute. Moves his hand like a variation of sign language.

Ernesto is silent, but animated. Boy senses what Ernesto is sensing, and interprets.

> *"Wallace was in trouble,"* Boy says. *"Somebody kidnapped him and shot him in the back of his head."*

I'm unsure whether Boy is getting his information from Ernestus or directly from Wallace.

> "The bullet exited his temple."

Well, there are several problems with that scenario. First, there is no record of Wallace having been kidnapped. He put himself into self-imposed exile many times, but that's different, surely. And, if he had been shot as Ernestus describes, he surely would have been killed immediately, yet we know that Wallace died peacefully at home in 1913, age 90.

Boy changes the narrative. He self-corrects.

> "He didn't die. Just hurt his head."

I change the subject. "Wallace, do you know what happened to Ali after you left him in Singapore?"

I find two things curious.

First, Boy assumes Wallace's spirit is in England, and has taken pains to explain to Wallace where we are in the world. This surprises me because I would have thought that spirits float about like Instagram photos—they are not tethered to a particular location.

And the fact that the mediums have trouble because they don't speak English confuses me as well. Surely there is a single Psychic-Energy Esperanto that spirits and mediums use to communicate.

I repeat my question about his relationship with Ali.

There is no answer to my direct query.

> "He goes to another island, a place with fossils."

Oh dear. Is there no such thing as a concrete answer to a question?

> "He says you are looking for something. He says you should tell the Ali story."

This contradicts what Rita said, in which Wallace said I should forget about the Ali story.

> "Wallace died holding something hard, like iron, or stone. Maybe a fossil."

Again, a fossil. On my desk at home I have a fossil given to me by the current owner of the house in Usk, Wales, where Wallace was born and where he lived until the age of five. Perhaps Wallace started his love of natural history by collecting a similar fossil? No doubt he was fascinated by fossils, but he wrote relatively little about them. And in the later years of his life he lived in Broadstone, Dorset, near the Jurassic Coast of southern England that is famous for fossils.

> "He was holding this fossil or stone and researching it, but died before finishing his research."

It's time to stop the séance. Maria and Boy have to get to work. I have a plane to catch. Yes, I do consider asking Silviana to delay the flight, but figure she has done enough work today.

"I don't agree with the shooting and kidnapping story," I tell Boy as we drove to the airport.

Then he said something that makes sense.

> "I think Wallace was holding his head because he was sick, not because he was shot."

Now, here's wild speculation on my part. It's well known that Wallace suffered from regular bouts of malaria. During one of the most serious attacks, while on the island of Halmahera, near Ternate, Wallace conceived of the mechanism of evolution by natural selection, what later became known as the "survival of the fittest." His "faithful companion" Ali nursed him back to health and, when back in Ternate, Wallace wrote a ten-page scientific paper detailing his theory, commonly called the Ternate Paper. He then sent this ready-for-publication paper to Charles Darwin for comment.

Malaria provokes severe headaches. Could malaria, as opposed to a bullet, be the cause of the extreme cranial suffering that Ernestus experienced while channeling Wallace?[52] Another possible but similarly implausible explanation is that during one séance with Mrs. Guppy, the spirits were playing a guitar that had been placed on the table. During the performance, Wallace received a severe blow on his temple and blood flowed. "It was my own fault entire," said Wallace. "I broke the conditions—the orders were to join hands; and I was very curious to know what sort of hand was playing the guitar, and that was the cause of the blow."

I thank Boy for his hospitality and energy in helping me with my quest. Once again, I am overwhelmed by the generosity of Indonesians to help a stranger with strange requests.

"You know my Auntie Silviana was expecting you."

"What do you mean?"

"She had a dream that an important foreigner would be coming to our home."

I demur. Just a bit of flattery.

> "She recognized you when you walked in. Gave her a shock."

Well, I do that to some women.

> "This isn't over, you know," Boy says. "Sometimes the spirit comes back at night. Now that we've made contact, it's likely that we'll be in further contact with Wallace."

"That would be great, Boy. Send me an email if you get more information."

> "No need for email. I'll send it to you via a dream. That way you can speak directly with Wallace."

Part III – Wallace Rambles Along Regent's Canal

As I had with Rita Congera, I find Nasrin Moazenchi through the recommendation of a friend in London. "She's terrific," he had said. Enough endorsement for me.

We meet at the Camden Town tube station and walk to the path adjacent to the nearby Regent's Canal, a lovely tree-lined stroll through London.

Unlike Brigitte Favre (Part IV) or Rita Congera, who are comfortably mainstream, Nasrin has esoteric interests and regularly refers to the Akashic Records and the Knowledge Book, sources of ancient, perhaps alien, only recently revealed truths and wisdom. She invokes Archangel Gabriel and is a fan of Donald Trump, who she says is a descendant of Saint Germain, a legendary Theosophical spiritual master of ancient wisdom. Nasrin, a thin, attractive woman with a sparkle of energy and curiosity, shows me some of the paintings she created while speaking with spirits and extraterrestrial beings. Two things strike me. The first is that her artwork is evocative and professional. The second is that each of the dozens of paintings she shows me is different. Usually when a medium paints such images she creates variations on a theme; each of Nasrin's paintings are unique.

It is a weekday, but nevertheless the path is busy with strollers and joggers. We pass permanently moored houseboats and Georgian-styled mansions. Quiet electric tourist boats cruise past. It is a lovely place to escape the hustle of London, but I am concerned it is too busy for psychic communication. "Won't there be too much disturbance for you?" I ask.

"Should be okay," Nasrin says. *"Let's sit on that bench over there."*

The setting is surprisingly tranquil, with foliage and trees on both banks. Almost tropical. But I get distracted by people walking just in front of us. I would have preferred a quieter, more secluded spot for this attempt to speak with Wallace. It doesn't seem to bother Nasrin.

Like Brigitte Favre (see Part IV—"Wallace, the Social Reformer, in the City That Hosts the United Nations and Hundreds of Humanitarian and Environmental Action Groups"), Nasrin doesn't want any information about Wallace before we begin. And, like Brigitte, Nasrin doesn't go into a trance. Wallace speaks to Nasrin in snippets of information, spurts of words that are open to various interpretations. I've edited the transcript to put a bit of structure into the dialogue.

"Tall, young man. Long hands. Kind. Long face like a triangle. Hair is short, wavy, dark brown. Eyes dark brown. Stylish, dressed in white shirt, brown suit. No tie. He keeps one hand in his pocket. Shiny shoes."

"Short, wavy hair?" Brigitte Favre also mentions "curly" hair. Looking at photos of him at various ages I'd go along with "wavy." But Nasrin's wrong about the brown eyes; Wallace had blue eyes.

I ask Nasrin whether she can actually see Wallace and Ali.

> *"They make themselves look human when they want you to see them, because they are energy."*

So, if I understand correctly, Wallace and Ali have no form, no substance as spirit, but just as the Invisible Man wrapped himself in bandages when he wanted to be visible, Wallace has dressed in an appropriate manner for such an auspicious encounter with Nasrin and me.

"He seems quite elegant," I say.

> *"Not all spirits are beautiful,"* Nasrin cautions.

Might as well get stuck in. "How did Wallace come up with the Theory of Natural Selection?"

> *"He had a dream, asked 'where do we come from?'"*

Ah, Wallace's famous dream. As Wallace describes it, during a malaria dream, drenched in sweat and almost delirious, he dreamt of Robert Malthus and his ideas about the limits of population growth. From that philosophical reverie, Wallace recognized the key to the Theory of Evolution by Natural Selection. It's one of the most famous productive nightmare episodes in history. But Nasrin was totally unaware of this event. So where does Nasrin get the image of a dream? Nasrin has no way of knowing about this incident. Extraordinary.

> *"In the dream he saw another dimension."*

Another dimension. Is Nasrin referring to the revolutionary impact of Wallace's theory? Or more like she is simply adding her own personal spin to the conversation? She is a firm believer in multiple dimensions and extraterrestrial influences.

> *"Thinking about a theory, but wasn't sure."*

"And his relationship with Darwin?"

> *"Mister Wallace said he answered your questions before."*

What?! *He answered your questions before.* Is she referring to the séance I had with Rita some months earlier? Did I tell Nasrin that I had "spoken" with him previously?

But then something else strikes me. And it bothers me. Am I becoming a nuisance? An unwanted groupie? Is Wallace getting tired of me asking the same questions via different mediums?

> *"But again, he says he admires Darwin as a teacher and scientist and they can meet over there whenever they want to as they both are from the same galaxy."*

Other mediums have used similar terms, but I am still too restrained and mainstream to be comfortable when I'm told spirits are living in a different "galaxy." But who's to say? Maybe aliens *did* help the Egyptians build the pyramids.

"Be more specific."

> *"Wallace and Darwin were together when alive.*

> *Wallace had big affection for Darwin, a big fan, but it wasn't all right.*

Now, this is interesting. What to make of the statement "wasn't all right." My interpretation: Although Wallace had a legitimate case to claim priority for the Theory of Natural Selection, he ceded the fight to Charles Darwin, who Wallace felt, perhaps, was better placed (both in terms of status and temperament) to promote the concept. Wallace dedicated *The Malay Archipelago* to Darwin, and even titled his own book on evolution *Darwinism*. For his part, Darwin only grudgingly acknowledged Wallace's work, and then only at the insistence of his friend, the geologist Charles Lyell.

> *"Both of them made big mistakes. Misunderstanding about philosophy and theory. Like Big Bang. We wanted to help humanity."*

Nasrin is shifting between third person observer—"Both of them," and first-person Wallace—"We wanted to help humanity." Confusing.

Nevertheless, this comment resonates with what Rita said. And there's no way that Nasrin would have known this. My interpretation is that the "misunderstanding" relates to some basic differences in how the evolution works. And indeed, the two men disagreed about several things, including whether natural selection applies to people (see The Setup of this chapter). Or am I reading too much into it?

I asked about Wallace's interest in Spiritualism.

> *"He came again to this world, he incarnated as a woman. He doesn't say where."*

Not a direct answer to the question. And impossible to verify.

> *"Now he's not on earth, in another galaxy, still in spirit. Studying and researching in another dimension."*

Elsewhere in Indonesia I had criticized the Ternate mediums for imposing a cultural veneer on the conversation (see following chapter: "The Search for Ali"). Here Nasrin is doing something similar. She firmly believes in distant galaxies, other dimensions, and reincarnation, and is attributing those beliefs to Wallace.

Does Wallace have anything to say to me?

> *"Just wait to have more information. Don't depend just on us* [Wallace and Ali?]. *Not everything we say is true, not true as written in books, always some part missing."*

Good advice for any historian.

> *"He likes you, but asks why do you want to write a book about him?"*

I fumble for an answer. "He's an interesting, kind guy." A useless response.

> *"Wallace says 'thank you,' sends kisses, and gives you a theatrical bow with a flourish."*

Curious. Astounding, really. This resonates with the comments of Brigitte and other mediums who say Wallace said goodbye with a similarly theatrical gesture.

> *"He will come to you if you need him, just ask three times and thank him."*

And the instruction to call him "three times" resonates with the invitation offered by Kanjeng Ratu Kidul (see the chapter "An Invitation to Meet the Mermaid Queen"). Other mediums—Rita, Brigitte, Boy—have also indicated that just as I'm a fan of Wallace, he's a fan of me. Reassuring, great for the ego. But do I dare to believe this? Part of me senses this is more of a generic feel-good medium-speak emotional message than a specific message from a spirit.

> "Wallace and Ali can both help in so many ways."

Then Nasrin jumps back to first person.

> "Even if you just open a book, if you are smart enough you will get it."

> "You have to earn it."

These Hallmark card-like aphorisms remind me of the Joseph Campbell archetype of the Wise Old Man-Mentor figure in the hero's journey.

> "I sense they are very humble."

Nasrin isn't the first to offer this feeling.

Then Wallace surprises me again.

> "What have I done to honor this visit?"

Again, I repeat the platitudes. "I admire him, I think he deserves to be better appreciated."

> "Thank you Nasrin for connecting us," Wallace says.

> "They don't always come," Nasrin says to me.
> "They know me, I know them."

Part IV – Wallace, the Social Reformer, in the City That Hosts the United Nations and Hundreds of Humanitarian and Environmental Action Groups

I have lunch with Christian, an old friend who is a psychiatrist based in Geneva. I explain my desire to contact Alfred Russel Wallace and he suggests I speak with Brigitte Favre, who is both a clinical psychologist and a medium. It is an intriguing combination of two disciplines that resonate, but are rarely professionally practiced by the same person.

Brigitte has two conditions, similar to some other mediums. First, she will not give any guarantee that she will be able to make contact. Second, she doesn't want prior information about him—she prefers to work with a clean slate. Whoops. By the time she tells me this, I had already sent her the following information about Wallace, and his photo.

"Alfred Russel Wallace (1823–1913). British explorer, naturalist, "bug collector," geographer, socialist, spiritualist who explored the Amazon (1848–1852) for four years, and Southeast Asia (1854–1862) for eight."

In that initial email I had added that if time permits (and obviously if the spirits were willing), I'd like to speak with Ali.

I send her this information about Ali, again perhaps more than she wants. I hope this information, full of clues that an intuitive medium can build on, doesn't skew the conversation with Wallace.

"While in Borneo Wallace hired Ali, then 15, as a cook. Ali traveled with Wallace throughout Southeast Asia gaining self-confidence and stature, becoming Wallace's camp manager and main collector. This photo is the only one we have of Ali, taken in Singapore in 1862 when Ali would have been around 22."

Brigitte works out of her home in a leafy Geneva suburb. To me, her consulting room resembles her psychologist persona more than her medium persona—there is a large window looking out to her spacious garden, and on one wall she has hung a painting of Masai warriors and an underwater photo of a lion fish. Brigitte has long curly dark hair, round glasses, and is quietly elegant, articulate, and patient, all that one could ask for in a psychologist or a medium.

Before we begin, I ask Brigitte how she got her gift, how this process works, and what happens when she contacts a spirit. Her answers are similar to comments from other mediums.

> "When you go to spirit our filters go as well. The personality stays and the sense of who you are stays."
>
> "You feel the energy of the spirits, it's a different vibration."
>
> "We don't have the vocabulary to describe what happens. Just feel another presence, try to follow, not to involve my mind."
>
> "Spirits respond to openness."
>
> "I had some ability to feel energy when I was small, but shut it out. I didn't know what to do with it. But things came back as an adult—I was able to do automatic writing, and kept getting messages of unconditional love. I tried to shut it out, but it kept coming back. Then I had a mysterious experience about a friend who had died fourteen years earlier. But it didn't occur to me at the time it was mediumship."

"Do you use mediumship in your psychological counseling?"

"Only if the patient asks for it."

"But surely your ability might help you to understand the patient's situation, particularly during bereavement counseling."

"If I let those things in, then yes, I get some insight to ask better questions."

Brigitte starts.

"Can I link to your energy?" she says to me. *"You can feel energy. You have a quest for spirituality. You say you are skeptical but you are being pushed into the spiritual."*

This is lovely and reassuring, but I've heard similar thoughts from other mediums. I still am not convinced that I have psychic ability. I'm simply dabbling on the fringes of something I don't understand.

"You have a link with people from outside America."

Unclear if she refers to immediate ancestors (eastern Europe) or life experiences. If the latter, then this is a no-brainer; at the most basic level she can see that I'm an American living in Geneva, not to mention my globetrotting lifestyle.

Brigitte explains once again that there are no guarantees she can speak with Wallace. Yet, she goes straight into a conversation with him. She retains consciousness; she is not in a trance, but speaks lucidly, like Nasrin in London, like June in London, and like Rita at the beginning of our session—before she went into a trance.

"Beings of a Like Mental Nature to Ourselves" | 77

> *"Wallace has an understanding about spiritualism. He fought it for a while because he has a scientific mind and took quite a while to accept it. He wanted proof."*

Well, she gets right to the point. Did she pick this up directly from Wallace, or from my thoughts, or from the short description I sent her? I had mentioned his interest in Spiritualism in my earlier note, but hadn't mentioned that Wallace spent decades trying to find scientific evidence for Spiritualism.

> *"I feel a very strong man. He could get obsessed by something and wouldn't stop until he got it. He would go anywhere if there was something to discover."*

Absolutely. But how much of this is intuition from the 26-word summary I sent her?

> *"Spent lots of time on boats. Also enjoyed writing—he wrote journals."*

Yes to both observations.

> *"He asked questions."*

Again, he was a scientist and an explorer, and I had told her that. Explorers ask questions, don't they?

"Brigitte, do you see him? Or how do you get this information?"

> *"No, I don't see him. I feel him. Feel his energy through clairsentience."*

Then Brigitte opens up a new theme, one I hadn't considered.

> "Link with slavery. Not him directly but people he was involved with. He met people who weren't free."

This seems unlikely, but later I did some checking. Wallace wrote about the evils of slavery, perhaps spurred by his friendship with Maarten Dirk van Renesse van Duivenbode, a Dutch merchant who was dubbed the "King of Ternate" because of his wealth, social standing, and influence. Van Duivenbode, it turns out, owned some one hundred slaves, a fact never mentioned by Wallace.

> "Affectionate bond with natives—he had someone, maybe a woman?"

There is no evidence that Wallace had a romantic liaison. But he very well might have. He never mentioned it, and no reason he should have written about such a liaison. Victorian reserve, and all that.

> "Developed love for the people—first thinking the people he met were objects, but he developed a respect and fondness. Learning from them, shift from studying people to interacting with them."

Now this is getting interesting. None of the other mediums approached this theme, and I wonder whether Wallace is telling these things to Brigitte because he thinks that she will understand and interpret his thoughts correctly. A fascinating concept—spirits have different chemistry with different mediums and filter their conversation accordingly. Just like people.[53]

> "Interested in different breeds of people, different bodies and colors, understanding racial backgrounds, wanted to know if body physiology is related to race."

Brigitte and Wallace are entering territory that all the other mediums have ignored—in fact most biographers focus almost entirely on Wallace's achievements in natural history and evolution, and don't look at his interest in ethnography. She is correct—Wallace was intensely interested in culture and characteristics of different races of people. He devoted many pages of *The Malay Archipelago* to describing physical and behavioral differences between people of the Malay race and the Papuan race. While in Asia he collected 57 vocabularies of obscure tribal languages of which he believed "more than half are quite unknown to philologists." He was interested in how language developed and the process of "civilizing the savages," and he was impressed that the villages of rural people in which he was welcomed were more peaceful, safer, and better run than British villages of similar size.

Then, through clairvoyance, she offers a physical description:

> "Long, curly, dark hair, round glasses, quietly elegant. Quite tall."

Pretty close. Interesting that she used the term "elegant." June-Elleni (Part V) says something similar.

> "Studied nature. He shows me tropical plants—triangle shape, big leaves. Certain sap he was interested in. He asked people about their knowledge of plants."

Other mediums, including Rita and Nasrin, also focused on Wallace's interest in plants, while neglecting his interest in insects, birds, and mammals.

> "He wrote a book."

Well, he wrote 23 books. And one of the books was specifically about plants—*Palm Trees of the Amazon*. That this book exists at all is almost a miracle—he lost most of his specimens, notes, and drawings when the ship on which he was sailing back to England from Brazil caught fire and sank in the mid-Atlantic. The sinking ship was carrying thousands of specimens of insects, birds, mammals, and plants that he had collected during his four years on the Amazon and Rio Negro rivers. Before escaping the burning ship, he managed to grab a handful of notes. He and the crew members came close to death during the ten days they spent in a small lifeboat before they were rescued. He wrote the book, as well as an important travel book—*Travels on the Amazon and Rio Negro*—largely from memory.

> "He got sick, some disease, couldn't travel as much as he wanted."

Absolutely. In the next chapter, "The Search for Ali," I document how he was regularly ill or injured, as was Ali.

> "Died at age sixty."

"No, he was ninety," I say. A serious error.

But then Brigitte autocorrects.

> "Where did I get sixty? Mediumship is a translation," she says.

Most mediums say something similar whenever they hit a roadblock. The medium acknowledges that the conversation is not necessarily logical and straightforward, and it's up to the sitter to link the dots.

But then, if the spirit is living as ethereal energy, why should we expect it to speak in logical, grammatically correct sentences?

> "Sixty was a turning point for him. Something happened, couldn't travel as much as he used to. At around sixty he had to spend more time in Asia."

No, at age 60 he was living in the UK; he never returned to Asia. Brigitte tries to regain traction.

> "OK, rephrase. It wasn't clear. At age sixty he had work with laws and government. Fighting for something, to help other people. Trying to change society, laws, and convince people. He didn't succeed as he wanted, he sees it as a failure."

Ah, Brigitte has made a quick and graceful recalculation. More important, Brigitte is the first medium to speak about Wallace's social actions.

Without realizing it she has opened a Pandora's box of themes to explore. Wallace had opinions about an exhausting list of social issues, and was in his sixties when he devoted much of his energy to humanitarian and environmental causes. Not only did he speak out about his solutions for improving the world, he joined (and sometimes led) numerous groups, and he wrote hundreds of articles and opinion pieces on subjects that interested him.

Wallace was hugely prolific and outspoken. Without stopping for breath he wrote about land nationalization, phrenology, glaciation, the evils of slavery (but the benefits of wise colonialism), government aid to science, climatology, land reform, the suffragette movement (he was in favor), smallpox vaccination (against), disarmament, the status of teachers, the possibility of life on Mars (no way, he argued), the age of the Earth, the causes of the ice age, and even that eternally vexing question of whether the Earth is an oblate or prolate spheroid. He argued that explosives should be stored under water, for greenbelts to be created in cities, that historic monuments be protected, the creation of a minimum wage, the need for all manufactured goods to carry labels specifying their component materials, the horror of eugenics and militarism. He wrote about the advantages of implementing a paper money standard, suggested changes in the means of dealing with inherited wealth and trusts, and wrote essays on how to re-establish confidence in the House of Lords and how to revitalize the Church of England.

I'm exhausted just listing his interests. I wonder where he got his energy.

> *"After that he kind of gave up, or he did it in another way."*

It's possible that Wallace might have lost interest in some ideas and continued with others. But he remained opinionated to his death.

I am mindful that mediums say spirits only come when they want to come. I ask Brigitte, "Was it difficult to make contact with Wallace? Why did he come?"

> *"He knows you tried to speak with him previously."*

> *"He came for you."*

> *"You want to rehabilitate something about him."*

> *"He's excited about that, like you could take some of his work further."*

> *"He's excited."*

Again, this is similar to the feel-good feedback that Rita and Nasrin received. I'm flying! Seriously. We're pals!

"Does Wallace have any advice for me?"

> "Go back to same places he went to—to Asia."

Well, I've been doing that for fifty years. And the next trip is planned for four months from now.

"Where is Wallace now?"

> "Now he lives in a place where he can follow his interests, keeps on writing. Not Earth. House with books, like where he used to live."

What a nice view of a parallel universe.

> "He's still very interested in what's going on now and here. Still trying to do things that have an impact on us today, still a scientist trying to help us now, interested in technology."

Now this is fascinating. At the end of *An Inordinate Fondness for Beetles*, I imagine a conversation with Wallace. He's picking up on that and expanding it. And in the conversation with June-Elleni (Part V), Wallace speaks at length about modern technology and scientific advances.

> "Fascinated by modern 'ease of travel.'"

I imagine many things about today's world would fascinate Wallace.

> "He's surprised by the wealth of the planet and worried how things are going, especially pollution. Doesn't understand that with the technology we have why we don't do more for the planet, especially pollution in Asia."

This sounds just like Wallace. And in the 19th century he was already fighting against pollution. It was a time when England suffered severe air pollution, causing Dickens to write in *Bleak House*: "Smoke lowering down from chimney pots, making a soft black drizzle, with flakes of soot as big as full-grown snowflakes—gone into mourning for the death of the sun."

> *"He is honored by your interest. He gives you a 'little bow and touches his forelock,' as a mark of respect, and is pleased that you share his interest and can take his ideas further."*

Absolutely fascinating. How to account for the fact that three mediums have reported that Wallace gave me a theatrical bow and tip of his hat.

And then Wallace goes on a riff about writing.

> *"He could not not write."*

Correct. He wrote 747 published articles and papers (508 of which were scientific papers), and 23 books. Those volumes including topics as diverse as island biology, races of man, spiritualism, palm trees of the Amazon, travel stories, evolution, history, miracles, and memoir.

> *"He was a fan of writing—you can ask his help."*

This is ambiguous, but my ego chooses to believe that he says he's a fan of *my* writing.

> *"He knows you've tried to speak with him."*

Several mediums have mentioned that Wallace knows I've contacted him. Is he flattered that I've tried to contact him, or getting annoyed? He doesn't *have* to answer, after all. Perhaps he really does like me? I sound like a besotted teenager.

"You are both writers."

"I want to thank him."

"He heard you."

❧

I have lunch with Brigitte a few weeks later.

"I've got a present for you," she says.

Brigitte attends a "medium circle" and asked the group to try to obtain information about Wallace. She gave them the same small photo and short description I had given her earlier. She didn't tell them about her earlier contact with Wallace. Based on fleeting images and "feeling," a member of the group tells her the following:

"He wanted to validate theories about origins and evolution. Adamant about his ideas."

Correct, and Brigitte's colleague wouldn't have known this based on the short description she had given them.

"Humanist. Even avant-garde. Ideas ahead of his time. Interested in 'savages,' but not colonialist."

Yes.

"Had a different vision to Darwin regarding evolution."

Absolutely. Again, unlikely she would have known this. This is uncanny; his statement is almost verbatim to what Rita said Wallace told her. Neither Rita nor Brigitte's colleague know about the complexities of the Wallace-Darwin relationship.

The reason I continually ask about Wallace's relationship with Charles Darwin is because the two of them had a wary and complicated bromance. Darwin was older—he departed on the *Beagle* voyage when Wallace was just seven. Darwin was one of the respected elders of the British scientific establishment. Darwin came from a prominent, wealthy, and respected family, while Wallace was middle-class and always had to scrape for money. Darwin went to Cambridge; Wallace left school at the age of 13. And perhaps most important, Darwin and his friends denied Wallace priority for the *Theory of Evolution by Natural Selection*. Wallace never asserted his right to priority, and it is unclear whether he bore a grudge against Darwin. It would appear not (at least not in public), since Wallace dedicated *The Malay Archipelago* to Darwin, titled his own book about evolution *Darwinism*, and was a pallbearer at Darwin's funeral.

"Had personal wealth, but not good with money."

Wrong about the personal wealth. His father graduated in law, but never practiced law; he regularly made bad investments. His mother was from a middle-class English family. The family scraped through. Wallace always had a precarious financial position; later in his life he was in such a dire strait that Darwin had to use his government contacts to get Wallace a state pension. Wallace never got the jobs he applied for (and for which he was admirably suited). And he had no head for finance—he lost a substantial sum (for him) by investing in shady railway stocks.

> "Frustrated about not being published as much as he wanted."

Quite possible (I share his frustration), but his output was nevertheless prodigious.

Part V—Good News. Wallace Is My Spirit Guide

I find June-Elleni Laine through a mutual friend at the College of Psychic Studies in London.

I am careful to tell her only that I want to speak with a 19th-century historical figure. I do not give her names or other information. "Can you help?"

She suggests a preliminary Skype conversation, during which we talk about how she works, there are no guarantees, her worldwide group of clients, her ability to access automatic drawing to sketch portraits of dead folks and, intriguingly, her ongoing conversations with Leonardo da Vinci.

And then, out of nowhere, June-Elleni says:

> "This gentleman you want to speak with. He's your spiritual guide."

I tell her that I thought a spiritual guide was the intermediary between the sitter and the spirit. The one who makes the contact with the spirit, who ensure that both parties want to chat, who protects the sitter if the vibes aren't positive.

> "No, that's a gatekeeper. This gentleman is your spiritual guide."

This is a new, more intimate version of Wallace's role. But it aligns with what other mediums have told me—I have a connection with Wallace, and vice versa, and that Wallace is like a "soul brother" (or Mentor to use Joseph Campbell's terminology) who will guide me through life. But they all stress that this assistance is only available if I ask.

> "I'm picking up a man who is a humanist. I think you told me that," June-Elleni says.

"No, I certainly didn't tell you that," I say. "I was extremely careful only to say he's a 19th-century personage. But yes, you could call him a humanist."

> "He wants to come through to you. Together you can make a difference."

Sounds like another joint venture opportunity, similar to when Moses gave Yan Mokoginta and me instructions to negotiate peace in the Middle East.

> "Great sense of moral obligation."

That sounds like Wallace.

> "I recall reading something: 'The way human beings torture themselves is funny as hell. No, it's funnier.' Would your friend be amused by that?"

"Absolutely."

> "He dressed like a gentleman. Some kind of boarding school attire."

Now this is interesting. First, both Rita and Nasrin commented that Wallace was "elegant." But I don't think he was too concerned about being *elegantly* dressed (for one thing he rarely had enough money to buy elegant clothes). He was, however, very concerned with being *improperly* dressed. In his autobiography he remarks how embarrassed he was when, as a gawky, rapidly growing youngster, he used his sleeve cuff to clean his school slate. This so irritated his mother that she made calico over-sleeves. He refused to wear them until his mother asked the teacher to order him to do so. This shame, in front of the entire class, was "perhaps the severest punishment I ever endured," he wrote. Wallace specifically used the term "loss of face."

We talk a bit about science and spirituality.

Like Brigitte Favre, June-Elleni is a stickler for honesty and transparency.

> *"I'm a skeptic myself. I can't do any work that can't be validated."*

I ask her permission to record the session and use excerpts in my book. She agrees, and adds that she has been misquoted in previous published pieces and asks me to be accurate.

We agree that I will pay her fee by PayPal and speak again in a few days for a full-fledged session.

I look forward to that, because, intriguingly, June-Elleni says that while we peak with Alfred she will draw his portrait.

> *"I trust that's okay."*

"Terrific."

June-Elleni looks relaxed, sitting in a simple room, family photos behind her. She has a long, attractive face, wears a simple gray and white cable-knit sweater, and her dark curly hair is loosely tied behind. She wears a minimum of jewelry, but what she does wear is simple, refined, and elegant—what appears to be gold and diamond stud earrings, a thin necklace, and a discrete ring.

> "Just so you're clear. I'm not sure who will appear. Do you want to give me a name to try to zero in?"

Up to this point I have not given June-Elleni any clues except my desire to speak with "a historical figure." I don't want to give away Wallace's name, in case she has knowledge about him. I simply say "Alfred."

> "Now, this is interesting. Mothballs?"

"No idea."

> "As before, I see him in a tweed jacket. One of my favorite teachers wore a tweed jacket, Mister Elliott. So possibly Alfred was a teacher?"

Well, Wallace taught when he was younger, for a brief period, but more important he was a teacher in the larger sense of opening people's minds and forcing them to think about themselves and their world. But, of course, that description could apply to almost anyone.

> "He's been trying to contact you. I get the number fifteen. Could be fifteen years or months?"

I suppose I could make either number work if I twisted and strained, but nothing jumps out at me.

"Did he live in the 1800s?"

"Yes."

"He was a pioneer, writing about new ideas that were later validated."

"Absolutely."

"I am hearing the word 'whales.'"

"The animal? That doesn't ring a bell."

June-Elleni corrects.

"Could be the animal as a metaphor for something large and almost mythical. Or it could be the sound of the word, maybe the nation Wales."

Ah, the power of homonyms. Wallace was born in Usk, a small village in Wales, just across the border from England.

"Good singing or speaking voice."

She admits the Wales connection got her thinking of the singer Tom Jones.

No idea. No one has ever written about Wallace's spoken voice. But he lectured worldwide, so it's likely he had some stage presence.

June-Elleni is busy drawing. She continues to draw during our hour-long conversation.

"Ooh! Quick spurt of energy just now. I'm getting a hairy face."

"Could be." I don't want to give too much away. I think, but don't mention, that Wallace had a big beard for most of his adult life.

> "Not a big man in stature, average or below average height."

Here June-Elleni makes her first big error. Wallace was tall, six-foot one-inch (185 cm).

Then she self-corrects. June-Elleni stresses, as most mediums do, that sometimes the information she receives is not to be taken literally, but should be viewed as metaphors.

> "Were there times when people disagreed with him or made him feel small?"

Her self-correction makes sense. "Yes."

> "And this resulted in anger, disappointment. No, it was more frustration than anger."
>
> "He couldn't understand the mentality of people who wanted to bicker just for the sake of arguing."

She returns to the hairy face.

> "Are you aware of a beard?"

"Yes."

> "I smell smoke. Did he smoke? Or was he around people who smoke?"

No idea, but I don't think he smoked. If I want to stretch things, I could imagine an open cooking fire while he was living rough in Asia.

She's back to the hair.

"Thin on top?"

"Not especially. He died with a full head of hair." Of course, Wallace might have *thought* his hair was thinning. How literal, or how liberal, should I be when given information like this?

"*Fairly long life. Into his seventies.*"

"No, longer. He died at ninety."

Then things start to get really interesting.

"*Have you done automatic writing?*"

"No."

"*Perhaps you have and not realized it. Alfred's inspired you to do automatic writing. He's already been trying to help you to do that. You may think it's your own ideas you're writing, but you're being inspired.*"

June-Elleni is basically reinforcing ideas suggested by Boy, Nasrin, Brigitte, and Rita—that Wallace is helping me, supporting me, even inspiring me in ways that I might not be aware of. My emotional right brain is thrilled. The question for my ever-present logical left brain niggles—is she telling me what I want to hear? Something that will make me happy? Or should I accept it in good grace, especially since other mediums have made a similar claim? I probably should give Wallace co-authorship credit for this book.

"*Stubborn. Wasn't very agreeable. Liked to cooperate but had his own ideas.*"

"Yes."

> "I'm getting a long-suffering wife."

"No, he had a happy marriage."

Then June-Elleni self-corrects.

> "Maybe he had a good marriage and this was his way of teasing; he could only say this if his marriage was good, tongue in cheek."

She's good at this self-correction. And she's such a nice person, I want to believe her winding turns are done in good faith and are true to her contact with Wallace.

> "Urge to know different cultures and religions and different ways of living in the world.

Now this is interesting. My left brain tells me that June-Elleni is picking up this concept from *my* interests. Perhaps she uses telepathy (which in itself is a wonderful, magical gift). Perhaps she picks up clues by looking me up on Google. And we're on Skype and she can peer into a corner of my study, which features numerous Ganesha statues, meters of books, old lithographs, and, most prominently from her point of view, two rare and dramatic African masks.

> "He was fascinated by psychic ideas, but wasn't sure about whether he could trust his instincts. Some eminent people around him. Not sure he would have put his name to Spiritualism. Maybe he was a closet Spiritualist, not like Conan Doyle, who went public. Alfred hemmed and hawed before declaring himself. But once he was in, he was in."

"Beings of a Like Mental Nature to Ourselves" | 95

Okay, where does this come from? I've given her no clues that Wallace was a Spiritualist. He probably did prevaricate before coming out of the closet, but once he did he was a full-fledged believer. And Conan Doyle was a pal.

I ask, "Does the name 'Ali' mean anything?"

> "Feels familiar. Was Ali some kind of mystic? Ali was a teacher of Wallace?"

If I want to, I can twist and turn and make June-Elleni's Ali answer sound feasible. But it would be a stretch. Once again, Ali chooses to remain a mystery.

"And does the name 'Darwin' mean anything?"

And here June-Elleni shudders. Suddenly. I can see it in her face—surprise, anxiety perhaps.

> "All the hairs on my arm just stood up. I have goosebumps all over. Rival. That's the first thought that comes to me. Non-cooperation. Frustration. Hand-wringing frustration. An exchange of information that was incorrect. Some information deliberately incorrect. Not a lot of cooperation coming from Darwin, he even sent 'red herrings'—put Alfred on a wild goose chase."

Okay, this is crunch time. Let's give June-Elleni the benefit of the doubt that she has no idea we're talking about Alfred Russel Wallace, or that she is aware of Wallace's relationship to Charles Darwin—polite, even warm on the surface, but perhaps riddled with doubt and distrust. Her reaction, via Wallace, is impressive and disturbing. On reflection, perhaps I should have said "Charles" instead of "Darwin." *C'est la vie.*

"Where does his spirit live?"

June-Elleni starts a long explanation.

> "It's different for everybody. Alfred lives in a mindscape, he can choose anything and anywhere that he's experienced, any age, any situation. He seems to know about remote viewing."

She talks about ley lines, time travel, resonance, and vibration. Fascinating, but no room to explore in this chapter.

"Our time's limited, can we return to Alfred?"

> "I see the masks on your wall. They embody energy you don't have. Put a mask on and you will be imbued with mask energy. In the West, we hide behind masks, but the shamans will tell you that they wear masks to channel the energy within the mask."

Yes, there *is* energy in my masks. They're the real deal, used by shamans in villages in the Congo and Gabon, imbued with wood-fire smoke and ancient miracles. We're off the track, though.

> "A terrible toothache. Two children, a boy and a girl."

No idea about a toothache, but he had countless fevers, infections, and other physical ailments. He was a brave explorer, but a bit fragile.

And he had three children, not two—two boys and a girl.

> "Very private, doesn't like to speak about his personal life."

Could be.

> "Had many, many interests, some very obscure. Not a nine-to-five kind of guy."

Absolutely. (See the previous Part IV—"Wallace, the Social Reformer, in the City That Hosts the United Nations and Hundreds of Humanitarian and Environmental Action Groups" for a long list of his interests.)

> "Sometimes wanted to escape and stay on a beach. Watch the mist on the sea, the phases of the moon."

While I can't imagine Wallace lying on a sun chair on the Costa del Sol, I can easily imagine him sitting in his garden in England and daydreaming that he was back on a tiny obscure island in Indonesia—isolated, calm, intrigued, tired, eating rice for all his meals, and puzzling over the taxonomy of a new beetle he collected before breakfast.

> "A friend. George. Lost a finger on his hand. Alfred relied on George for a bit of sanity, to check his thinking. They shared a kind of black humor."

One of Wallace's best friends was George Silk, in London, and Wallace wrote from Indonesia that when he returns to London: "There will you be seated on the same chair, at the same table, surrounded by the same account books, and writing on paper of the same size and colour as when I last beheld you." Wallace's letters to George illustrate a good friendship but also mark a difference between Wallace's exuberant, disordered, insecure lifestyle with the safe and boring existences of his stay-at-home friends. Wallace is perhaps gently saying, "When I return to England, I will have changed; you, probably not." I have no idea whether George Silk lost a finger.

And then June-Elleni switches back to Ali.

> "Ali was an alchemist, changing people's minds. There's more to that character than meets the eye; his way of giving information through a back door."

And so June-Elleni doubles up on Ali as a wise teacher. Maybe he was. In the following chapter ("The Search for Ali") I point out that while Wallace was an important Mentor for Ali, the reverse was also true."

> "He is keen to feed you more information via automatic writing, and to tap into Ali's character."

This is different to what Nasrin and others have told me, which was basically to leave Ali alone.

And June-Elleni comes back to Darwin.

> "I'm getting twelve percent. Alfred has a twelve percent trust of Darwin."

And then she comes back to her oft-repeated refrain.

> "Alfred is your spiritual guide, you will uncover things that have been covered up."

I will take that as a confirmation of the work I'm doing with my old friend David Hallmark to prove that Darwin was guilty of plagiarism of Wallace's theory of evolution. David and I have written about this controversy for various magazines, and have given presentations on Darwin's questionable behavior for dozens of groups in the UK and internationally. In a few months we will suggest to the members of the Athenaeum, Darwin's gentleman's club, that he be disbarred for character unbecoming a member of that august group. Onward and upward. To the universe and beyond.

And what of June-Elleni's "automatic" drawing of "Alfred?" Here it is.

In June-Elleni's version, which resembles a police sketch, she's got his abundant beard right, also the very slightly thinning hair. But I point out to her that she hasn't given Wallace the spectacles he wore throughout his life.

> "They're there. Look closely," she says. "Alfred mentioned them to me, but I wasn't aware I was drawing them."

And indeed, her drawing shows the faint outline of glasses with thin wire frames.

For comparison, below we have Alfred Russel Wallace at a comparable age.

June-Elleni sends me an email.

She explains a serendipitous conversation she had with Gill, the principal of the College of Psychic Studies.

> "I was at the College and mentioned to her that I did a reading with a man named 'Alfred.' I told her that I had a feeling he was associated with the College. So I showed Gill my drawing. She was stunned and said, 'come with me.'"

On the fourth floor of the College, where June-Elleni had never been, the principal showed her a portrait of Alfred Russel Wallace, one of the early members of the College.

I ask June-Elleni if this incident happened before or after I had told her Alfred's full name or given her any information about his interest in Spiritualism.

> "Before you gave me his full name. Definitely before. This was when I only knew him as "Alfred,"" June-Elleni says.

We Skype again, a week later.

> "I got several visits from Alfred," she says.

"How do you know it was Alfred?"

> "He said, 'This is Alfred, friend of Paul's. We spoke the other day.'"

Once again, my easily massaged ego is pleased that Wallace considers me a "friend."

"I'm glad you have a new buddy," I say. Then I add, "This happened once or several times?"

> "Several times. Sometimes he comes in the evening, during the moment between waking and sleep."

I venture a joke. "Careful, he might be a psychic stalker."

Thankfully, she laughs.

"What did you talk about?"

When June-Elleni recounts their conversations, she is as vivacious and exuberant as the first time we spoke.

> "One rainy afternoon, Alfred ordered me to look out my window 'right now.' I saw an intense blue light on the house behind mine. He told me to take a photo immediately, then another in thirty minutes. At the thirty-minute mark, the blue light disappeared."

"How do you interpret that?"

> "He knows I'm a skeptic. He had to get my attention somehow. He wanted me to have validation. He said the blue light will help my DNA."

Putting aside for a moment the idea that Alfred knew about, or even caused, the blue light, what I find interesting is that Alfred, who died in 1907, is aware of modern cell phone technology and understood that June-Elleni had the ability to easily take photos.

> "Well, how about this?" she says. "Alfred then told me that at 1:15 exactly I should take my lunch outside, because the sun would be out for twenty minutes. At the time he said that, there was horrible wind and rain. But at 1:15 the sky cleared, for just twenty minutes. I ate my lunch on the terrace in bright sunshine."

Is Alfred a weatherman? How does he know what's going on in England at any given moment? I remind June-Elleni that it's March, and weather changes constantly, from hail to bright sunshine in a few moments.

June continues to talk, like an excited teenager. She and Alfred obviously have a thing going.

> *"Remember I told you that Alfred's interest in spiritualism was not like that of Conan Doyle, and you were skeptical. He corrected me about that— almost like teasing a friend. He said he had told me that his interest* is *like that of Conan Doyle."*

Alfred then gave June-Elleni a long, rambling lesson on metaphysics, modern science and genetics, and the healing power of color. June-Elleni's recounting of their conversation takes up several pages of notes. I will summarize:

Alfred analyzed the flashes of black and white triangles that June-Elleni sees in the periphery of her eyes, and explained that this is light energy sent to help her heal. He pointed out the importance of ferro-magnetic elements in our sinuses that help us orient ourselves (just days later, the newspapers carried a story about how humans may have an internal compass that can tell which way the earth's magnetic field is pointing). He gave her the chemical formula Fe_3O_4, iron oxide, and pointed out that crystals of this in the brains of whales helps them orient to the North Pole.

We both agree that her earlier comment about "whales/Wales," which I had thought referred to the nation of Wales, might indeed have referred to Alfred's new comment about the navigation ability of whales.

June-Elleni reminds me, as have most other mediums, that you have to be prepared to make an effort to interpret messages from the beyond; they are seldom clean and neat.

Alfred seemed to be voluble and enjoying the fact that he had such a receptive partner in June-Elleni. I feel like a successful matchmaker.

June-Elleni continues. The blue light she saw the previous day is designed to repair her DNA, Alfred told her.

"He said I'm getting a DNA upgrade."

"What in the world is a 'DNA upgrade?'"

June-Elleni offers a vague answer.

"He's upgrading DNA codes. Because we don't follow natural laws."

By itself this doesn't make sense. But yes, our DNA can get damaged and altered by environmental factors.

"He's worried about hybrid barriers that upset brain chemistry."

This is the Alfred I love. Curious to explore anything and everything, and quick to express an opinion.

"Hybrid barriers are there for good reason, in plants, animals, and insects. He is worried that the violation of hybrid barriers upsets brain chemistry."

This might be warped science, but it is exactly the type of speculation that Alfred enjoyed while alive. What makes it particularly interesting is that the field of biological hybrids, sometimes called chimera, is a relatively modern, often controversial area of genetic engineering. This has been going on in agriculture for decades: think of genetically modified crops. A true chimera is an organism that contains cells or tissues from two or more different species, let's say implanting human cells into a gorilla. A hybrid would be an offspring of two different species (which in theory aren't supposed to easily produce offspring); an example is the sterile mule resulting from the breeding of a horse and donkey. All these ideas are modern. Does Alfred have a subscription to *New Scientist?*

"June-Elleni, could he be reading your mind?"

> *"Well, spirits can tap into your psychic filing cabinet."*

"And there's more?"

> *"Alfred told me about the healing powers of colors—red for warmth and safety, yellow for information flow, white for harmony, blue for repairing DNA codes. That's why he alerted me to the blue light on the rainy afternoon."*

Well, it's been known for a while that colors affect emotions.

> *"He told me not to eat grains. And that my body needs fulvic acid and humic acid to clean our internal crystals."*

I joke with June-Elleni that she already has an ongoing relationship with Leonardo da Vinci. Now she has *two* famous men to speak with.

> *"I took a salt bath, like he suggested. I feel totally different."*

"I can see it in your face." Indeed, she looks bright and alive.

THE SEARCH FOR ALI

Can eager shamans solve the mystery of Wallace's "faithful companion"?

Ali, age about 22, in an 1862 photograph taken in Singapore. This is the only photo we have of the young man. I've been using mediums to try to locate his descendants.

TERNATE, Indonesia

"Why don't I just go to the source?" I asked.

I was having a seafood dinner with Ofa Firman, the son of the sultan of Ternate. I was telling him my frustrations about trying to find the descendants of Ali, the young man who accompanied Alfred Russel Wallace through Southeast Asia. I thought that if we could find Ali's descendants, then it might spur a new burst of support for conservation in the region.

I explained to Ofa Firman that on several previous visits, I had encouraged university professors to ask a graduate student to take on the search for Ali's descendants. I spoke with officials in the tourist office, and with folks in the local historical society, about starting a public awareness campaign. I offered to write a newspaper article explaining who Ali was and why we're looking for him. All these friendly people had agreed—*Yes, very interesting. Yes, we can do something.* And each time, after I left, nothing happened. I was frustrated about my seemingly Quixotic quest, defeated by the black hole of enthusiastic Indonesian inertia.

Perhaps it was personal—they didn't like me, or the idea of following up on someone else's idea. Or perhaps Wallace's star was shining less brightly—the small street where his house was ostensibly located, which had in the early twentieth century been renamed *Jalan* Alfred Russel Wallace (Alfred Russel Wallace Street) had been downgraded to Lorong A. Wallace (Alfred Russel Wallace small alley).

"And by 'source' you mean what?" Ofa Firman said as he passed me the plate of tamarind prawns.

I suggested that together we create a new form of historical research. Rather than examining academic tomes, instead of sifting through dusty Dutch records, instead of going door to door in the Malay settlements, why not talk to Ali himself? Ali has passed on, which means he's a ghost. A *hantu* in Indonesian terms.

"Ternate is full of mediums," I said, passing him a platter of chilli crabs. They were a specialty of Royal's Resto & Function Hall. "Let's talk to Ali himself and get the true story."

Let's call it History by *Hantu*. If my History by *Hantu* works, what might we learn? Will we unravel the "mystery of Ali?" (On a broader scale, could such investigations answer the great historical mysteries? What if we could speak with Lee Harvey Oswald and ask if he acted alone, and for what reason? Or get into the head of Napoleon, or Cleopatra, or Genghis Khan? Wouldn't scholars love to ask Shakespeare if he wrote all those plays and sonnets? Or ask Mary, mother of Jesus, about that virgin birth story?)[54]

"I know just the guy," Ofa Firman said.

The Setup

Why Ali?

The Borneo newspapers in 1858 sported a large headline: "Local Borneo lad helps develop theory of evolution."

The local reporters told how a teenaged cook from Sarawak named Ali assisted Alfred Russel Wallace on his eight-year adventure in Southeast Asia, culminating in Wallace's development of the Theory of Natural Selection, written while Ali and Wallace were living in Ternate, a picture-postcard beautiful island in eastern Indonesia that was the original source of cloves, and therefore one of the most legendary of the Spice Islands that spurred European exploration, trade, and colonialism.

The Borneo newspapers revealed how Ali nursed Wallace during a malaria fever, giving the older Englishman strength and moral support to write the theory that changed the way we view ourselves and our place in the scheme of things.

The Borneo newspapers, of course, said none of these things. Ali was then, and remained, a footnote, a historical afterthought written in small type.

Searching for Ali was just one of my Asian quests.

I seek tiger magicians in Sumatra. Snowmen of the Jungle in Flores. I seek reasons why people believe in the power of magic amulets and influential mermaids and white elephants. I seek the secrets of growing healthy, juicy tomatoes. I seek a writing voice that makes people sit up and take notice—I don't expect them to leap and shout "huzzah!" but a satisfied smile once in a while would be welcome. I seek someone who can explain the Higgs boson. I seek the answer to why some people believe in a stern Hairy Thunderer, while other people bow to a benign Cosmic Muffin, while other people value spirits in the trees and waterfalls, and still other folks consult astrological charts and brightly designed tarot cards while others scoff at metaphysics and choose to rely on their own judgment and inner values.

I have spent forty years trying to find out more about Ali. Who he was, why he went with Wallace, what his contribution was, and where he ultimately settled.

I clearly needed spiritual intervention.

Western history treats famous explorers as bigger-than-life individuals who braved the elements alone—stoic, unflappable, with immense strength of character and fortitude. But actually, all explorers, the famous as well as the overlooked, relied on often unheralded people to assist in their odyssey. Lewis and Clark had Sacagawea, Edmund Hillary had Tenzing Norgay. Ferdinand Magellan had Enrique, a slave he bought in Malacca and whom he encouraged (I use the term advisedly) to renounce Islam and convert to Catholicism. Enrique became Magellan's interpreter, guide, and assistant; he may also have been among the first people to complete the circumnavigation of the globe, since Magellan, who gets the credit, was killed in the Philippines before finishing the epic journey, while Enrique might have continued the voyage to its conclusion.

British naturalist and explorer Alfred Russel Wallace had Ali, and without Ali's assistance it is unlikely Wallace would have been as successful as he was.

That's about all we know.

Alfred Russel Wallace spent the first six months in the Malay Archipelago exploring the outskirts of cosmopolitan Singapore and the hilly region around Malacca, now in Peninsular Malaysia. While in Singapore Wallace renewed his acquaintance with James Brooke, the famed "White Rajah" of Sarawak, who invited him to Borneo.

Wallace's prior four-year Amazon adventure had helped him immensely in learning to survive in alien environments and cultures. But in Asia he was a stranger in a strange land. Nevertheless, he was a quick learner and rapidly gained competence in Malay, the lingua franca of the region.

While in Sarawak, in late 1855, Wallace hired Ali.

Ali accompanied Wallace on most of his subsequent Asian travels. Starting out as a cook, Ali himself evolved—he learned to collect and prepare specimens, particularly birds. He took on more responsibility for organizing travel (imagine the negotiations with self-important village chiefs, unreliable porters and laborers, and greedy merchants, whose eyes no doubt grew large when they saw a white man like Alfred come to buy supplies). Ali became both a friend and a valuable assistant; Wallace called him "my faithful companion."

There's an awful lot we don't know about Ali. We speculate on where he came from. How Wallace met him. Whether he went to school. Where he settled after he parted ways with Wallace. And most interesting, what did Ali think of the tall, awkward, bearded Englishman who spent his days collecting innumerable insects and his nights writing in a small notebook by the dim light of an oil lamp.

Christopher Vogler is a Hollywood screenwriter whose book *The Writer's Journey* explores how a classical mythic structure is used in popular films such as *Casablanca*, *The Wizard of Oz*, *Star Wars*, and *Close Encounters of the Third Kind*. "All stories consist of a few common structural elements found universally in myths, fairy tales, dreams, and movies," Vogler says. "They are known collectively as The Hero's Journey."

One essential archetype in the hero's journey is the character Vogler calls the Mentor (and which philosopher Joseph Campbell refers to as the Wise Old Man or the Wise Old Woman), who teaches and protects heroes and gives them gifts. In classical mythology, as well as contemporary novels, the Mentor is a sage adult—Merlin guiding King Arthur, the Fairy Godmother helping Cinderella, or a veteran sergeant giving advice to a rookie cop.

If you wish to plot Ali's hero's journey in this way, then Wallace was clearly the Mentor, and Ali took the role of a keen, but initially naïve, son who grows in competence and confidence as the story progresses. We can assume that when Wallace met Ali, the Malay teenager had never left Sarawak, probably had never had a serious conversation with a European, and had a limited worldview. Wallace took him on a magnificent journey lasting almost eight years, and by the time Ali and Wallace parted company, Ali no doubt had grown considerably.

"Ali would have been one of the most widely traveled Malays of his age," according to Jerry Drawhorn of California State University, Sacramento. "He would have seen most of what is today modern Indonesia (Papua to Sumatra). He would have seen the ancient Hindu temples of Java; the modern metropolises of Batavia and Singapore; the primitive villages of the people of Dorey and the stylized royal courts of central Java. He tasted modern science and medicine and yet retained his beliefs in ghosts and men who could transform into tigers."

The reverse is also true.

Just as Wallace taught and guided Ali through new adventures, perspectives and skills, Ali was similarly Wallace's guide. The Englishman was a good pupil and Wallace's steep learning curve, abetted by Ali, included mastering the Malay language, understanding the vagaries of dozens of cultural groups (Wallace compiled 57 vocabularies during his travels in Asia), and becoming comfortable with an Asian worldview in which female vampire ghosts, crocodile whisperers, bird omens, and kings who consort with mermaids danced an intricate waltz of life as seen through a spectral prism.

Under what circumstances did Wallace hire Ali? My theory:

Wallace formed a friendship with Rajah James Brooke and Brooke's secretary and friend Spenser St. John. I figure that one night, over brandy, James Brooke said, "Look here, Wallace, here in Sarawak people know you're my friend and they will tolerate your curious behavior and listen to your baby-talk Malay and won't cheat you too much. But out there [no doubt he was pointing south to the maze of thousands of Indonesian islands where Wallace was heading] they're going to eat you alive." Brooke then asked one of his Malay assistants if he had a young relative who would be willing to go off on an adventure from which he might not return. The result was the Wallace-Ali partnership.

Here's how Wallace described his engagement of Ali as personal assistant:

> When I was at Sarawak in 1855 I engaged a Malay boy named Ali as a personal servant, and also to help me to learn the Malay language . . . He was attentive and clean, and could cook very well.[55]

Wallace described how Ali grew into the job, growing from cook to collector to preparer of specimens to manager of an often changing team of laborers, hunters, and boat crews—over eight years, more than one hundred men worked for Wallace.

> [Ali] soon learnt to shoot birds, to skin them properly, and latterly even to put up the skins very neatly. Of course, he was a good boatman, as are all Malays . . . He accompanied me through all my travels, sometimes alone, but more frequently with several others, and was then very useful in teaching them their duties, as he soon became well acquainted with my wants and habits.[56]

Wallace made no secret of the fact that many of the 125,660 specimens he obtained in the Malay Archipelago were collected by his various collecting assistants (perhaps some thirty men over the years), including an English assistant named Charles Allen. Earl of Cranbrook, a leading ornithologist and mammalogist, and historian Adrian G. Marshall, wrote that Wallace regularly "bought trade specimens [and] was always ready to recruit casual help in collecting, whether small boys with blowpipes or local hunters and bird traders."[57, 58]

Yet it was Ali who saw himself as the senior collector, taking pride in his work and collecting a bird that became one of Wallace's most prized specimens:

> Just as I got home I overtook Ali returning from shooting with some birds hanging from his belt. He seemed much pleased, and said, "Look here, sir, what a curious bird!" holding out what at first completely puzzled me. I saw a bird with a mass of splendid green feathers on its breast, elongated into two glittering tufts; but what I could not understand was a pair of long white feathers, which stuck straight out from each shoulder. Ali assured me that the bird stuck them out this way itself when fluttering its wings, and that they had remained so without his touching them. I now saw that I had got a great prize, no less than a com-

pletely new form of the bird of paradise, different and most remarkable from every other known bird . . . This striking novelty has been named by Mr. G.R. Gray of the British Museum, Semioptera Wallacei [today it's known as *Semioptera wallacii*], or "Wallace's Standard-wing."[59]

Ali was so proficient that he might have been responsible for collecting a large number of Wallace's total of 8,050 bird specimens, which included 212 new bird species.

Within a year of hiring him, Wallace described Ali as follows:

> Ali, the Malay boy whom I had picked up in Borneo, was my head man. He had already been with me a year, could turn his hand to any thing, and was quite attentive and trustworthy. He was a good shot, and fond of shooting, and I had taught him to skin birds very well.[60]

And Wallace eventually trusted Ali to go by himself to buy natural history specimens. Note that Ali was ill (poor health dogged both Ali and Wallace throughout the journey) and that he was trustworthy and respected by outsiders:

> My boy Ali returned from Wanumbai, where I had sent him alone for a fortnight to buy Paradise birds and prepare the skins; he brought me sixteen glorious specimens, and had he not been very ill with fever and ague might have obtained twice the number. He had lived with the people whose house I had occupied, and it is a proof of their goodness, if fairly treated, that although he took with him a quantity of silver dollars to pay for the birds they caught, no attempt was made to rob him, which might have been done with the most perfect impunity. He was kindly treated when ill, and was brought back to me with the balance of the dollars he had not spent.[61]

Ali showed that he had pride in his work; it was more than a job—he seemed to enjoy his role as a trusted bird collector and was willing to endure pain and discomfort to obtain a rare creature.

Soon after we had arrived at Waypoti, Ali had seen a beautiful little bird of the genus Pitta, which I was very anxious to obtain, as in almost every island the species are different, and none were yet known from Bouru [now Buru]. He and my other hunter continued to see it two or three times a week, and to hear its peculiar note much oftener, but could never get a specimen, owing to its always frequenting the most dense thorny thickets, where only hasty glimpses of it could be obtained, and at so short a distance that it would be difficult to avoid blowing the bird to pieces. *Ali was very much annoyed that he could not get a specimen of this bird*, in going after which he had already severely wounded his feet with thorns; and when we had only two days more to stay, *he went of his own accord* one evening to sleep at a little hut in the forest some miles off, in order to have a last try for it at daybreak, when many birds come out to feed, and are very intent on their morning meal. The next evening he brought me home two specimens, one with the head blown completely off, and otherwise too much injured to preserve, the other in very good order, and which I at once saw to be a new species, very like the Pitta celebensis, but ornamented with a square patch of bright red on the nape of the neck. [italics added][62]

And in due course Wallace trusted Ali to scout locations that might be sufficiently productive for Wallace to go to the expense and trouble of moving his camp.

It became evident, therefore, that I must leave Cajeli [on Buru] for some better collecting-ground . . . *I sent my boy Ali . . . to explore and report* on the capabilities of the district [Pelah] . . . [after an account of a difficult walk that occupies two pages of text, Wallace continues] I waited Ali's return to decide on my future movements. He came the following day, and gave a very bad account of Pelah, where he had been. [italics added][63]

I don't want to overstate Ali's involvement, since his role was supportive rather than intellectual, but the young man was present when Wallace made his most important scientific breakthrough in his quest to understand the process of evolution.

Ali had not yet been hired in February 1855 when Wallace wrote his Sarawak Law ("On the Law Which Has Regulated the Introduction of New Species"). This paper, published in September 1855, was an important first step toward Wallace's Theory of Natural Selection and includes the statement: "Every species has come into existence coincident both in space and time with a pre-existing closely allied species."

Ali, however, played an important supporting role in Wallace's second breakthrough, which came three years after the Sarawak Law.

Wallace wrote that, while in Jailolo (Halmahera) in eastern Indonesia in February 1858, Ali cared for him during the periods when he was "suffering from a sharp attack of intermittent fever." During one particularly severe malaria attack, Wallace had a breakthrough that explained the mechanism of evolution by natural selection. Within days of the fever subsiding, on his return to nearby Ternate, he had written "On the Tendency of Varieties to Depart Indefinitely from the Original Type," sometimes called the Ternate Paper, which contained the idea that later became known as "survival of the fittest." Wallace then sent his paper to Charles Darwin, who up to that point had not published one word on evolution or natural selection.

Much has been made of Ali's nursing skills. Yet Wallace wrote that he in turn cared for Ali on various occasions when the young man was incapacitated by often serious illnesses and injuries. Wallace and Ali both suffered, and they helped each other overcome continuing episodes of fevers, inflammations, suppurating sores, accidents, shipwrecks, and general misery, not to mention the exasperation of trying to manage a string of often unreliable, sometimes larcenous, hired hands.

While on the island of Lombok, for example, Wallace asked his host for "a horse for Ali, who was lame."[64] Apparently the horse never appeared, and Wallace noted:

> I gave Ali my horse, and started on foot, but he afterward mounted behind Mr. Ross's groom, and we got home very well, though rather hot and tired.[65]

In another passage, from Macassar (now Makassar), Wallace wrote about his concern for Ali's health, mixed with his annoyance at not having a regular cook.

> Although this was the height of the dry season, and there was a fine wind all day, it was by no means a healthy time of year. My boy Ali had hardly been a day onshore when he was attacked by fever, which put me to great inconvenience, as at the house where I was staying nothing could be obtained but at meal-times. After having cured Ali, and with much difficulty got another servant to cook for me, I was no sooner settled at my country abode than the latter was attacked with the same disease, and, having a wife in the town, left me. Hardly was he gone than I fell ill myself, with strong intermittent fever every other day. In about a week I got over it by a liberal use of quinine, when scarcely was I on my legs than Ali again became worse than ever. His fever attacked him daily, but early in the morning he was pretty well, and then managed to cook me enough for the day. In a week I cured him.[66]

And Wallace sought medical help for Ali in Maros, north of Makassar (and again bemoaned the inconvenience).

> My boy Ali was so ill with fever that I was obliged to leave him in the hospital, under the care of my friend the German doctor, and I had to make shift with two new servants utterly ignorant of everything.[67]

And again near Macassar, Ali once more came down with fever, and again Wallace was annoyed that his routine was disrupted:

> My Malay boy Ali was affected with the same illness, and as he was my chief bird-skinner I got on but slowly with my collections.[68]

⁓

I wonder what we might learn by flipping things around and looking at the Wallace-Ali relationship from Ali's point of view. What did Ali think about all those characteristics (well educated, science-influenced, relatively wealthy, curious, much traveled, openminded, meticulous, living far from his family, willing to sacrifice comfort for the sake of the quest) that intrigues us about Wallace? Can we speculate on how Ali judged his tall, gawky, bearded (beards are a constant source of fascination, and often fear, to many rural Asians) employer? At times Ali might have been confused—Wallace was his boss, but he cared for Ali when he was sick, almost as a father might have done. How did Ali try to make sense of this Englishman, who, with all the wealth and status that designation implies, deliberately chose not to live like other white foreigners but instead insisted on spending miserable weeks camped out in the forest, in palm leaf shelters that leaked, fighting rats, dogs, and ants that tried to devour his specimens. And my word, those specimens. Often, they were dull in color and to Ali without interest. Yet Wallace seemed as happy to collect a miserable gray-brown beetle as tiny as a rice grain with the same enthusiasm as he collected a big, bold hornbill. And what mental illness drove Wallace to spend long periods huddled over his journal writing intently about an ant. A miserable *semut*! And so many of them! Wallace said they were all different, but Ali couldn't see much beyond the fact that some were big and some were small and some were black and some were red. And Wallace smelled. Even in the forest, Ali took pride in his hygiene, washing his clothes and himself at every opportunity with buckets of rain water or in a nearby stream. But, he had to admit, some of the butterflies and birds *were* attractive. However, all told, if Ali was in control of the shotguns, he might better have used his time and ability to shoot deer for the dinner table.

⌒

Wallace was traveling independently—he had no government or military support system. He also had little cash—he was a self-described "beetle collector" who earned enough to survive by sending natural history specimens to Samuel Stevens, his beetle agent in London, who then sold the critters to enthusiastic collectors. (Darwin, on the other hand, during his famous voyage on the *HMS Beagle*, lived onboard in what was, in effect, a floating base camp, with Royal Navy sailors on hand to provide security, logistics, laundry, and food. He had a permanent, dry place to write his notes and mount his specimens. (The downside: Darwin shared a cabin with the captain, Robert FitzRoy, who, Darwin noted, had a quick temper that resulted in behavior sometimes "bordering on insanity.")

Wallace moved camp some one hundred times during his eight years in Southeast Asia. Ali probably reduced the amount that Wallace was overcharged, and helped in negotiations with self-important village chiefs: *Hello, good sir, do you mind if I set up a camp in your forest and shoot your birds and collect your butterflies?* Ali hired and fired porters and laborers and organized the thousands of annoying details of travel.

⌒

In 1862, after some seven years traveling together throughout the Indonesian archipelago, Wallace and Ali made their way to Singapore. Wallace was getting on a ship to return to England. Wallace took Ali to a photographer; the picture (the only one we have) shows a full-mouthed, serious, dark-complexioned lad with wavy hair, thick eyebrows, and a broad nose, dressed in a dark European-style jacket and under-jacket, white shirt, and a white bow tie. Wallace remembers the farewell:

> On parting, besides a present in money, I gave him my two double-barreled guns and whatever ammunition I had, with a lot of surplus stores . . . which made him quite rich. He here, for the first time, *adopted European clothes, which did not suit him nearly so well as his native dress*, and thus clad, a friend took a very good photograph of him. I therefore now present his likeness to my readers as that of the best native servant I ever had, and the faithful companion of almost all my journeyings among the islands of the far East. [italics added][69]

The small community of Ali scholars ponder two basic questions. These questions have little import in the bigger scheme of things, but they keep a few people busy exchanging academic papers and snippy emails. And for me they are the basic questions I intend to ask Ali, assuming I can find a suitably skilled medium.

First, *where did Ali come from?* Was he born in Sarawak (the general assumption) or did he originate in Ternate (the view of some historians and several Ternate-based mediums).

Second, when Ali parted ways with Wallace, *where did he "retire?"* The two options seem to be either Sarawak (the choice of some Sarawak-based mediums), Ternate (the general consensus), or a ludicrously distant country (an imaginative London-based medium).

Ali's Birthplace

Option I—Sarawak

Let's examine the first claim, that Ali was from Sarawak.

That conclusion fits with the fact that Wallace hired Ali in Sarawak, described Ali as "my Bornean lad," and, in an 1867 lecture in London, referred to Ali as "a native of Borneo."[70]

Kuching residents Tom McLaughlin and Suriani binti Sahari claim that Ali's patronym was (Ali) bin Amit (Ali, son of Amit),[71] that he was born around 1849, was the youngest of five children, and came from Kampung Jaie, today about two hours' drive from the Sarawak capital of Kuching.[72] McLaughlin and Suriani, who have spent years speaking with Sarawak historians and residents, suggest that Ali worked in Rajah James Brooke's household under the tutelage of his elder brother Osman, later known as Panglima (General) Seman,[73] and subsequently moved to Osman's residence in Kampung Panglima Seman. McLaughlin and Suriani consulted a *bomoh* (local shaman) who indicated that Ali met a man named Edward at James Brooke's palace, who taught him English.

John van Wyhe, of National University of Singapore, and Gerrell M. Drawhorn, of Sacramento State University, similarly say:

> "It is likely that Ali was from the groups of Muslims living in various small villages of houses on stilts along the Sarawak River. He may also have come from the village of Santubong . . . Ali was perhaps about 15 years old, dark, short of stature with black hair and brown eyes. He would have grown up on and around boats. He would have spoken the local dialect of Malay and was probably unable to read or write."[74]

Option II—Ternate

Another view suggests Ali was *not* from Sarawak.

Cranbrook and Marshall suggest that Sarawak has not been confirmed as Ali's birthplace.

They offer circumstantial evidence that Ali was "a roving youth of Malay race born and raised outside Sarawak, and it is plausible that Ali's 'own country' was Ternate, where he had grown up hearing the Dutch style of Malay, where he found his wife with surprising alacrity and where he chose to settle permanently."

Their arguments are that "Ali's domestic abilities—'he was clean and could cook very well'—denote independence from his family, and possibly some previous experience as a servant. His evident capability to organise his employer's affairs, with a level of command over other men, implies maturity and self-reliance. Ali's language, his skills and his self-confident authority are wholly inconsistent with the image of an unsophisticated Sarawak lad . . . Ali's prowess as a boatman could have been gained through serving on inter-island voyages."

Cranbrook and Marshall offer another argument that Ali wasn't from Sarawak. They note that in one passage in *The Malay Archipelago*, Wallace quotes Ali; this is the only time we hear a direct quote attributed to the young man. Wallace wrote that he and Ali were staying in a house on Arru (now Aru) island in 1858 containing

> about four or five families & there are generally from 6 to a dozen visitors besides. They keep up a continual row from morning to night, talking laughing shouting without intermission . . . My boy Ali says 'Banyak quot bitchara orang Arru' [roughly *The Aru people are very strong talkers*] having never been accustomed to such eloquence either in his own or any other Malay country we have visited." Cranbrook and Marshall say that

the phrase "is far from the vernacular of Sarawak Malay and shows that, early in his employment, Ali addressed [Wallace] in the Bazaar Malay typical of the area of Dutch control."[75, 76]

Just to review.
We know Wallace hired Ali in Sarawak.
We think, but aren't certain, that Ali was born in Sarawak.

Where Did Ali Retire?

Where did Ali go after saying goodbye to Wallace in Singapore in 1862?

This is the second (and to my mind, more important) question, which took me to Ternate several times to speak with Ali's spirit. The only accurate answer is that we aren't sure. The few people who have pondered that question certainly have ideas. We have theories, we have snippets of evidence, we have a bunch of clues and a jumble of hunches. But we don't have a smoking gun. Or do we? We're not certain. The search goes on.[77]

Option I—Sarawak

Malaysia has two states on the island of Borneo—Sabah and Sarawak. I have a particular fondness for Sarawak, since that is where, in 1969 at the age of 22, I began two years working as an education adviser for the U.S. Peace Corps. Although the state has become more sophisticated in the years since, it retains a semi-rural rural vibe enhanced by strong cultural traditions. It is a good example of an ethnic, linguistic, and religious melting pot, with residents from all the major religions and some dozen or so ethnicities, including various tribal groups, all living in relative harmony. Also, like much of the rest of Southeast Asia, Sarawak has diverse and fascinating natural diversity that is being hammered by oil palm plantations encouraged by the toxic cocktail of corrupt politicians, greedy businessmen, and apathetic consumers. My novel *Redheads* explores this dynamic.

People of Sarawak have a modest awareness of Wallace, and almost zero awareness of Ali.

Among the few people in Kuching who care about the Ali saga is Tom McLaughlin, an American historian, and his Sarawak-born wife, Suriani binti Sahari.

McLaughlin and Suriani base most of their case on interviews with elders (including one prominent *bomoh*, or Malay shaman) living in Malay communities around Kuching. McLaughlin and Suriani believe that following his Singapore farewell to Wallace, Ali boarded a ship for a two-day passage and returned to Sarawak. They say Ali "built a 20 post house on stilts at Kampung Jaie. . . . He became involved in processing of palm sugar . . . he smoked palm cigarettes and loved coffee . . . [he purchased] sweets for the children [and walked] with a cane."

McLaughlin and Suriani were told Ali had a black sea chest of British origin, which they say contained a "picture of Ali with a European gentleman [and] papers with British seals." The box was evidently haunted because it "became alive each Thursday night making noises. Because of the belief in ghosts, the box was taken out and placed in the sea."

For several months in 1859, while Wallace was traveling in Indonesia, Ali seemingly disappeared from Wallace's chronicle. Some observers call this Ali's Gap Year; I call it his Agatha Christie period. McLaughlin and Suriani believe that during this year, Ali "probably returned to Kampung Jaie to check on his nephews" and to return for the Hari Raya (Eid) celebrations.

McLaughlin and Suriani also state that according to local folklore, after Ali returned to Sarawak he married a woman named Saaidah binti Jaludin.[78] And McLaughlin and Suriani quote a long *pantun* (a form of traditional song often used to relate mythical and historical events) sung to them by Jompot bin Chong, the grandson of Panglima Osman (Seman) who they say was Ali's elder brother. Verses include statements like these (in translation from Sarawak Malay): "How are you, Wallace the white man/Wallace and brother Ali are good friends/Unfortunately this year our teamwork has ended." McLaughlin told me that he was skeptical himself with the "*bomoh*'s observations until Jompot came up with the *pantun*. He didn't even have to think about it . . . just spouted it out. Then I checked with an 86-year-old '*pantun* expert' here in Kuching and she said she had heard of it. The *pantun*, in itself, is very strong evidence that Ali was here."[79]

And finally, they were told that "[Ali] died just after the Japanese invaded Kuching," which would have made Ali about a hundred years old at the time of his death. They visited what they were told was Ali's grave in Kampung Jaie. In an attempt to "test" the authenticity that this was indeed Ali's grave, McLaughlin and Suriani brought a *bomoh* and local official to the site. They said that the government official was so overpowered by the spirit of Ali that he collapsed on top of the grave.

～

And then there is the curious story of Ali Kasut ("Ali of the Shoes"). In 1863 two young British brothers, Arthur and Frederick Boyle, hired a Malay guide named Ali to help them explore the interior of Sarawak. Curiously, Ali wore western clothes instead of traditional Malay attire, including "two or three pair [of shoes] made of black English leather, without which he was never visible."80 This shoe-wearing Ali worked for the young men as a capable camp manager and boat captain. He spoke reasonable English. Ali Kasut, as they named him, had recurrent outbreaks of fever, which is consistent with "Ali Wallace," whom we know was seriously ill no fewer than six times on his journey with Wallace. Jerry Drawhorn, a Kuching-based historian, notes that "Frederick Boyle never mentions that 'Ali Kasut' was 'Wallace's Ali,' but then again Wallace had not yet become the famous writer of the 'Malay Archi-pelago.'"81

When the Boyles left Sarawak, they gave Ali Kasut a "large sampan." Frederick Boyle suggested that Ali Kasut perhaps had "Visions of trade with the simple Dyaks at a profit of 1,000 per cent . . . a hundred Malay pleasures became tangible in the near future, and possibly the wealth and influence of a real Nakodah showed themselves at the end of the vista, with, maybe, half a dozen honestly purchased wives, and a steeple-crowned residence like that of the uxorious merchant at Muka."82

Jerry Drawhorn told me he thinks Ali Kasut is "most likely" Wallace's Ali.83

So, if Ali returned to Sarawak to work with the Boyles, did he remain there? Or after his responsibilities with the Boyles were completed, did he move back to Ternate?

Option II—Singapore

Perhaps Ali stayed in Singapore? I put the question to various historians in Singapore and was greeted with polite interest and zero desire to follow up. There is no evidence, and no one suggests that Ali stayed in Singapore; I think we can discount this possibility.

Option III—Ternate

There are several convincing morsels of evidence that Ali settled in Ternate.

Wallace and Ali spent a long time in Ternate; Wallace used the town as his eastern Indonesia base camp for some three and a half years, where he recovered from voyages to distant islands and prepared for their next adventure. Wallace wrote fondly about the creature comforts he enjoyed in Ternate—"a deep well supplied me with "pure cold water . . . luxuries of milk and fresh bread . . . fish and eggs . . . ample space for unpacking, sorting, and arranging my treasures . . . delightful walks."[84]

Wallace twice refers to Ali's having married and established a family in Ternate; Wallace refers to Ali's marriage in a letter to Samuel Stevens from Ceram on November 26, 1859:

> [Ali] is married in Ternate, and his wife *would not let him go* [with Wallace to Ceram]; he, however, remains working for me and is going again to the eastern part of Gilolo.[85]

Many years later, in his autobiography, Wallace again refers to Ali's marriage and suggests that Ali's wife had loosened her grip on her husband's travels.

> During our residence at Ternate he married [probably in early 1859], but his wife lived with her family, and it made no difference in his accompanying me whenever I went till we reached Singapore on my way home.[86, 87]

Earl of Cranbrook and Adrian G. Marshall agree that Ali returned to Ternate, stating unequivocally "After ARW [Alfred Russel Wallace] departed from Singapore, Ali returned to Ternate to rejoin his wife and, perhaps, a young family."

There is a particularly tantalizing piece of evidence that Ali settled there.

In 1907 American naturalist Thomas Barbour visited Ternate and claimed he met Ali. We know that Ali was about 15 when he met Wallace in 1855, so he would have been around 67 when he met Barbour, a relatively old man but well within the limits of possibility.

Three times Barbour mentions meeting Ali.

In 1912 Barbour, director of the Museum of Comparative Zoology at Harvard University, wrote in a scientific paper: "I showed a Ceram specimen of *L. muelleri* [*Lerista muelleri*, common name: wood mulch-slider] to many intelligent natives of Ternate, including indeed Ali, the faithful companion of Wallace during his many journeys, now an old man, and all agreed that they had not seen such a lizard before."[88]

In 1921, in another scientific paper, Barbour wrote: "On the day of my walk to the Ternate lake an old Malay spoke to me; he had long forgotten his English, but he tapped his chest, drew himself up and told me he was Ali Wallace. No lover of 'The Malay Archipelago' but remembers Ali who was Wallace's young companion on many a hazardous journey. After my return a letter from Mr. Wallace speaks of his envy of my having so recently met his old associate."[89]

And in his autobiography of 1943, *Naturalist at Large*, Barbour wrote the most detailed account.

> Here came a real thrill, for I was stopped in the street [in Ternate] one day as my wife and I were preparing to climb up to the Crater Lake. With us were Ah Woo with his butterfly net, Indit and Bandoung, our well-trained Javanese collectors, with shotguns, cloth bags, and a vasculum for carrying the birds. We were stopped by a wizened old Malay man. I can see him now, with a faded blue fez on his head. He said, 'I am Ali Wallace.'[90] I knew at once that there stood before me Wallace's faithful companion of many years, the boy who not only helped him collect but nursed him when he was sick. We took his photograph and sent it to Wallace when we got home. He wrote me a delightful letter acknowledging it and reminiscing over the time when Ali had saved his life, nursing him through a terrific attack

of malaria. This letter I have managed to lose, to my eternal chagrin.[91, 92, 93]

This should be sufficient evidence, but one historian notes that there are questions about Barbour's claims and "we should perhaps be wary." Barbour's letters to Wallace have never been found, the historian argues, so we are relying on Barbour's recollection and Wallace's single letter, which we *do* have. Barbour said he sent Wallace a photo of Ali, but Wallace's reply indicated that he hadn't—an archivist at the Harvard University archives, where Barbour's papers are housed, terms this an example of Barbour "misremembering." No such photo has been found in either Wallace's or Barbour's archives. Perhaps instead of meeting Ali, Barbour actually met one of the Ternate-based "collectors" who traveled with Wallace who said "I *knew* Ali and Wallace." Perhaps Wallace's very polite statement that he would have preferred a photo of Ali ("Thanks for sending me news of . . . my 'boy' Ali—a photograph of whom would have been more interesting to me than those of the men of Dorey, who are pretty nearly as I left them 50 years ago.") indicates that Wallace desired confirmation of Ali's existence in Ternate. Wallace doesn't ask Barbour for any news about Ali, or how to contact him, which might indicate he was skeptical about Barbour's claim. Wallace did not include the Barbour information about meeting Ali in the New Revised Edition of his autobiography that came out in the Autumn of 1908 (the Wallace to Barbour letter dates 21 February 1908). Clearly there was time to include the Barbour information in a footnote. Or in the reprint of *The Malay Archipelago* in 1913.

Conclusion? My money's on Barbour, but there is no definitive proof that he met Ali on a Ternate street.

Nevertheless, since Barbour's report is the only shred of hard evidence we have that Ali had settled in Ternate, I went to the island and spoke to the mayor and various officials to encourage them to find Ali's descendants. After leaving Wallace in Singapore, Ali would have returned to Ternate as an important and relatively wealthy man. He had traveled widely and been friends with a tall, respected, undeniably quirky Englishman. He had his photo taken wearing European clothes. He had tall tales to tell and wasn't shy about recounting them to anyone who would listen. Wallace recalled that while in Singapore, Ali had "seen a live tiger [and] made much of his knowledge when we reached the Moluccas, where such animals are totally unknown. I used to overhear him of an evening, recounting strange adventures with tigers, which he said had happened to himself. He declared that these tigers were men who had been great magicians and who changed themselves into tigers to eat their enemies . . . These tales were accepted as literal facts by his hearers, and listened to with breathless attention and awe.[94]

People, especially family members, would have heard his stories and repeated them as part of family history.

I suggested to Ternate government officials, royal family members, journalists, and academics that they could place an article in the local paper; I even volunteered to write it. "Let's show Ali's photo and story to the village elders," I suggested. "Let's get a university student to write a thesis on the search for Ali." I pointed out that this search could generate national, even international news, and be a stimulus for the tourist business and a catalyst for conservation. It would certainly help build local pride, which is always a good thing for elected officials to bask in. *Bagus*, everyone said. Good idea. Lots of enthusiasm, no action. Indonesian apathy? A dearth of intellectual curiosity? A reluctance to pursue a "foreign" idea?

In a fit of frustration, I went on what I knew would be Quixotic quest. Surely, I thought, someone would have a memory of great-great-granduncle Ali.

I gave lectures to history and biology students at universities in Ternate and neighboring cities and encouraged them to seek Ali. A few students I spoke with privately expressed polite interest, but quickly zoned out when I explained that for their research they would have to speak with old folks in the villages and go through dusty records. "But that sounds like . . . field work!" they would explain, before politely excusing themselves.

It seems as if Ali is destined to remain an enigma, a lost soul in the large filing cabinet labeled: People Who Did Important Things But Never Got Any Credit. I suspect we all have a bunch of Alis in our memory banks and karmic stockpiles, folks who have helped us in innumerable ways, folks to whom we rarely raise a glass. We don't know Ali's birthday. But perhaps we might declare January 8, Wallace's birthday, as Global Ali Day to give remembrance to those who nursed us, did us unexpected favors, and who, sometimes, without our awareness, eased our paths.

The Conversation with Spirits

Part I – The Three Shamans

Scratch Indonesia's cosmopolitan surface and you'll see a plethora of shamans, mediums, psychics, and soothsayers, all of whom claim some ability to speak with *hantu*, the Indonesian term for ghosts and spirits.

Ofa Firman, and a few other friends, recommended I meet Nurdin Amin, commonly known as Ohm (Uncle) Udin, a noted *dukun* (shaman) whose uncle was related to an earlier sultan of Ternate. *He's very good. Well known. He lives behind the Muslim cemetery. Bring him some cigarettes.*

With a couple of friends, I easily found his simple but comfortable house that indeed was just behind the Salero cemetery that adjoins the sultan's palace.

"I'd like to speak with Ali," I said, showing Udin the only extant photo of Ali, taken in Singapore in 1862 when Ali would have been about 22.

Udin, 50, a slender man with an impressive moustache, long thin hands, and large eyes that shifted quickly between a warm gaze and an intense stare, opened one of the packs of *kreteks* I had brought, placed one of the clove cigarettes in a black holder, and took a few puffs before replying. "I'll need some help with this one."

We walked a few hundred meters to a similarly simple and comfortable house on the main road. This was the home of Ibu Ratna, 61, a carefully dressed woman of a certain age with a gentle, calm appearance. She wore a black hijab and a bright batik dress.

We were soon joined by a third medium, Ibu Dayu, 37, originally from Bali and married to a man from Ternate. Ibu Dayu has a small business selling decorative stones from nearby Bacan island. I asked if she deals in magic stones. She laughed. "Just normal jewelry." She showed me some of the rings she has designed.

The three mediums work together, concentrating their efforts toward Ratna, who sometimes asks Dayu or Udin for clarification. I appreciate the idea of having multiple mediums focusing on Ali, and, since we know the power of triumvirates (Musketeers, Tenors, and Stooges), in my mind Ratna, Dayu, and Udin become the Three *Dukuns*.

Ratna clearly has the power. She closes her eyes, and almost immediately begins coughing. It is a sharp, high-pitched cough. Her hands tremble. She starts crying.

"Sad. So sad."

Ratna's voice is thin and high-pitched.

She relates Ali's story over the next fifteen minutes. It is not a logical story in which incident A is followed by incident B. But why should I suggest otherwise? Virtually no one tells a story in a clean chronological timeline; this is particularly true when one is chatting with a spirit for whom time has little meaning.

"*Ali had a problem with a girl in Ternate.*"

"*She broke his heart.*"

Who broke his heart?

"*A girl. His wife. He doesn't want to talk about it.*"

"*Very sad.*"

Ratna is crying.

"*Ali and Wallace were good friends.*"

No points for Ratna, I had mentioned Ali and Wallace were friends when we first met.

> "Ali is a romantic man. He likes scenic places. He likes to take his wife to Akah Rica beach in Ternate where they watched the sunset."

> "He is not too tall, not too fat."

Ratna continues to cough. Her arms shake.

> "His wife is from the royal family of Jailolo."

This is interesting. She's referring to neighboring Halmahera island, where Ali nursed Wallace during his bout with malaria, and where Wallace wrote the outline of his Theory of Natural Selection. Wallace later refined and mailed the essay to Darwin from Ternate, hence its common description as the Ternate Paper.

> "She looks Arabic. Her father is Arabic."

I want to shout. Her name! What's her name?

> "Her name: Shinta Qomariah Kaulana."

This is huge. We have a name for Ali's wife.

> "She and Ali have one son: Ahmad Kaolan Ibrahim Djafar."

And a name for their son!

> "They lived in Foramadiahi village."

I know the place. It's one of the four original villages of Ternate. Not too far away.

Ratna continues crying.

"Why are you crying?"

> "Wallace asked Ali to accompany him to Singapore."

Loss of credibility for Ratna—this isn't a psychic breakthrough, since I had earlier mentioned that Ali and Wallace separated in Singapore and Ali subsequently returned to Ternate.

> "Ali asked Shinta to go with them to Singapore. She refused."

This is news. I wonder what reason she had for refusing? Afraid of travel? Stubborn? Unwilling to endanger her son? Or perhaps she saw this as a chance to escape a loveless marriage? I recall Wallace's contradictory comments about the relationship. He wrote that Ali's wife "would not let him" travel with Wallace to Ceram, then noted that "his wife lived with her family, and it made no difference in his accompanying me wherever I went till we reached Singapore on my way home."

> "When Ali returned to Ternate he was broken-hearted that Shinta and their son had disappeared."

Shinta abandoned Ali! I wonder. Maybe I should channel Shinta?

> "Ali never saw them again."

"What!?"

> "They were gone when he returned. She disappeared. Left him. He was heartbroken."

That could explain the crying. So sad, as Ratna says repeatedly.

Ratna regularly loses contact with Ali; it's almost like having a dodgy internet connection or a broken radio signal at the far end of the broadcast range. It's as if Ratna is sitting in the dark on a stormy night, waiting for a burst of lightning to illuminate her surroundings for a brief moment. During the disconnect time she remains calm, sometimes sitting quietly while waiting for the contact to be restored, occasionally chatting with Dayu.

"Ali died at around the age of forty."

Big problem with this answer. This contradicts Thomas Barbour's report that in 1907 he met Ali in Ternate, when Ali would have been around 67.

The connection is broken again. Ratna pauses to ask Dayu a question. She re-enters her trance.

I ask, "Where is Ali buried?"

"Foramadiahi. He was a follower of Sultan Babullah."

Ratna has gone off-piste. She's referring to Sultan Babullah Datu Shah, one of Ternate's most prominent sultans—the Ternate airport is named after him. He reigned from 1570–1583, some three hundred years before Ali lived in Ternate.

This is another example of Ratna's cultural bias. She has accorded Ali a noble status that is almost certainly bogus, simply because she (perhaps in good faith) feels it is correct. I am a foreigner, with perceived status myself, and I think she feels that Ali should also have a respectable social position.

Ratna is exhausted, and the connection is broken. I ask if we can visit Ali's grave.

My interpreter goes out to hire an *oplet*, a public minivan. The cost is about $20 for half a day. We all pile in and drive half an hour to Foramadiahi village, on the other side of the island. The *oplet* goes partway up a steep, narrow, paved path, then the path becomes too steep and we are forced to walk in the midday sun. At the top of the hill we turn left and walk another twenty minutes to the grave of Sultan Babullah. It's a historic site in Ternate, well maintained, with a gate and signboards at the entrance. The sultan's grave, under a mature banyan tree, is surrounded by half a dozen other graves. Some graves have worn headstone markers, but they offer no hints about the occupants because Muslim graves do not have inscriptions identifying who is buried there. We sit down around a grave that has been renovated with white bathroom tiles within the past decade or so. The grave is prominently placed, in the shadow of the banyan tree and just below the grave of Sultan Babullah.

We sit around the grave. Dayu's young daughter is bored and wants her mother to hold her.

Ratna goes into a trance.

"Sad. Sad."

I ask why Ali, a commoner, is buried here, next to a great sultan.

"Ali was a tariqat."

Ratna is referring to a person who has studied a mystical form of Sufism.

But my Western brain, always seeking a logical explanation, still can't figure out why Ali would be buried in this particular site.

> "He became a holy man and God gave permission for him to be buried here."

This is unsatisfying. Ofa Firma later confirms that the grave around which we sat is occupied by one of Sultan Babullah's relatives.

We are at the point of diminishing returns. We are all tired. I think we have asked all we can of Ratna.

Along the coast road we stop and buy a few bottles of water. I give a tip to the mediums and retreat to the comfort of my air-conditioned hotel room to take a headache tablet and realize I didn't ask the single question that might have helped us find Ali's descendants: His full name. Tom McLaughlin and Suriani binti Sahari in Kuching (who received their information from local shamans) had provided Ali's full name—Ali bin Amit—but I am skeptical of their information and desperate to have a second opinion.

While this particular intervention didn't result in a big breakthrough, Ibu Dayu said we should try again, that sometimes the signals get crossed. And if that fails, well, there are plenty of other *dukuns* in Ternate.

On a subsequent visit to Ternate, I meet again with the Three *Dukuns*. They say they have new information that Ali's descendants live in Halmahera. I don't have time to go with them, but Emelya, a guide from the Ternate mayor's office, offers to accompany them. The Three *Dukuns* say they will need two days, with a budget of a couple of hundred dollars. I'm tempted, but am uncertain how the results would be communicated to me and would prefer to go with them myself. However, after I leave Ternate, Emelya continues the negotiations and the Three *Dukuns* tell her the search will take about a week, and that the budget for their time and services has increased to nine hundred dollars. Through Emelya I tell them not now, maybe when I come back to Ternate.[95]

Part II – The Spirits That Keep Office Hours

I climb into the front seat of the air-conditioned taxi at Ternate airport. After a few words of greeting—*May I know your name? How's life? Will it rain this afternoon? Who won the election for governor?*—I ask the driver, Irjan, if he knows any good mediums.

And that's one of my criteria for choosing which places in the world to visit. Not just the presence of mediums, but the reality that I can ask a total stranger for his recommendation of a high-quality medium as easily as asking where I can find the best seafood in town.

With just a moment's hesitation (*Who is this foreigner who just entered my life?*), Irjan replies that his cousin might be suitable. She's famous and works with many of the important people in Ternate, a claim I've heard about most of the Ternate mediums I've met. He'll arrange a meeting; we'll see her the next day.

Amalia is in her thirties, wearing a pink *jilbab* (the Indonesian term for an Islamic hijab), a black T-shirt, and jeans. She speaks in a soft voice. Perfectly ordinary in appearance and demeanor. With a couple of Irjan's curious friends, who are present either because they have some psychic abilities themselves or simply because they are curious and bored, we drive out to a simple seaside recreation area. It's a weekday afternoon and the place is almost deserted. We sit on benches under a thatched-roof shelter and drink fresh coconut water. I explain that I'm looking for Ali. Can she help?

"*We'll do it next Wednesday night. Or Thursday night if you prefer.*"

Well, the day we meet is a Saturday, and I explain I have a flight out of Ternate on Tuesday.

"*Sorry.*"

I'm not sure if she's busy or has suddenly changed her mind.

"*The spirits only are available on Wednesday and Thursday nights.*"

I had heard of mediums not being available due to other engagements or illness or needing time to prepare. But I've never heard of spirits of dead people having strict office hours like a bank or government office. I've learned that in Indonesia it is good to be optimistic, to spread your net widely, and hope for the best but be prepared to be disappointed. This is one of those times when I need to take a deep breath.

"Too bad," I say. "Next time I'll come back on a day when the spirits are working."

Part III – The Medium of Transformation

The most dramatic of my *dukun* experiences in Ternate occurs when I meet Iis Ariska Abdullah.

As with many of my encounters, this meeting involves some legwork and a bit of serendipity.

My Kuching friends Tom McLaughlin and Suriani binti Sahari told me that when they visited Ternate (also in search of Ali), they employed a taxi driver and guide named Mansur, who had a relative named Iis who was a medium. Unfortunately Tom and Suriani did not keep their phone numbers, full names, or addresses.

After asking other taxi drivers, guides, and hotel staff for several days I finally locate Mansur, a talkative fellow who enjoys telling me about the important people he has ferried around the island. He is happy to introduce me to his "cousin" Iis (exact family relationships can be fluid).

Iis gives readings to the Ternate royal family and is well known in Ternate spiritual circles. She is a normal-appearing young woman, works in a government office, and lives in a comfortable, spotless, solid middle-class house. Family photos adorn the walls; the furniture is, to my taste, too heavy and formal for the tropics. I'm welcomed by her proud parents. If they are nervous it's perhaps because it's unusual for them to welcome a foreigner, not because they are apprehensive about their daughter's upcoming trance.

I explain briefly that I want to speak with Ali and find his descendants. I try not to give too much away.

Iis slips away to her room and returns wrapped in a Muslim prayer shawl, a *mukena*. This garment, a form of *chador*, is usually a sober white or pastel color. Iis's *mukena*, however, is muted gold with a motif of embroidered red flowers.

It is as if Iis has donned a magic cloak. She undergoes a transformation as dramatic as any I've seen. The sweet, quiet young woman becomes a crone, scrunched and jittery, with a high voice that conveys a feeling of deep sadness.

Iis wiggles her fingers, twists her body to make herself even smaller in the large chair, rocks back and forth, and cries out. Her face is in extreme pain. She looks like she is paralyzed and she has trouble speaking; her mouth is twisted and she chews her words. She later explains she was channeling her grandmother, who would speak with Ali.

She suddenly laughs, not the giggle of a young woman or the response to a joke, but a cackle I would imagine coming from one of the witches in *Macbeth*.

Her eyes are closed, then she opens them. But even though she faces me and my friend Rinto, she doesn't seem to see us. Yet she responds to questions.

"*You are a traveler,*" she says to me.

What a disappointing first comment.

"*You are the most popular man in the world for Ali.*"

I think I understand her meaning—that I've taken an inordinate interest in the man. Nice, but still an empty bit of praise.

I ask her the usual questions about Ali's background.

> "Ali is not from Sarawak."

She explains he is from Ternate, and was sent to Sarawak as an ambassador for trade and to promote Islam.

He would have been a young boy, I argue.

Iis tries to clarify. Has she been caught in a wrong guess and needs to talk herself out of trouble? But she's clearly in a trance, so I have no idea what's going on in her head. How does she come up with this stuff?"

> "Ali went with older relatives because they sensed he was bright and that travel might be enlightening for the lad. They were all from a 'normal' family that was nevertheless related to the sultan [that would have been Sultan Muhammad Zain, who reigned 1823–1859]."

I subsequently checked with my friend Ofa Firman, son of the late sultan; he does not believe this story.

This seems to be another example of exaggerating Ali's importance, similar to how Ratna of the Three *Dukuns* told me that Ali was a holy man and therefore deserved to be buried next to Ternate's most famous sultan.

I want to clarify whether Ali was from a noble family or was a commoner, but Iis is rushing ahead, clenching her fists, making whimpering sounds, tightening her body into an awkward posture.

> "Ali had conflict with other people. He had a different perspective."

I have no idea what that means.

> "You are on a holy mission."

Nice of her to say, but I disregard it as a culturally biased compliment. Iis then gives me a piece of information that appeals to my left-brained quest for data.

> *Ali's wife's name is Siti Humairah.*

Although I'm skeptical, perhaps this will turn out to be a vital clue to help find Ali. "Please continue," I say.

> *"She might be mixed Ternate Malay and Arabic."*

Interesting and perhaps important. Although the name is different, this corresponds to the Three *Dukuns* who said Ali's wife was Arabic.

> *"Ali and Siti had six children, three girls, three boys."*

And she returns to the story that Ali was sent to Sarawak with older relatives.

> *"The sultan of Ternate sent Ali, who was then a boy, and five adults to Sarawak. In due course Ali met Wallace."*

This opens an entirely new concept of Ali, which relates, with a bit of imagination, to the Three *Dukuns'* claim that Ali is buried next to Sultan Babullah Datu Shah, in Kampong Foramadiahi, Ternate, because he was a holy man.

But Iis clarifies that Ali wasn't a holy man but a *kapitalao*, the admiral of the sultan's fleet.

This is completely new information, and quite unbelievable. But before I can ask for clarification, Iis is off on another tangent. She gives me more information than any other medium has.

> "The mother of Sultan Mudaffar Syah wrote a book about Ali. She dictated it to a scribe named Naida in the Melayu [Malay] language and it exists as a handwritten manuscript."[96]

This is an example of a medium inflating a response. After the conversation with Iis, I check with Ofa Firman. The truth is that there *is* a book titled *Naida*, but it was written by a prime minister of a Ternate sultan around 1800 (decades before Ali was born). And Ofa Firman says that his grandmother (Sultan Madarfasyah's mother) never wrote a book and no such manuscript exists.

Is Iis lying? Misinformed? Unconcerned about accuracy? Concocting a story that sounds plausible in order to appease me? All of the above?

Then it gets even more interesting. She returns to the *kapitalao* story.

> "Ali returned to Ternate and rose through the ranks to become the admiral of the sultan's fleet, the kapitalao."

And then Iis tells me something that mirrored what Sultan Hamengku Buwono IX of Yogyakarta said about his relationship with the Mermaid Queen. Happy coincidence? Is Iis reading my mind? Or is this international medium-speak?

> "We cannot look at Ali using logic. Even though he was a cook, the sultan felt that Ali was special and sent him to Sarawak, and then made him kapitalao."

So, the young inexperienced Malay boy has morphed into

a proud, high-ranking military officer. Another example of cultural embellishment.

> *"Ali is wearing his military uniform. He looks like a gentleman. He wears a gold turban. He introduces himself to me, saying: 'I am Kapitalao Ali.'"*

Lovely image, but a lot of new and dramatic information for me to digest. But I'm intrigued by the image of Ali as a man who liked fancy dress. He seemed proud to be photographed, in Singapore in 1862, shortly before Wallace returned to England, wearing a stylish European suit; I can accept the idea of Ali being proud to dress up. The Malays, both women and men, of the archipelago are known to be proud of their personal appearance and take pleasure in dressing elegantly. Also, we know from Wallace's writing that Ali was garrulous and liked to be the center of attention. So, the concept of an idealized Ali dressed in full military regalia makes sense, but the reality is ridiculously far-fetched.

"He looked Arabic."

Well, according to that single photo we have of Ali, taken in Singapore in 1862, Ali had dark skin and could well have been, at least partially, of Arabic descent.

"He was tall."

And here we come unstuck. Wallace said Ali was short. The 1862 photo shows a young man of about twenty-two, but gives no indication of his height. When Barbour met Ali decades later, he describes him as "wizened," meaning hunched over like an old man (Ali would have been around 67). This "tall" description surprises me.

> "Ali learned cooking from his mother, who worked in the sultan's household."

I wonder, did I mention to Iis that Wallace first hired Ali as a cook? Or is this new information?

Suddenly, Iis's posture changes—she becomes less cramped, more fluid and expansive. Her voice shifts register—it becomes deeper, more masculine. She is now in touch with her grandfather (she explains later), and Iis demands a cigarette. We pass her a lighted clove cigarette, which she puffs hungrily.

A missed question. Does Iis smoke in normal life?

Iis smooths her chin, as if caressing an imaginary goatee. Her posture becomes less cramped; she seems more contemplative.

> "There was a conflict between Ali and other people."

I recall Ratna's comment that "Ali had conflict with other people. He had a different perspective." I wonder if all of Ternate's mediums regularly get together for coffee and share experiences they've had with curious clients.

"What kind of conflict?"

Iis doesn't respond to the direct question. She puffs her cigarette, which she holds like a man.

> "Your book has many problems."

A true mind-reader.

> "Many different perspectives."

What does this woman know about writing, or my book?

But she's right, of course. Problems. Perspectives. I've got them all.

"You are on a holy mission."

Again, a holy mission. A quest. Where does this stuff come from? Is this a generic comment made by Indonesian mediums, like the assurance "Your grandmother loves you and protects you," given by British mediums?

"Ali plays games."

The Indonesian language is less precise than English. And Iis is speaking in standard Indonesian mixed with dialect. It's unclear whether she is saying "Ali *was* playing games" (a historical observation) or "Ali *is* playing games" (referring to the current conversation.) Either statement requires clarification. Playing games with whom? For what ends? I want to shout, "Come on, woman, speak in simple, complete, illustrative, declarative sentences."

"You have to work for it."

That's a message for me from Iis? Or life wisdom offered by Ali?

"He was nothing. But special."

And she repeats her earlier comment.

"Ali was nothing special. Sometimes ordinary people are special. Don't use logic."

And it's over. Iis shakes, grunts, and slowly comes out of her trance, a touch dazed, as if awakening from an afternoon nap in a sweaty place. She leaves the room to remove her *mukena*, and returns as just another normal-appearing young Indonesian woman. She has no idea what just took place. Her parents, who had watched the session, offer us tea and biscuits.

Part IV – Hard-to-Digest Statements in London

While speaking with Wallace via Nasrin Moazenchi in London (see chapter "Beings of a Like Mental Nature to Ourselves"), I naturally ask about Ali.

❦

Nasrin's comments are curious. I've conflated the information that Nasrin gave me while we sat on the walking path next to Regent's Canal with additional information she provides me a few weeks later.

> "Ali did not tell me where he was born, but I think he said it was a small village near Sarawak."

Had I mentioned to her that Ali came from Sarawak? I must have. It's not a location known to many people outside of the region. Unless she got it from Ali?

> "He is buried near Sarawak in a little church in a family private section. He showed me the church but I did not see any name, but the triangle shape on the church had a dark blue color with a cross on top."

Now, about his being buried in a church. By all accounts, and by all logic, Ali was Muslim, and the idea that he is buried in a church (and in a special family plot), is ridiculous. In a follow-up discussion, Nasrin self-corrects.

> *"I see a small building, with a steep roof and a yellow and red circle on the gable. A weathervane. It's similar to some of the graveyard memorials we find in Persia."*

Well, Nasrin is originally from Iran, so she is putting a cultural spin on this reading.

"Where did he go when he left Wallace?"

> *"When he separated from Mister Wallace he went to Burma and started his life."*

Wow. Where to begin with this exchange? *Ali went to Burma?* Ridiculous.

> *"[In Burma] he continued to do his own research."*

He continued to do his own research? Hmm. A number of mediums have given Ali qualities and expertise he didn't have. They exaggerate his importance, perhaps to please me —if a European arrives suddenly, expressing an interest in a man named Ali, logically, that Ali chap must be important. But Ali wasn't a scientist. He wasn't a researcher. Nor was he part of a high-level diplomatic delegation, later an admiral serving the sultan, as Iis in Ternate said, nor a holy man, as Ratna suggested, nor a scientist as Nasrin said. He was a simple, good-natured, helpful, underrated lad.

> *"He exchanged letters with Wallace, but as the time passed this contact got less, as he had children and was busy with his own life."*

Absolutely no evidence of this. Ali was probably illiterate, and there is no evidence that Wallace ever wrote him a letter. Nasrin is speculating like the others, who grossly inflated Ali's abilities and career path. Nasrin is culturally biased and guessing that Ali was an educated Christian scientist.

> "He kept those letters in a wooden box. However, he didn't say where they are now."

Tom McLaughlin and Suriani binti Sahari mention that Ali kept valuables in a now-haunted black sea chest. Let's give Nasrin the benefit of the doubt and say that it's possible that Ali kept valuables (but not necessarily letters from Wallace) in some form of wooden box.

> "Ali is with Wallace in a distant galaxy."

His birth?

> "Born in Malaysia, some village. Was working on a farm. He was young."

Where did they meet?

> "Somewhere in Malaysia. I see a restaurant."

One of the big mysteries is where and how Wallace met Ali. A restaurant? They didn't have modern European-style restaurants in mid-19th-century Sarawak. But if Ali was a cook, they could conceivably have met at a dinner at someone's house, or a coffee shop or food stall in the bazaar, or even (my speculation) while Wallace was dining with Rajah James Brooke. In my filmic scenario Brooke might have said to Wallace, "My junior cook Ali comes from a good family and is curious about many things. He's honest and good-natured. Why don't you take him along on your travels?"

> "Ali is dark, slim, short."

Yes. "And his name?"

> "They're not telling me Ali's full name. They don't say. I have a problem when I ask about the name."

Hmmm.

> "Ali is curious to learn. They had a teacher–student relationship. Ali had a dream to learn."

This idea of Ali as a keen student was repeated by June-Elleni Laine while speaking with Wallace. Other mediums have imputed serious scientific abilities to the young man.

> "Ali says he wants to live his life journey. He says he wanted to do a lot of things."

Interesting. Here Nasrin is describing an Ali who is a keen student, not an unsophisticated youth.

> "Had a wife and children."

When Nasrin asked this of Wallace and Ali earlier, she says Wallace chimed in and joked, "Go to the archives."

> "One of Ali's ancestors was from China. Maybe grandfather."

Highly unlikely.

"Ali's children?"

> "Descendants. One, a son?—is in Norway."

Wheee! And Nasrin is off into never-never land.

She adjusts her story, sticking with Nordic countries but shifting from Norway to Finland.

> "One of his children is in Helsinki. He said his family is named something like Parsavalus or Parsavarus. I am not sure."

All of his children would surely be long dead. And to claim that he has a descendant in Norway or Finland (with a vaguely Finnish-sounding name) is implausible, but not impossible. Nasrin's responses are convoluted and improbable; I am inclined to discount other information she has given me. But let's speculate. Maybe by "children" she means great-great-grandchildren. Maybe one of Ali's distant female descendants married a man from Finland (or Norway). It would have been highly unlikely during Ali's lifetime, but in the early 21st century it would not have been unusual for such an international, intercultural marriage to take place. Or am I giving her too much of a benefit of the doubt?

> "Wallace liked to test him. Because they didn't trust others, they started to talk among themselves."

I like the idea of Wallace and Ali as co-conspirators.

> "Ali doesn't want to talk. It's really hard to get information out of him."

Other mediums have said something similar, noting that while I have an emotional bond with Wallace, I do not have a strong connection to Ali. He can choose whether or not to converse, and in general chooses to remain incommunicado. Is this his decision based on my vibrations? Does the talent of the medium come into play? What about the personality and ability of the medium's Spirit Guides? So many co-conspirators, I sometimes feel like I'm entering a psychic world with a flow chart created by the Robert Mueller investigation.

Part V – Ali Remains Elusive in Geneva

During the conversation with Alfred Russel Wallace described in the previous chapter, Brigitte Favre tries to connect with Ali. Based on the given information, she cannot establish to her satisfaction that it is really Ali she is connecting to, so she stops the reading.

I ask: "Why do you think you can't make the same kind of contact as you did with Wallace?"

For Brigitte this is obvious.

> "You have a connection with Wallace, and he has a connection with you. Wallace wanted to speak with you. You have no real connection with Ali, and vice versa."

Part VI – Ali, a Seated Skeleton

Barbara Kohler is a well-known German medium. On my behalf a friend asks her to contact Ali, giving her only the information that Ali was an assistant to Alfred Russel Wallace. The only clarification Barbara asked was, "Wallace, the explorer?" We can safely assume that Barbara had no prior knowledge of Ali.

These are the answers she receives.

> "Ali was born near the sea, small coastal village on an island, perhaps Sumatra?"

Well, Borneo, but Sumatra's a pretty good guess.

> "He was indigenous, grew up in poor conditions, underprivileged."

Likely true, but this could also be Barbara's cultural bias creeping in.

> "Alfred Russel Wallace offered Ali a job . . . as a simple mate first, hauling boxes, cooking . . . then he worked his way up."

Extraordinary, not the fact that Ali was lugging boxes, but that he was cooking, and most important, "worked his way up."

> "Ali could write, you can find Ali's handwriting [marginal notes] on Wallace's papers!"

Ridiculous. No evidence Ali was literate.

> "So he kept lists, cataloged."

Like most other mediums, she's inflating his importance and skill by giving him more credit than he deserves. There is absolutely no evidence Ali was involved in cataloguing or written administration.

> "He got more and more knowledge."

Now this is interesting and accurate.

> "He is extremely loyal, faithful . . . position of trust . . . scientific tasks were handed over to him."

True, although it is an exaggeration that Wallace handed him "scientific tasks." Collecting and skinning birds, yes. Does that count as "scientific?"

> "Ali never intended to travel with Wallace, but that's how it worked out."

And then Barbara comes up with a bombshell.

> "Ali's contribution was a caring support . . . he nursed Wallace during a serious illness."

If we accept that Barbara had no prior knowledge of Ali, and little knowledge about Wallace, how could she know that Ali nursed Wallace in Ternate during the malaria attack during which Wallace conceived the Theory of Natural Selection?

> "Ali was paid with silver coins, with it he supported his family, and his tribe."

Possible.

> "Ali had no family of his own, no children!"

This is untrue, at least if we accept Wallace's repeated comments that Ali had a family in Ternate. Not to mention the many (and conflicting) reports by other mediums that Ali had a wife and children.

> "After leaving Wallace, Ali returned to his village and lived with his brother or cousin . . . in any case blood relationship, until his death."

There is evidence against this—remember, Barbour recalls meeting "Ali Wallace" in Ternate.

> "Ali died rather young, between 40 and 50 years. Although he ate mostly fish he died due to blood-vessel obstruction, and heart disease."

This contradicts Barbour, who met Ali Wallace in Ternate when Ali would have been about 67 years old.

> "No one in the village knew about his merits."

Unlikely, from Wallace's notes Ali was voluble and a keen storyteller, often self-aggrandizing himself when recounting stories of his voyage with Wallace.

Where did he die?

> "No one can say, Ali died anonymous, unnoticed."

But then Barbara adds:

> "I see a seated skeleton in a cave."

Now we're in the fascinating realm of Indiana Jones and gruesome funerary rituals. It's starting to get a bit woo-woo, and I love it.

I'm impressed by Barbara. She got some of Ali's story arc correct, particularly the bit about nursing Wallace. And, to be honest, I relish the "seated skeleton" image, improbable as it is.

Ali remains in the shadows, a mostly hidden, largely reticent, illusionary spirit.

ALI: A LIFE STORY FULL OF SUPPOSITION

Ali's biography is based on a confusing jumble of facts (precious few), supposition (plenty), and information sourced from mediums in several countries (contradictory and unreliable). The source of the information is noted in parentheses.

1. ALI'S FAMILY NAME/PATRONYM:

    - Unknown—Wallace never mentioned it, there are no contemporary records
    - Ali bin Amit—Ali, son of Amit (McLaughlin and Suriani)
    - Ali Doja Khan, from clan Soamole—this is a clan name in the Sula islands, North Maluku Province (Iis)

2. ALI'S WIFE:

    - Shinta Qomariah Kaulana (Three *Dukuns*)
    - Siti Humairah (Iis)
    - Saadiah binti Jaludin (McLaughlin and Suriani)
    - No family (Barbara Kohler)

3. ALI'S SIBLINGS:

    - Four older brothers—Chek, Osman, Tad, Lon. (McLaughlin and Suriani)

4. ALI'S CHILDREN:

    - Two sons—Said (who died childless), and Rajak, who fathered seven children (five girls and two boys) (McLaughlin and Suriani)

- Six children—three girls, three boys (Iis)
- One son—Ahmad Kaolan Ibrahim Djafar (Three *Dukuns*)
- A child/descendant lives in Norway or Finland (Nasrin)
- No family (Barbara Kohler)

5. ALI'S BIRTHPLACE:

- Kuching (region), Sarawak (Wallace, McLoughlin and Suriani, van Whye and Drawhorn, Nasrin)
- "Coastal village," perhaps Sumatra (Barbara Kohler)
- Ternate, Indonesia (Cranbrook and Marshall, Iis, Three *Dukuns*)

6. AFTER WALLACE DEPARTED, WHERE DID ALI SPEND THE REMAINDER OF HIS LIFE?

- Sarawak, Malaysia (McLaughlin and Suriani, also Boyle who wrote that he met "Ali Kasut" in Sarawak, with modern interpretation that this man was indeed "Ali Wallace." In any case, this does not prove Ali *stayed* in Sarawak.)
- Ternate, Indonesia (Barbour, Three *Dukuns*, Iis, Cranbrook and Marshall, van Whye and Drawhorn, Wallace—implied since he did not express surprise that Barbour met Ali in Ternate in 1907)
- Burma (Nasrin)
- Returned to his village, lived with brother or cousin (Barbara Kohler)

7. ALI'S BURIAL SITE:

- Unkown (No contemporary records, and Wallace had no further contact with Ali after they parted ways in 1862.)
- Kampung Jaie, Sarawak (McLaughlin and Suriani)
- Kampong Foramadiahi, Ternate, adjacent to grave of Sultan Babullah Datu Shah; or Ini Susupu, Jailolo, Halmahera (Three *Dukuns*, who gave two answers)
- Hate Bicara, Jailolo, Halmahera, or the Chinese cemetery—Kubur Cina—in Ternate (Iis, who gave two answers)
- Buried anonymously, in a cave (Barbara Kohler)

8. ALI'S DESCENDANTS CURRENTLY LIVE IN:

- Ini Susupu, Jailolo, Halmahera (Three *Dukuns*)
- Sarawak (McLaughlin and Suriani)
- Finland (Nasrin)

AND MY BEST GUESSES?

1. Ali's family name: Unknown

2. Ali's wife's name: Unknown

3. Ali's siblings: Unknown

4. Ali's children: Unknown

5. Ali's birthplace: Around Kuching or nearby Santubong, Sarawak

6. After Wallace departed, where did Ali spend the remainder of his life? Initially Sarawak, with the Boyle brothers, then Ternate. Died some time after meeting Barbour in 1907 (when Ali would have been around 67).

7. Ali's burial site: Unknown, likely on Ternate or neighboring islands

8. Ali's descendants currently live in: Unknown, could be anywhere

NB: I am on a continuing quest to know more about Ali and locate his descendants, and I welcome information. Please contact me via my website: www.sochaczewski.com

"Are You Strong Enough to Go Through with This?"

Conversations with a female vampire spirit in a city built on a ghost story.

Pontianak tales form an important horror film genre in Malaysia and Indonesia. That's well and good, but what happens when a female vampire spirit named Farida wants to follow me home?

PONTIANAK, West Kalimantan, Indonesia

If most Western mediums can be believed, the spirits of ancestors, even if abusive and cruel during their time on Earth, turn into cupcakes of affection and support once they "pass."

But some spirits can be downright nasty.

We're fascinated by evil-intentioned ghosts. And writers and filmmakers worldwide have stoked that fascination with campfire tales of scary things that go bump in the night and leave a trail of insanity and blood. These creatures have gruesome chips on their shoulders and inhabit the dark otherworld of nightmares and mayhem.

So it is in Borneo, where the *pontianak* reigns.

The Setup

In the Inter-World, in the twilight mist of gray rainbows, hovering between dusk and dawn, joy and sorrow, life and death, dwell the ghosts. Wisps of smoke, certainly, but all too real for those who believe.

And the best place in the world to look for ghosts is the western edge of Borneo.

Not just any kind of ghost, but a very specific type of spirit that gives this city its name: Pontianak. The only city in the world named after a female vampire spirit who is eternally angry at men.

According to legends, and there are many, a *pontianak* is a misandrist for good reason: she is the spirit of a woman who died in childbirth, alone, abandoned by the child's father.

She preys on men, indiscriminately. She is pale, dressed in white and horribly ugly, except for those interludes when she chooses to be an alluring seductress. Her hag phase isn't necessarily permanent; some people say you can make a hideous ghost beautiful by hammering a nail into the hollow on the nape of her neck; the spirit will then become a comely and dutiful wife.

A note on nomenclature (apologies, this gets a bit confusing). In the Malay language, used in Malaysia, Singapore, Brunei, and parts of Indonesia, the term for this particular spirit is *pontianak*. In the closely related Indonesian language (the difference between the two languages might be compared to the difference between American English and Australian English), the term is *kuntilanak*. Even though the town of Pontianak is in Indonesia, they use the Malay word, *pontianak*, for their city and use the Indonesian term, *kuntilanak*, for the ghost. For simplicity I will refer to the ghost as *pontianak*, regardless of whether it appears in Malaysia or Indonesia.

Additionally, the Malay term for a shaman/medicine man/magician/ healer is *bomoh*, while the Indonesian term is *dukun*.

~

I met the sultan of Pontianak during a 2014 visit.

I was having dinner with two friends who are related to the royal family. While we were enjoying grilled prawns and fish soup, one of my friends, a cousin of the sultan, said, "You're asking so many questions about the royal family, do you want to meet the sultan?"

"But it's already eight-thirty. Isn't it too late?"

"No problem."

So, we forgot about dessert, walked to the nearby harbor, and boarded a comfortable wide-beamed boat that served as a semi-permanent café. Rustammy asked the other patrons if they minded a little river cruise, I forked over a few dollars, and the boat untied from the mooring and chugged across the river to the sultan's *kraton* (palace) where I would meet Syarif Toto Thaha Alkadrie, the tenth sultan of his line, the successor to a man who was Pontianak's first ghostbuster.

In 1771 a prince named Syarif Abdul Rahman al-Gadri, burdened with a dodgy reputation among seafarers and hassled by a nasty ongoing family feud at home, wanted to have a new start to his life and settle somewhere without being burdened with the baggage of his past. He sailed along the west Borneo coast and anchored near an empty stretch of land 17 kilometers from the sea where two major rivers meet. It was a strategic place for a settlement, but had been left empty because it was a swampy jungle believed to be a place of bad spirits—the *pontianaks*.

Local historian Din Osman recounted one of many tales of the founding of Pontianak. He said that for three days and three nights the ghosts mocked the intruders, making an eerie "hee-hee-hee" laughing sound that infuriated Abdul Rahman.

Legend has it Abdul Rahman scared the *pontianaks* away in the same way he usually fought his earthly enemies, with a large bombardment of cannons. History is not an exact science here; myth and fact are joined at the hip. Some legends say that the spirits fled. Other myths say that the sultan never got rid of all the ghosts and was haunted for the remainder of his life.

Either way, Abdul Rahman became the first sultan of Pontianak, and the town was given the name it has to this day. Every October the local tourist office celebrates the event with the Pontianak Ghost Festival.

∽

The busy town of Pontianak has 600,000 people, a large university, shopping malls, traffic jams, and luxury hotels.

But the ghosts remain. Pontianak probably has more ghosts per capita than any other small city, and virtually everyone I spoke with has a ghost story to tell. It doesn't take long before I imagine the entire population leaping out of their schools, cars, and offices and bursting into an Indonesian *Rocky Horror Picture Show*, with people and ghosts alike singing "ooh-eee . . . one-eyed, one-horned, flyin' purple people eater."

Spirits are everywhere, and I challenge a visitor to find a citizen of the town who *doesn't* have a *pontianak* story.

Ghosts, sprites, and demons are rampant. They're in the

banana trees. They're in the restaurants: *"Don't eat the soup at Auntie Aminah's, she might put a spell on you."* In cellphone towers, in dreams and, most definitely, in schools. You might hear: *"There is a particularly nasty* pontianak *that lives in the old house near the cemetery, where my sister-in-law's ex-boyfriend's motorcycle mechanic's grandfather was killed; just before he died he ran gibbering into the yard shouting, "I'm not the one who killed your baby. Go back to your own world."*

Din Osman's *pontianak* encounter is typical. One evening in 1984 he was on a motorcycle crossing the bridge over the Kapuas river. It is no ordinary bridge. For a start it spans the swampy site where the first sultan encountered the ghosts. And, on one end of the bridge, a small road leads to a riverside cemetery. Osman was stunned to see a *pontianak* walking alongside his motorcycle carrying a gravestone. He watched her for a while, and then decided that safety was better than curiosity and he sped away.

That doesn't mean that everyone believes in the ghosts. Many of the folks I spoke with speculated that the ghosts are spirits of dead women who are stuck between earth and heaven. "So you believe it," I would prod. "Not really," they would reply. "I don't believe in ghosts. But I saw it. I can't explain it. If it's not a ghost, then what is it?"[97]

∽

When an AirAsia flight from Surabaya to Singapore disappeared near Kalimantan in late 2014, Jakarta Governor Basuki "Ahok" Tjahaja Purnama referred to the high density of ghosts and mystical phenomena in the area. He joked that djinns (supernatural creatures in Islamic mythology and the origin of the English "genie") might be responsible for the disappearance of the plane. His statement was poorly received.[98]

The discipline of ghost classification is still in its infancy, and the spiritual world could certainly use someone like 18th-century Swedish botanist Carl Linnaeus, who was to taxonomy what Brigitte Bardot was to the bikini.

One might argue that nature (and the spirit world) is, by definition, chaotic and disorderly. But Linnaeus, who liked to say "God created, Linnaeus organized," strove for structure and logic. Linnaeus lamented that there was no common, easy-to-use, universal system of nomenclature for different species, citing the case of the common tomato, which was described as *Solanum caule inermi herbaceo, foliis pinnatis incises*—the solanum with the smooth stem, which is herbaceous and has incised pinnate leaves.[99]

Ghost taxonomy is similarly chaotic and imprecise.

In his work *The Malaysian Book of the Undead*, Danny Lim catalogues 126 different types of ghosts, vampires, *hantus*, demons, were-tigers, evil spirits, goblins, and other creatures you don't want to meet on a dark and stormy night. Malaysia has plenty of faults, but you've got to love a nation with enough ghosts to make up more than ten football teams.

I met Lim at a Kuala Lumpur café. Like a taxonomist, he suggests various classifications.

There are the "class of disease-causing ghosts" like *hantu cika*, which causes colic, or *hantu sawan*, which causes convulsions in young children.

He names nature spirits that inhabit snakes, rivers, and wind.

He writes about men who turn themselves into were-tigers, were-pigs, and were-crocodiles.

There is even a conservation spirit, *hantu songkei*, that undoes snares "to release trapped animals."

One ghost that takes up a large space in the Malaysian/Indonesian psyche is *orang minyak*, "greasy man," who is a take on the Hunchback of Notre Dame. *Orang minyak*, who wanders around naked, is covered in oil and preys on beautiful young women.

But it is the female ghosts that steal the show.

The *pontianak* is the most prominent of a large sisterhood of female ghosts that are descended from women who have died in childbirth or who have been abused by men. If you have the patience, gather together some Malay friends and ask them to name and describe the characteristics of the various angry female ghosts. There is considerable overlap and confusion. They are beautiful and entice young men to messy demises. They are old hags with pendulous breasts. Or they exhibit both personas, depending on the situation and who's telling the story.

Here are some of the more well-known forms of female Malay ghosts identified by ghost taxonomists:

- The classic female vampire ghost is called *pontianak* in Malaysia and *kuntilanak* or *matianak* (death of a child) in Indonesia. It is the ghost of a woman who died in childbirth, and sucks blood of virgins and men who have wronged her.
- *Sundel bolong* is the spirit of a woman who has been raped and abandoned to die. She has a deep hollow in her back. She is very angry, and hence a nasty piece of work.
- *Langsuir* has the ability to fly, like a *pontianak;* she is sometimes associated with the owl, called "ghost bird," in Malay.
- *Hantu tetek*, also known as *hantu kopek*, is a huge old hag with drooping breasts who preys on children, thereby encouraging kids to get home in time for *maghrib* (dusk prayer) or risk being captured by her and smothered to death. Many cultures have this kind of Big Momma Witch—the cannibalistic forest-dwelling sorceress in *Hansel and Gretel* comes to mind.

- *Churel* is another female ghost with oversized, sagging breasts, a consistent feature of their kind. And, like other female ghosts, she can also appear as a beautiful young woman who can charm any man. Because young men caused her death during childbirth, the *churel* drinks their blood, beginning with the man she loved in life. There are numerous ways to get rid of a *churel*, including burning a ball of thread along with the corpse in the belief that the woman's spirit will be so preoccupied with unwinding the ball that she won't bother to haunt anyone. The term *churel* is also used in Bangladesh, India, and Pakistan to describe a *pontianak*-like spirit.

- *Penangallan*, which Danny Lim describes as having long flowing hair, penetrating red eyes, and a long protruding tongue, feeds on human blood and flesh, with a preference for the taste of a newborn infant. When she goes out on the town, she is able to separate her head and digestive organs from the rest of her body; she leaves the remainder in a container of vinegar to preserve it until she returns. As Lim says, "A woman smelling of vinegar is not to be trifled with." This head-and-intestines creature seeks houses where women are about to give birth. The way to prevent her entry is by hanging pineapple or pandan thorns around the house; the sharp points will hook the *penangallan's* flailing intestinal tracts and entrap the spirit.

Maya Satrini doesn't look like a woman who could beat up a *pontianak*. She's a thin, neat, serious grandmother who lives in Singkawang, a small town two hours north of Pontianak.

But Maya has steel in her character.

She runs a non-governmental organization that tries to stop the trafficking of women from the region to men in Hong Kong, Taiwan, and Malaysia. "Young girls from the villages are promised jobs as maids or think they're going to get married," she explains, "but often they wind up as 'family whores,' forced to service many men. They're promised salaries but they receive nothing after the down payment of a few hundred dollars. Eventually they get HIV and are sent back. Sometimes I get a call in the middle of the night," Maya says, "to rescue a girl left in the middle of some rural road."

Maya believes the origin of the *pontianak* myth is based on the widespread (and not incorrect) belief that men don't take responsibility for fatherhood.

The first sultan of Pontianak encountered *pontianaks* when he wanted to make a settlement in the swampy forest. Similarly, Maya's house abuts a forest and she thinks that could be one reason why her son and two grandchildren saw *pontianaks* in front of the family home, since demons are well known to live in forests.

"*Pontianaks* are spirits that haven't had a chance to settle," she says, explaining that most people die because their contract with Allah is finished. "But some spirits don't go back to Allah immediately; they're waiting for a promise that has yet to be kept."

Several *pontianaks* appeared to Maya a few days before my visit.

"It was 8:30 in the morning," she recalls. "I was in my bedroom. They looked like normal adult women except I could see through them—they were transparent." Maya told me that one of the ghosts was angry with her. "She knew you were coming and said I mustn't talk with you, that you had no business delving into such things." She said that she told the ghost they had no such agreement and ordered the spirit to leave. And then the *pontianak* spit at her.

Maya's face became red and a rash immediately appeared.

Maya spit back. "The *pontianak's* face became red and her eyes looked like they would burst out of her head," Maya recalled.

The ghosts disappeared. Maya treated her rash, which she described as being "like a bee sting," with an herbal remedy made of charcoal, garlic, onion, and dried chilli. The swelling went away after fifteen minutes.

Wherever there are ghosts, there are surely ghostbusters.

A *dukun* has to know not only how to call a spirit, but how to get rid of one.

My friend Amalia is a Singaporean spirit guide who makes a decent living flying around the world cleansing homes and businesses of bad spirits. I never quite know how serious she is when she tells me about her achievements. You would recognize the names of some of her Beverly Hills–type clients.

At the village level, shamans "cleanse" the victim. The concept of cleansing has a special place in Indonesia's Islamic community, and Muslim prayers are often invoked to rid the individual of malevolent spirits.

But is there a deeper intention?

The term "catharsis" derives from the Greek for purging or cleansing. One controversial etymology of the word, suggested by Bruce Chatwin, derives from the Greek *katheiro*, to rid the land of monsters.

Isn't that what a shaman does? He or she helps us banish the demons within. We all tango with our demons—weaving, posturing, conquering and submitting, seducing and sometimes conquering. Demons are our dark sides, our uncontrollable desires, our regrets over actions taken, or not.

Vampire movies sink their teeth into theaters in most countries. A quick check of the IMDb database gives some 200 results with "vampire" in the title, including *Jesus Christ Vampire Hunter, Vampire Hookers, I Bought a Vampire Motorcycle,* and *A Polish Vampire in Burbank.*

Pontianak- and *kuntilanak-*themed films have been box-office favorites in Malaysia and Indonesia since 1958 when the Malaysian film *Anak Pontianak* (Child Pontianak) was released, followed three years later by the Indonesian film *Kuntilanak.* A spate of female vampire ghost films ensued, followed by a three-decade hiatus. The industry picked up again in the 2000s.

Lakshmana Krishnan, one of the pioneers of the Malaysian film industry, is now in his nineties and living in Thailand. His films include some of the classic Malaysian ghost films, such as the 1958 *Serangan Orang Minyak* (Attack of the Orang Minyak).

"No, I don't believe in ghosts, but the people who go to the cinema do," he explained over lunch at a Bangkok café. "There were times when the film was shown in a cinema and the film burned because the projectionist hadn't said the proper prayers."

Shankar Punjabi is another leading horror film director who doesn't believe in ghosts. "No, I've never seen a ghost and I never got possessed. If you believe in ghosts you will see them. It's the power of suggestion, as if I ask you, 'Do you feel the wind on your arms?' People go into self-induced trances. Imagination works best in a dark room. If you believe, you will feel; if you feel, you will see."

Over coffee in a Jakarta restaurant, Indonesia-based Shankar added, "But I've had actors who got possessed, and we always have an *ustād* [Islamic spiritual teacher] on call during the shoot to treat the crew and actors who get haunted."

Prem Pasha, a Malaysian filmmaker (who is Lakshmana Krishnan's son), recalled that when he was about seven he visited the set of one of his father's films, being shot at night at an old English bungalow in Kuala Lumpur. "I remember that Nordin Ahmad, the star who played the *orang minyak*, approached the camera. I looked up and saw a 'real' *orang minyak* watching the proceedings from the balcony where Nordin had just come from."

Teenage boys like to tempt fate, and when Prem Pasha was sixteen he and two friends went to a cemetery to spend the night. He recalls they were approached by a woman who glowed like she was covered in diamonds. Prem went into a coma for two days, and when he awoke he was suffering a high fever and his frantic grandmother was rubbing Indian holy ash on his forehead.

I asked if they had called a *bomoh*. "No, 99.9 percent of *bomohs* are fakes," he said. "But what about spirits and ghosts?" I asked. "Ah. They're real."

Are the *pontianak* films sexist? Singaporean Glen Goei, who co-authored and directed the 2015 film *Pontianak*, thinks they represent the 1950s Malaysian society when men were men and women were women. He didn't say so, and I'm not suggesting he thinks this, but the extension of this idea is that in rural Malay societies, women are closer to the spiritual world than men; they have special, sometimes nasty, powers and are fickle about whom they choose to befriend and whom they elect to curse. Perhaps this is male resentment (or acknowledgment) that Malay women, like women throughout most of Asia, bear the brunt of the domestic labor, take a large chunk of familial responsibility, and are generally the stronger and more reliable of the two genders.[100]

Danny Lim, the ghost cataloguer, agrees that ghost stories and films reflect rural, village life. "You don't have many urban ghosts," he says, although some modern ghost films feature sophisticated urban men (usually spoiled playboys and businessmen) encountering traditional spirits.

I wanted to speak with an actress who played a vampire ghost. I was introduced to Indonesian actress Julia Perez by a mutual friend, a leading Indonesian film producer. I was in Jakarta, and she was in a Singapore hospital. I was surprised she bothered to exchange SMS messages with me to set up a phone interview; the day before our talk she had undergone an operation for cervical cancer.

Known by her nickname Jupe (pronounced Joo-Pay), her career rose due largely to her energetic portrayal of a range of sexy and nasty ghosts.[101] She has starred in some of the most famous Indonesian *kuntilanak* films, such as *Jeritan Kuntilanak* (Scream of the Kuntilanak), *Kuntilanak Kesurupan* (Trance of the Kuntilanak), *Kuntilanak Kamar Mayat* (The Mortuary Ghost), and *Beranak Dalam Kubur* (Birth in the Graveyard).[102]

"Acting in a horror movie is not difficult," Jupe said. "They're the same as any action movie."

But has she seen ghosts while making her films?

"Not clearly, not in front of my face, but I've seen strange shadows. My grandmother told me they exist."

I didn't know how hard to push a woman who had just had major surgery, but I asked whether she believed in these spirits.

"I believe fifty percent. There are mystical things we have to respect. But the other fifty percent is just human behavior." It was a similar answer to the question I had been posing so frequently—*maybe, who knows, I'm not sure, I saw something I can't explain, better not examine it too closely*.

༒

Why do ghost stories linger in so many countries?

Some people feel the *pontianak* is an enforcer of morality, a creation of Malay wives who wanted to discourage their husbands from engaging in casual sex with women they might meet on the road at night. Be faithful, the man is told, and he won't have any supernatural complications.

Dimas Jayasrana is an Indonesian film producer who thinks that an encounter with a ghost is like meeting a superstar. "Seeing an old lady in a white dress who is dripping blood and laughing like a crazed little girl is the village equivalent of running into George Clooney," he explained. "After an encounter with this ghost you've got a great story you can tell for the rest of your life. And," Jayasrana adds, "ghosts are useful for disciplining kids."

How can you recognize a *pontianak*?

And, more importantly, what can you do when you are confronted by one?

My Indonesian friends offer this advice: A *pontianak*'s presence can sometimes be detected by an initial sweet floral fragrance of the frangipani (considered an unlucky cemetery flower by people in the region), followed by an awful stench afterward.

A *pontianak* kills its victims by digging into their stomachs with its sharp fingernails and devouring their organs. In some cases where the *pontianak* desires revenge against a man, it rips out his sex organs with its hands. It is said that if you have your eyes open when a *pontianak* is nearby, it will suck them out of your head.

Pontianaks locate prey by sniffing clothes left outside to dry. For this reason, some people refuse to leave any article of clothing outside of their residences overnight.

And most insidious, the *pontianak* announces its presence through baby cries. If the cry is loud then the ghost must be far away. If the baby's cry is soft, then she is close, ready to punish a man. It doesn't really matter to the *pontianak* whether the man she has targeted is good or evil; all men are same-same, which is to say all men, according to her definition, deserve to die.

The Conversation *with* Spirits

I am in the city of Pontianak. I have heard dozens of *pontianak* stories. Now I want to encounter one for myself.

A friend finds an urban shaman who is willing to hold a séance and, through a medium, introduce me to a "real" *pontianak*. The only hitch is that the shaman-for-hire has to pay the medium, buy offerings, cover his costs. "How much?" I ask. "About six hundred and fifty dollars," my friend says.

Time for Plan B.

The alternative to the expensive séance is provided by my friend Din Osman. One rainy afternoon we visit the home of one of his office colleagues, Rustammy. He runs a music café that is attached to his house, and in his home office I notice a few electric guitars lying about, like a poor man's Hard Rock Café.

"*Why do you want to speak with a* pontianak?" Rustammy asks.

I explain it's part of my quest.

"*Yes, but why? It's difficult.*"

Yes, and that's why I need your help.

"*But it can be dangerous.*"

That's okay. Din Osman is translating this exchange and I can sense he is concerned about what he's getting me into.

Rustammy tries again to discourage me.

"*And it's difficult.*"

I can handle it.

Rustammy looks at me closely. He appears skeptical. Finally he relents.

"*Come back tonight. Around nine.*"

When we get to Rustammy's house there are about ten people chatting among themselves. Two additional men stroll in.

"*Who are you?*" Rustammy asks.

"*We heard you were going to call a* pontianak *and we came over,*" the strangers say.

Rustammy is clearly annoyed.

"*I don't know you,*" he says to the men, angry, but in a polite Indonesian way. "*How did you find out about this? Please leave.*"

Rustammy explains the two options. I can "call" a *pontianak* myself and have a one-on-one experience with her. Or I can "speak" with a *pontianak* via a medium, a much easier option, he explains.

We could do it right now.

> "Are you really strong enough?"

He's still testing my resolve.

Send me in, coach.

> The shaman asks me again. "*Are you sure you want to do this?*"

I feel like I am back in high school again and my soccer coach, Charlie Koch, is looking down the bench to see who he can put into the game. "Put me in, coach. I can do it. I'm ready."

I am the first European to pose this particular challenge, which adds extra zing to Rustammy's decision whether I have the strength to handle what might take place if he is successful in calling the spirit.

Send me in, coach.

He is relentless in offering me a way out. He points to a thirty-something woman named Dewi, who is seated nearby, watching quietly.

> "*She's a medium. She can channel the spirit and you can watch. It'll be easier for you.*"

But I have come this far and can be stubborn when faced with a challenge.

Put me in, coach. I'm sure. I want to see a *pontianak*.

❦

Rustammy explains the procedure, what I must do and what I might expect.

Suddenly, one of Rustammy's friends, a man named Andi, starts shouting. His eyes bulge, then he arches his back and pounds the table.

> "*He's a foreigner,*" the man yells, looking in my direction. "*It's not right.*"
>
> "*Ah, that's Datuk Jangut* [the Bearded Lord]," Rustammy says. "*Datuk Jangut often speaks through Andi—he goes into a trance easily.*"

I find it refreshing that in a city named after a ghost, even the guests at a séance are mediums. Everybody can play a role.

> "*There are so many spirits in this room, and some of them don't want to be bothered,*" Rustammy says. "*Can you feel them?*"

No, I don't feel them. I have attended dozens of séances throughout Indonesia and other parts of Southeast Asia. I've seen men in trances speaking in tongues. Men in trances stabbing themselves with knives and broken glass. Men in trances claiming to be my father. One time a man in a trance said he was Moses and that he wanted me to go to the Middle East to stop the never-ending feud between the Israelis and the Palestinians.

Rustammy calmly tells the spirit that we aren't going to bother anybody, to just settle down and be cool. Datuk Jangut leaves Andi's body without another word.

Too many people. For a bit of privacy, four of us—Rustammy, Dewi, a translator, and I—go into a partly enclosed adjacent room. Din Osman and his wife are discouraged from joining and they agree to sit outside with the other guests. I feel bad not having them with me—they made this event possible, after all, and Din's a good friend. They watch Rustammy lead me away, almost like family members might watch an ill relative being led away for a difficult operation.

> "You're really sure you are strong enough to see a pontianak?"

Yes, coach.

> "Sit in a lotus position, close your eyes, and call the pontianak," Rustammy instructs.

I'm not comfortable sitting in a lotus position and sit against a wall.

> "Hold your hands out in front of you."

Which I do.

> "Close your eyes."

Which I do.

> "Now call the pontianak."

Which I will do. But I don't know if I need to say it out loud or just think it. I opt for a silent murmur. *Hello, Ibu*

Pontianak! Good day to you. Respected Miss Pontianak, where are you? I know you're here. Come to me. Mademoiselle Pontianak, I want to see you.

> "She's close, I can feel she's close," Rustammy says. "Order *her to come.*"

Get your vampire-ass over here right now.

> "She's right here," Rustammy insists. *"I can feel her."*

I don't feel her.

> "Be strong. Order *her to come,*" Rustammy says, insistent that his tactics will work.

I'm not sure that it's a good idea to boss around a female vampire ghost who hates men.

I mix the strategies of command and request. *Come closer, Madam Pontianak. Close to me, close to you. I order you. I command you. You're close. I want to see you. Come closer to me.*

And then my monkey-mind kicks in. I start to hum the Carpenters' song "Close to You." *Why do birds suddenly appear, every time, you are near?*

I want to giggle.

Do *pontianaks* have a sense of humor? Do they appreciate music of the seventies?

After about five additional minutes of unanswered entreaties and scraps of banal music, I open my eyes. "Nothing," I say.

It's late and we're tired.

"*You were so close,*" Rustammy says.

He reminds me of a baseball manager talking to a player who hits a long ball that is caught when the outfielder makes a spectacular leaping catch.

But actually, I wasn't close at all. I don't believe in this stuff.

"*Want to try again?*"

Rustammy instructs me to relax, repeat the body posture with hands extended, and this time he says I should ask the *pontianak* to shake my hands.

I've done this type of thing before. The power of suggestion is a strong power indeed. I hold my hands in front of me, keeping them still. Come on *pontianak*, make my hands jiggle.

I sit there for another few minutes. Nothing. I order the spirit to come to me, to make my hands shake. I command her in English. In Indonesian. In French. In Thai. I run out of languages. Oh yeah, German. That must be a good language for ordering a spirit to come hither. *Komm sofort her.* No, make it stronger. *Sonst,* I said with menace in my voice.

And just for fun I start to wiggle my hand.

And once the wiggling starts, the jiggle and jangle of my hands become stronger and my arms are bouncing around, like a small boat on a rough sea. But I am in control. I could stop it at any moment, but it is sort of fun. Let's see how this plays out.

Come to me. I order you. I humbly request you. Sorry to impose, but I'm only in Pontianak for a short time and it's now or never. I have a story to write.

What a great song Burt Bacharach wrote for Karen and Richard Carpenter.

Karen Carpenter couldn't be a *pontianak*. Could she? No, no way.

Monkey-mind goes wild. I'm shaking my arms and having a good old time.

Foreplay, but no climax. No ghost appears. After a few more minutes, I deliberately stop my flailing arms, take a breath, and open my eyes.

And then, Dewi, the quiet housewife in the maroon head scarf sitting opposite me, lets out a shriek that, excuse the cliché, could have woken the dead. It is a cinematic screech, worthy of the best (or the worst, it's hard to tell sometimes) *pontianak* movies. Her voice goes all husky; she lets out a high-pitched "ha-hee-ha-hee" laugh of maleficence that could equally be a cry of anguish.

Her voice can best be described by a phrase I would never allow my writing students to use: *blood-curdling*. Laughter. Screaming. Crying. Sobbing.

"*You people are bothering me.*"

Her gaze is distant and unfocused, her eyes hooded, her voice husky. Repeat laughter, screaming, crying, sobbing. Dewi starts to shake, jerks around and stands up. Her headscarf goes flying. It looks like she is having an epileptic fit. Softer laugh.

"Blood. See the blood!?" she shrieks.

Dewi quiets down a bit. Rustammy speaks to her, asks who she is.

"Farida," she spits out. "*My name is Farida. I was killed by a man. I want to go to Meester Paul. He called me.*"

Meester Paul. That is me.

"*I want blood. His blood.*" Laughter and sobbing.

"*I want to return. Don't bother me.*"

Dewi crawls into the next room, her sobbing mixed with a hysterical laugh.

Rustammy calms her down.

"*Go back. It's okay, Farida. Go back.*"

Then Dewi erupts again.

"*I was torn apart. I'll remember his face forever. I don't want to go home. I want to follow Meester.*"

Dewi collapses. She is lying on her back. She looks like she is in a coma.

Rustammy "wipes" her body to remove the ghost. It's a cleansing action in which he rapidly sweeps the negative energy from Dewi's head, her back, her stomach, her legs. Even Western massage therapists know this move.

After a few minutes Dewi opens her eyes and sits up. We all breathe easier.

Meanwhile, in the adjacent room a few meters away, Rustammy's wife Anni, who had been drinking tea and chatting with friends, becomes possessed. She doesn't shout, but her eyes roll up in their sockets and she is quietly sick. The spirits are up and about, targeting impressible women.

Just as Westerners are taught the Heimlich maneuver, most Indonesians seem to know how to ask a spirit to leave. Someone puts his hand on Anni's forehead and "sweeps" away the spirit while mumbling some Islamic prayers. Anni is an elegant woman, wearing a dress with a Burberry-style plaid. She calms down, embarrassed by the mess she has made.

I kneel down next to Dewi and ask if she has any recollection of what just happened. And she goes wild. It is a false calm. Farida has not left at all, but is lying in wait, like a hibernating bear.

Dewi screams and sobs and laughs. This time she looks straight at me.

> "I want to follow you. You follow me to the cemetery."

She picks up a plastic water bottle and throws it across the room.

Dewi holds out her hand, wants me to take it so she can guide me to the cemetery. I refuse. Her eyes bulge, unfocused.

> "*Meester,*" she says, using the expression Indonesians in an earlier generation used to address Dutchmen.
>
> "*Meester.* You called me. I am Farida. You wanted to see me. I am here for you."

Dewi crawls into the next room, knocks over a table with coffee cups, and then crashes into a computer printer. She huddles in a corner, then squats on a chair.

I don't get too close to her.

> But Dewi approaches me. "*Meeesterrrr,*" she says, rolling her Rs in a supernatural vibrato, drawing out the two-syllable word for several seconds. "*Mee-Sterrrr.* You called me. Fifteen years. I am Farida. You called me."

Fifteen years? I have no idea if that was her age when she died, or how long she's been in this place between two worlds.

Dewi then ignores me, like a small child who's bored with a toy. She shudders and Rustammy cleanses her once again.

Rustammy brings Dewi out of the trance, and this time it seems like Farida has genuinely left.

> "So, you saw a *pontianak,*" Rustammy says to me.

"But she didn't come when I called her myself," I say.

> "But that's exactly what did happen. You called her," Rustammy says, "and she came to you, through Dewi. You saw Farida. She'll be with you tonight."

I think about that for a moment and say, *"Never mind, that's okay. I got what I came for."*

Rustammy gets really pissed off.

> *"But you called her,"* Rustammy says, *"and she came to you. You made a deal with her."*

Now my monkey-mind recalls the story "The Devil and Daniel Webster." Faust and all that. I don't have a valid contract with a *pontianak*.

Or do I?

Of course I don't believe all this stuff. But I also don't want to insult my hosts by appearing to not take it seriously. *"What can we do?"*

Rustammy obviously is disappointed in my lack of commitment.

> *"You're not convinced, I can see that. But still, you called her, and she came."*

"And so?"

> *"Chicken blood should do the trick."*

I look bewildered.

> Rustammy explains: *"She wants your blood. But she'll settle for chicken blood."*

It is about midnight on a Sunday night. We are in a middle-class, residential neighborhood of Pontianak. You can't just go into the backyard and grab a chicken. And the live chicken market is surely closed.

But this is Indonesia, and everything is possible. I dig into my wallet and hand a few bills to a young man. Forty-five minutes later he comes back with an unhappy-looking red chicken strapped to his motorcycle handlebars.

"Do I need to kill it myself?" I ask.

"No, since you're not a true believer, we can do it. You can go home."

I don't like the religious connotation of whether I am a "believer," but perhaps I am overreacting.

To be certain I ask one last time. "So this will satisfy Farida and keep her happy?"

"It should be okay. She probably won't bother you tonight," Rustammy says. "But you never know."

⌒

I return to my comfortable hotel around one in the morning, have a shower, and hop into bed. I have no fear that a *pontianak* has followed me home. I don't believe in such stuff. I turn the air-con up and snuggle in for a good rest.

Just as I am hitting that never-neverland between consciousness and sleep, I hear a faint sound that jars me awake. I listen more carefully. It is the cry of a baby. Unmistakable. Coming from the next room. Damn, that meddling *pontianak* Farida *did* follow me home.

And then I remember. Earlier in the day I had heard a baby crying in the adjoining room. Parents traveling with a young child—so common in Indonesia as not to be worth a second thought. Surely that is the baby's cry that I hear. Of course it isn't a *pontianak*. Surely not. Just a normal human baby crying for a feed. Isn't it?

An Invitation to Meet the Mermaid Queen

Some relationships aren't meant to be analyzed too closely. "Accept it. Or not."

For half the month the Mermaid Queen is an alluring beauty, for the other half a frightening hag. She is arguably the most influential mythical spirit in Indonesia. I spoke to her; she invited me on a date.

SOLO, Java

I've tried to channel my ancestors. I've "spoken" with historic figures like Alfred Russel Wallace and Ali. And, in central Java, I had an encounter with a powerful mythological personage, the Queen of the Southern Ocean, whom I've dubbed the Mermaid Queen.

Such an adventure poses an enigma. According to legend, the Mermaid Queen is the spirit of a historical character who herself might have been a storyteller's creation. The Mermaid Queen's mortal persona (if there is one) has been transformed into a Super-Spirit.

The West has a rich pantheon of female goddesses that once held sway over various aspects of life—Gaia, Aphrodite, and Isis, as well as modern unidimensional comic book characters with limited spiritual gravitas—Wonder Woman, Xena, and Black Widow.

Java, however, has the Mermaid Queen, a potent, revered personage who millions of people today are convinced exists. It's hard to describe in Western terms what she is or the influence she wields. Not quite a god, but god-like. Powerful. Lives in the mysterious, dangerous sea. Capricious and selfish, yet generous to those she likes. More than the consort of kings, she determines who will be king and what power he will have.

In the central Javanese city of Solo I had a conversation with the Mermaid Queen.

THE SETUP

The instructions, given by a friend of Javanese nobility, were tantalizingly vague. If you look really carefully, and if the wind is blowing right and you are of good heart and you let yourself "switch mode" into a semi-trance, you just might see a tenth dancer. That would be the Queen herself.

My friend was referring to the *bedoyo ketawang*, a sacred court dance held once a year, in August, in honor of the ongoing love affair between the kings of Java and Kanjeng Ratu Kidul, a mermaid-like spirit who is considered the Queen of the Southern

Ocean. In this 90-minute ritual, nine dancers, all virgins by decree, weave an intricate and highly stylized ritual in front of the current king of Solo, Susuhunan Paku Buwono XIII. If a tenth dancer is seen, palace watchers say, that blink-of-an-eye appearance would be the Mermaid Queen herself, come to pay her respects and reaffirm her love for the monarch.

Through my friend's intercession, my wife and I were invited to witness this dance, which is not open to the public. We thought it would be a perfectly suitable honeymoon event.

The *bedoyo ketawang* reflects one of Asia's most magical *histoires d'amour*—the affair between Panembahan Senopati, a late 16th-century prince of Java, and Kanjeng Ratu Kidul, a princess who was turned into a mermaid goddess. Together, this unlikely couple begat one of the world's longest surviving regal lines—the royal families of Surakarta (generally called Solo), and Yogyakarta, in central Java, Indonesia.

In one of many versions of the myth, a beautiful princess from the Padjajaran kingdom was afflicted by leprosy as a result of a curse inflicted by her jealous stepmother. Her disfigurement brought shame to the kingdom, and in despair the unfortunate young woman went to Java's raging southern coast to meditate, where a divine voice enticed her to enter the ocean and become reborn as a beautiful aquatic queen.

Meanwhile, Senopati, a very real Javanese ruler, was having his own *crise de coeur* about how best to create a kingdom, and he too headed south for prayer and contemplation (some versions of the tale include a 40-day period of fasting and meditation, resonating with the rigors of Moses, Buddha, and Jesus). While sitting on a rock on the dramatic sea cliffs south of Yogyakarta, he watched the sea erupt with huge waves. It was a portent, and Senopati was lured into the ocean by the spirit who became known as Kanjeng Ratu Kidul, the Queen of the

Southern Ocean. During their three-day honeymoon bacchanal in her submerged palace, she taught him the secrets of love and the intricacies of good governance.

And so Senopati founded the sultanate of Mataram. People in central Java explain that the dynasty's 450-year longevity is because Senopati's bride, Kanjeng Ratu Kidul, promised to be the consort and power behind the throne for all of Senopati's descendants.

Javanese terminology is complex. In Solo (Surakarta) this powerful spirit is named Kanjeng Ratu Kidul. In Yogyakarta, she has various names, notably Nyai Loro Kidul (a somewhat lesser title). For the sake of simplicity (although I'll get scolded by Yogyakarta friends), throughout this chapter I refer to the Mermaid Queen as Kanjeng Ratu Kidul, regardless of whether the scene takes place in Solo or Yogyakarta. Or, if you wish, the Queen of the Southern Ocean. And, in my terminology, the Mermaid Queen.[103]

The central Java royal line, as with every major royal family in the world, has endured feuds, arranged marriages, power grabs, colonial imposition, Shakespearean intrigue, and soap opera–like family scandals. The line started by Senopati now consists of two royal lines in Surakarta, often known as Solo, and two royal lines in Yogyakarta. Preeminent are the Susuhunan (king) of Surakarta (from the royal house of Pangkubuwono) and the sultan of Yogyakarta (the royal line of Hamengku Buwono).

Of the two major sultanates, the senior in terms of lineage is that of the Susuhunan of Surakarta (Solo), a quiet city of 500,000 an hour's flight east of Indonesia's capital Jakarta.

An Invitation to Meet the Mermaid Queen | 193

However, the sultan of Yogyakarta, an hour's drive west of Solo, is generally more respected and has greater political as well as moral influence.

⌒

In the mid-1980s I interviewed Sri Sultan Hamengku Buwono IX of Yogyakarta about his relationship with Kanjeng Ratu Kidul (the Yogyakarta royal family refers to her as Nyai Loro Kidul). The sultan, who died in 1988, was a key figure in modern Indonesia's history; he played a vital diplomatic role during the Japanese occupation in World War II and helped to lead the fight for independence from the Dutch.

His love story with Kanjeng Ratu Kidul was made public every June 21, when the sultan traveled twenty kilometers to the dangerous surf on the slate-gray southern coast of Java. There he made an offering to the Mermaid Queen of a full set of women's clothing and his own nail and hair clippings to pay his respects.

In 1984 I was granted an audience. In his souvenir-filled Jakarta office we talked about politics and the role of culture in enriching society. He explained the mysteries of magic *krises* that could be sent by remote control to kill an enemy. Fascinating conversation with an erudite and wise man. But I wasn't sure how to phrase the single question that was the real purpose of my visit. I tried to pose it in a refined Javanese manner. How was it that a man as pragmatic and cosmopolitan as the sultan—he had been vice president of Indonesia and had also held various ministerial posts—could pay tribute every year to a mermaid queen?

Instead of answering directly, Sri Sultan Hamengku Buwono IX offered me sweet tea and told a story. "One night during the Dutch occupation of Yogyakarta, I, and others who were living in the *kraton* [palace], heard soldiers moving noisily about, as if wearing armor. It is said they were the soldiers of

Ratu Kidul protecting the *kraton*." I pressed him for details. "There was no one in the *kraton* except our family and staff," he said. "But we all heard the soldiers' drums."

I was more than a little skeptical at this. With astounding patience, he explained how Kanjeng Ratu Kidul changes form between that of an old hag and a beautiful young woman depending on the cycles of the moon. He gave examples of how her timely interventions changed the course of Indonesia's history. He gave me the Javanese equivalent of Hamlet's "There are more things in heaven and earth, Horatio/ Than are dreamt of in your philosophy." He concluded: "When I was four years old I was already living with a Dutch family, so my brain is in some ways a Western brain. But many things happen which can't be explained in a logical way."

I must have looked bewildered.

The sultan then told me not to get too caught up in a Cartesian view of the world. "You're asking a Western question, expecting a Western answer," he admonished. "You either accept it or you don't."

Throughout Java there is magic in the air. Accept it or not. One man's myth-enrobed fantasy is another man's hard-nosed reality. In the rainbow-hued world of shifting Javanese cosmology, reality can be as ethereal as a wisp—like religion, like a miracle, like love. You believe it. Or not.

Visitors to Java might like to spend a night at the Samudra Beach Hotel at Pelabuhan Ratu (literally "Queen's Harbor") on the south coast of Java, scene of a dramatic appearance of the Mermaid Queen.

The story, as told to me by K.R.T. Hardjonagoro, the regent of the Susuhunan's palace in Solo, went like this:

"In 1966 Sri Sultan Hamengku Buwono the ninth [of Yogyakarta] attended the opening of the Samudra Beach Hotel, on Java's southern coast, which of course is Ratu Kidul's home territory," Hardjonagoro told me one evening as we nibbled some of the fried chicken for which central Java is justly famous.

"In the morning, a few hours before the event, a local *lurah* [village headman] asked for an audience with the sultan. The old man prostrated himself and told the sultan that he had had a dream the previous night in which a lady said she wanted her offerings. She was dressed in green.

"The sultan, of course, knew that the villager had seen Kanjeng Ratu Kidul. His Highness thanked the humbled man but explained that he would not make an offering since he was attending the hotel opening in his civilian capacity as minister of defense, and he wanted to separate the affairs of the state from the mystical duties of the palace." We ordered more chicken and Hardjonagoro continued. "I was outside, near the pool, when the sultan said goodbye to the well-meaning old man. A short time later I heard the sound of a locomotive. The noise increased until it sounded like ten locomotives were coming toward the beachfront terrace where we were enjoying the hotel's hospitality. Then a ten-meter-high tidal wave erupted from the sea, which had been calm. It washed away the hotel's buffet table and soaked all the visitors. Some trees were knocked down. Someone ran to tell the sultan what had happened, and realizing what had occurred, the sultan put on his ceremonial clothes, said his prayers to Kanjeng Ratu Kidul, and made the appropriate offerings. The sea was calm once again."

I was incredulous. Hardjonagoro showed me the photos of the devastation. I said "come on," or something equally un-Javanese. Instead of arguing, he simply told me to go to the hotel and ask for Room 319. Sometime later, I did. This, it turns out, is the room in which Sultan Hamengku Buwono IX made peace with the easily irritated Mermaid Queen. It is kept locked and reserved only for her. For a tip, hotel staff will allow people access so they can pray to the Queen of the Southern Ocean. It is a good business.

◦───

Sightings, or at least encounters, with Kanjeng Ratu Kidul are not uncommon.

- Muhammad Sholikhin told me that as he was finishing writing his book about the role of Kanjeng Ratu Kidul in Javanese Islam, a series of extraordinary events occurred. The publisher lost the paper manuscript he had sent, and it had similarly disappeared from the publisher's computer and from his own laptop. He meditated about this problem and the Mermaid Queen appeared. He gave me a detailed description. "She was beautiful, tall, Asian with fair skin, large eyes, aged about 20–25. She wore a Javanese sarong, green, yellow, and white, with a *seledang* shawl; she danced, gentle movements, like soft sea currents." She told Sholikhin to give a special feast to his family and friends, which he did. The computer file was subsequently found, but the story doesn't end there. The editor made numerous corrections and improvements to the text, but when the book was published, somehow the text had reverted to the earlier, uncorrected version.

- Suparno, a taxi driver in Solo I regularly hire, took a group of pilgrims to the Langse cave, near Parangtritis. The difficult-to-access cave is said to be one of the locations where Senopati meditated before meeting the Mermaid Queen. It was Jum'at Kliwon, one of the monthly sacred nights in the Javanese calendar, a propitious time for prayer and unusual encounters. Suparno, who describes himself as a Catholic who also believes in Javanese mysticism, saw a ghost-like female figure wearing a green sarong and with long hair. She emitted the smell of roses.

- A friend who was the Indonesian liaison for an Asian Travel Forum in the 1990s visited the construction site of the Yogyakarta Convention Center, the venue for the meeting, and found it to be only half finished, with workers lounging around exhibiting little sense of urgency. My friend, who belongs to the Solo royal family, meditated and spoke with Kanjeng Ratu Kidul, giving her this message: "Important visitors from all over Asia are coming to Yogyakarta, and it is disgraceful that no one is taking this construction seriously. We will be greatly embarrassed if nothing is done, and soon. Would you please take action and kick the appropriate backsides to get these lazy people working?" The Mermaid Queen apparently heeded the advice, had a stern word with the right people, and the building was completed just in time.

Like other Asian mythological icons—like Ganesha, the White Elephant, Kuan Yin—Kanjeng Ratu Kidul is likely a compilation of cultural greatest hits. Historians (who enjoy scrambling for minutiae and esoteric clues in old manuscripts, crumbling temples, and the hidden corners of their own imaginations) have theorized that Kanjeng Ratu Kidul might be related to an Animistic nature spirit, a universal Earth Mother, a powerful Hindu goddess, or the Tantric goddess Tara. Maybe all of the above.

Culturally, the Javanese are a nation of hoarders, hanging on to dusty ideas and legends that just might, you never know, come in handy someday. Historian Roy Jordaan studied the architecture, inscriptions, and legends of Candi Kalasan, an 8th-century temple that is a short distance from Yogyakarta, and came up with the not-impossible idea that Ratu Kidul evolved from an Animistic spirit that evolved into the Hindu mother goddess Uma (or Parvati, or Durga), who morphed into the Green Tara of Tantric Buddhism.[104] Like Green Tara and Uma/Parvati/Durga, Kanjeng Ratu Kidul has a fearsome side and a benevolent side. (A cynic might suggest this indicates she is the ultimate female goddess, unable to make up her mind). And, like Green Tara, she changes form between a beautiful maiden and an old hag based on the moon's cycle. All the members of this cosmological sorority have relationship with the sea and with sacred Naga serpents, as well as a reputation as protector of navigators, and all share a proprietary fondness for the color green.

But these analyses are rarely clear-cut. We could be making this too complicated.

Kanjeng Ratu Kidul might be something simpler, a nature spirit given human form. In *The Religion of Java* Clifford Geertz says Ratu Kidul is "perhaps Java's most powerful single *lelembut*," referring to her origin as an ethereal spirit.[105] Or Kanjeng Ratu Kidul might be a marine version, separated by birth perhaps, of her twin Dewi Sri, the Javanese rice goddess who is unremittingly terrestrial.

She could be all of these things. Or none of them. The point is that Javanese accumulate beliefs like a chef cooks a curry. A bit of Animistic chilli? Of course, throw it in. Some Hindu cardamom, nicely grilled and pounded? Can't hurt. Some Buddhist turmeric, golden and subtle? Absolutely. Some Islamic prayers and Christian guilt? Sure, the more the yummier.

The *bedoyo ketawang* was originally performed as a six-hour marathon, all the better to put the dancers and audience into a trance-like state. Today, the occasional ringing of guests' cell phones reminds us that we live in a faster world, and the dance has been shortened to 90 minutes. Nevertheless, the atmosphere is both picaresque and otherworldly, as the royal gamelan orchestra pings and glongs a deliberate beat that accompanies a high-pitched singer, whose voice, to my ears, is screechy, atonal, and melancholy. According to Nancy K. Florida of the University of Michigan, the verses first recount Senopati's setting forth to battle (or to a romantic encounter), then evoke the depth of Kanjeng Ratu Kidul's passion for Senopati and his royal successors, and end with her praise of the metaphysical potency of her lovers.

In the wrong frame of mind, the *bedoyo ketawang* is as tedious as an Andy Warhol movie, but when I remembered my friend's advice to "switch mode," it became otherworldly entrancing and elegant. Just as western Baroque music has been shown to induce relaxation (and learning) by reducing a person's heart rate and decreasing blood pressure, I have the impression that the *bedoyo ketawang* music, played on sacred gongs and xylophones used only on this occasion, alters our consciousness. Let's call it a Ratu Kidul–enhanced altered state.

The problem is that although we were seated near the front of what might be called the "commoners' section," we had poor sightlines and had to crane our necks to see past two-meter-tall statues of Greek goddesses and semi-clothed angels, huge Chinese vases, potted ferns, wrought-iron rococo balustrades, and a handful of photographers.

Nevertheless, we saw nine young women wearing dark blue and white batik sarongs, colors that symbolize earth and ocean, light and darkness. They wore hair extensions pulled back in chignons entwined with golden filigree and jasmine garlands. I was mesmerized as the young ladies flicked their *selendang* sashes; it was a gesture that was both provocative, emphatic, and, in my semi-trance mode, gave the impression of an underwater current. They had been rehearsing for weeks, and were forbidden to dance if they were menstruating.

⁓

I am intrigued by the possibility that Kanjeng Ratu Kidul was present at the dance and put the question to one of the *bedoyo ketawang* dancers. Wuri, 23, is a soft-spoken English teacher at a local elementary school in Solo. She didn't find the question strange. "Yes, I had a feeling Ratu Kidul was there. One time I made a mistake in my hand movement and I felt her correcting me."

Another dancer, Putri, 21, acknowledged that toward the end of the performance she felt a breeze, as if Kanjeng Ratu Kidul was "going to the king."

⁓

The morning after the *bedoyo ketawang*, we ran into one of the Susuhunan's close relatives, who was staying at our hotel. Over croissants we asked the elegantly dressed woman about the previous day's performance and whether she thought that Kanjeng Ratu Kidul had appeared.

"Absolutely," she said. Her eyes started to get misty and a dreamy look, wonderful to see in a woman of a certain age, came over her face. "There was a rush of cool air. That was the queen, going to the king."

Again, I tried to ask a Cartesian question in a polite way. What did she make of all this?

In a wistful voice perhaps more suited to a love-struck school girl she answered, "It's a love affair for the ages."

The Conversation *with* Spirits

During the reception that followed the *bedoyo ketawang* performance, a man named Ki Radu Kusumodiningrat approaches me and asks if I want to "speak with Kanjeng Ratu Kidul." I'm not too sure what he means but accept his offer.

Ki Radu Kusumodiningrat, a relative of the Susuhunan, is a traditional healer. He introduces us to his colleague, Raden Ayu Retno Handayati, also from a noble family. Although she works as an acupuncturist and massage therapist, Raden Retno is also a medium who will channel Kanjeng Ratu Kidul. We stop at a market to buy fruit, candles, and incense, and go back to our hotel for the séance. The doorman busts us for the pungent-smelling durian, and out of respect for the no-smoking signs in the room, we cancel the incense, but Raden Retno isn't perturbed. She puts on her headscarf and intones an Islamic blessing. When her voice shifts to the timbre of that of a young woman, we suspend belief and imagine we are speaking with the Mermaid Queen herself.

We ask her about her love affair with Senopati.

> "The prince asked for my help. It is my duty to assist him."

I want to say something silly like, "So how did you two crazy kids meet?" Instead I try to get beyond the platitudes with questions about their relationship.

> "I'm always there for the King."

"What happened when you met Prince Senopati? Why did you go to him? Did you know who he was?" As soon as I ask these literal (and probably inane) questions, I realize it's probably better to limit my questions to one at a time.

Ibu Retno continues with romantic banalities, sort of Javanese Hallmark-card sentiments. She oozes loyalty and devotion.

I change tack and ask if she was present just now at the *bedoyo ketawang*.

Raden Ayu Retno Handayati, perhaps channeling Kanjeng Ratu Kidul, smiles and answers enigmatically:

> "I'm always present for the sultan."

After a few other specific questions and vague answers, we see she is getting tired. But just before the channeling ends, the Mermaid Queen offers me personal support and invites me on a date.

> "Just go to the southern coast [of Java], *call my name, stamp your foot three times, and I will be there for you.*"

I'm not sure what to make of this. Did Raden Ayu Retno Handayati really channel the spirit of the Mermaid Queen?

And what kind of reception will I get if I actually go to the beach and seek out Kanjeng Ratu Kidul? Stories are rife about men who wear green (Kanjeng Ratu Kidul's favorite color) while swimming in the Southern Ocean and who are never seen again—perhaps victims of the treacherous riptides, perhaps whisked away to her aquatic castle.

I venture to the southern coast some years later. I visit the shrine where some pilgrims are praying at the rounded stone said to be the one on which Senopati sat. I ask permission of Pak Suratso, the shrine's caretaker, if I can take a few grains of black sand. I stroll down to the nearby shore.

Aware of the dangerous riptide, I stay on the beach. The sky is milky gray, the weather is steamy and irritable, the surf looks like it has been spewed out of a blender—it's the John Cage of a seascape. I am not a diligent meditator even in the best of conditions, and I sit in a halfbaked *padmasana* for about fifteen minutes. I then stomp my feet three times and call for the Mermaid Queen. I await a sign—a tsunami, or a breaching whale, or a parting of the ocean. It starts to rain and I walk back to the car, not disappointed because I hadn't expected anything. But still . . .

The Trees Speak

Vital energy meets conservation imperative—the eloquent spirits of nature plead for their lives.

Do you see a tree or a nature spirit? Pareidolia is the psychological phenomenon in which the mind responds to a stimulus, usually an image or a sound, by perceiving a familiar pattern where none exists—such as when people see human figures and faces in non-human objects. The tendency to see a face in a tree trunk where others might see two knotholes, a wayward branch, and a gash. But who's to say where our imagination ends and enhanced reality begins?

YANGON, Myanmar
ZEE-O-THIT-HLA, Myanmar
HSITHE, Myanmar

In this book I've written about my encounters with mediums, shamans, and spirits—people and phenomena that defy rational analysis. However, writing, by its nature, is a cerebral, left-brained exercise. To write coherently, let alone attractively, you have to find the appropriate terms; clarify your writing voice; check facts, grammar, and spelling; and create a literary logic that helps the reader move smoothly from idea A to idea B.

The problem is that reliance on this skill is a huge hindrance when trying to understand the world of spirits.

This is especially true when trying to understand and communicate with nature spirits, the fairy-like entities that inhabit trees, flowers, waterfalls, oceans, rivers, and even rocks and volcanoes.

I spoke with Françoise, a friend who communicates with trees. "Do you talk with them?" I ask. She laughs. "No, you don't 'speak' with them as we're speaking now. We share energy."

I understand what she means when she mentions energy, but I'm at a disadvantage. I don't feel special energy, neither good nor bad, when I'm in a certain place. Françoise does, however, and senses vibrations everywhere she goes, as long as she's in the right frame of mind.

"It's your monkey-mind getting in the way. Do you meditate?"

"No," I say, almost embarrassed. People who ask that question make me feel guilty, as if I'm a fraud trying to write this book without taking the first step through regular meditation in search of "nothingness." Perhaps in order to write this book I *should* meditate to get in touch with other dimensions. I feel I *should* go to intensive shaman-training retreats, imbibe large quantities of LSD and ayahuasca, spend full-moon forested nights in a sacred stone circle participating in a Wiccan drumming ritual. And perhaps I will, someday. I've dabbled at this stuff, but that's all it is—playing at the tidal edges rather than diving in.

Writing is the wrong medium for this journey. This chapter should be transmitted by telepathy, or massage, or music, or art. But writing is what I do, so writing it is.

THE SETUP

I'm fascinated by what lies beyond the next hill. In Sumatra, one of the larger Indonesian islands, I wanted to meet magicians who could tame wild tigers. In the cities I was told, "You'll have to go deep into the forest to find those guys." Then people would add "Be careful. Those rustics use magic." I would then ask my urban friends if they'd like to come. They'd decline, pointing out in words or intonation, "The forest is dark, and dangerous, full of spiders and demons. There's no Starbucks in the forest. Why don't you go shopping in Singapore instead?"

So, I'd set off by myself and fly to a remote town, take a wooden-seat bus to the end of the road, ride pillion on a junky motorcycle driven by a bored teenager in need of some spending money, then walk in the heat and rain until I would arrive at a village where I had been told such sorcerers could be found.

And I met lovely people, rural, without much in the way of material goods or infrastructure, who said, "It ain't us, but we've heard about such folks. They're over the next hill. But be careful, they practice powerful magic." Sometimes I found the tiger magicians. Sometimes other wonders appeared. Sometimes I got malaria. Sometimes I ate termite omelets. I met spiders, but no demons.

This isn't the place to analyze how the sophisticated urbanites in the capitals of Jakarta, Kuala Lumpur, or Manila denigrate the hill tribes. The urbanites speak the national language (and a few others), follow the national religion, are well educated and well clothed, know all the players on Manchester United. Their ancestors built empires by mastering wet rice agriculture, as opposed to the less productive dry rice agriculture of the hill tribes. The city folks go to "real" doctors and get their medicines at the drugstore, instead of consulting a shaman who wields rattles, feathers, and amulets. It's a cultural gulf that one finds throughout the region, although it's becoming less common as the rural people are increasingly exposed to the civilizing influences of missionaries, education, government propaganda (often described as "nation building"), communications, and consumer goods.

And because the rural folks are considered somehow "lesser," it is easy for the city dwellers to seek to "give our poor naked cousins the benefits we enjoy," as one environment minister told me. And, by extension, it's easy to rationalize the benefits of "civilizing" the dangerous and primitive rainforests by converting pristine environments into oil palm plantations.[106]

But I have a fondness for these distant people. Perhaps it's a silly romantic vestige of the old European "noble savage" paternalism.

But perhaps it's also because the rural folks believe that spirits inhabit the rivers, trees, and volcanoes. I set out to speak with some of these nature spirits.

⌒

I soon realize that it's ridiculous to try to "speak" with nature spirits. Françoise reminds me that one needs to be in the right frame of mind to sense vibrations. "That's all there is?" I ask. Sounds easy.

Like many things, less is more. Scientist and self-described friend of nature Chris S. Hetherington gives this advice:

Nature spirits are not celebrities, they don't invite exposure. But if you find somewhere that feels right to you . . . then the chances are that any nature spirits will notice you as much as you notice them and over time they will remember you and become curious (as they did with me).

Don't be pushy. Don't be expectant. Just be in this space, without invading it, but by being part of it. You could say that this is about starting a friendship.

Imagine the tales your new nature-spirit friend would be able to tell. Time perhaps moves too quickly. Consider a tomato plant, which is born, reaches glory quickly, then withers away, all in one season—and existence is paced like a Roadrunner cartoon.

Sometimes time moves too slowly—a sequoia takes centuries to rise to the sky.

There are invading armies (alien fungus! caterpillars! locusts!), and friendly, tickling new friends—bees! butterflies! hummingbirds!) that come for a quick touch and go. God-forces (storms, floods, drought, housing developments, fracking) that force an easygoing plant to ask, "What am I doing here?" Group migrations. Endless chats with an extended family. Does the day lily long to see the moon? Does one type of nocturnal water lily dream of seeing the sun? Does the sour crab apple wish it could wind up in a *tarte tatin* like its sweeter cousin Golden Delicious?

And since this is a book about life after death, consider the fact that a tree becomes even more productive *after it dies*.

The ambrosia beetle, for instance, is attracted to the alcohol of rotting wood. The little creature, let's call her Maude, excavates and sows bits of fungus. The fungus eats the wood; a beetle eats the fungus. As Richard Powers writes in *The Overstory*, "There's a kind of vole that needs old forest. It eats mushrooms that grow on rotting logs and excretes spores somewhere else. No rotting logs, no mushrooms; no mushrooms, no vole; no vole, no spreading fungus; no spreading fungus, no new trees."

The forest drama plays out in random time, a Stockhausen unpredictability, rarely a rhythmic Strauss waltz. Growth, community, pain, rebirth. Mangled plot lines, a Tarantino or Godard film, not a Disney animation with a predictable story arc. We humans would like to make the cycles of life clear and linear, but they are not so easily defined.

We cannot catalogue all the countless complex interactions that nature handles quite well, thank you, as long as nature is left alone.

Is the hedgerow proud to host thousands of squirming, hustling, life forms? Is the elephant grass desolate because it is so dense, untasty, and inhospitable that it hosts few life forms of consequence? Are plants reassured when there are other plant friends to chat with? But then those friends might suddenly disappear. However, if the plant is lucky and patient, new friends might surprisingly emerge.

And that's just the stuff with chlorophyll. How I'd love to chat with an orangutan ("What do you think about oil palm? Be honest, now.") Or an octopus. ("People say you're really clever. Got any comment about plastic in the ocean?"). I wish I had the intelligence to speak Avian. What are the birds singing? (Clever Noel Coward lyrics? The libretto from *Don Giovanni*? A click language like the Kalahari Bushmen? Morning news—*Hey, Mrs Smith next door just filled the bird feeder!* Morning warnings—*Don't go to the farm to the north, the idiot son there has a new shotgun!* Maybe the bird equivalent of "Oh, What a Beautiful Morning," from *Oklahoma*?)

It's easier for me to get my brain around the idea of speaking with the spirit of a dead person than it is to comprehend speaking with a fig tree or a small waterfall. But in a way, the concept of engaging a fig tree or a waterfall is more intriguing. Trouble is, well, the trouble is my left brain says to me, "Hey dude, if you think speaking to Alfred Russel Wallace is spacey, then wait until you hear what an oak has to say. Good luck, bro."

The Trees Speak | 211

In March 1996 environmental anthropologist John Studley organized a two-truck convoy of clothes, food, and medicine to help isolated ethnic Tibetan communities suffering from a series of blizzards. He had the support of local government officials in the nearest town of Shiqu, in China's western Sichuan province. The rural roads were in a miserable condition to begin with, and now they were frozen and snow-covered.

As Studley describes it, soon after they left the town trouble began. One truck broke a shock absorber and slipped off a narrow bridge, just missing tumbling hundreds of meters to the frozen river below. They had to unload the truck and ease it across. Another vehicle, a Pajero, broke through some ice and cracked the front axle. Then its engine froze.

That night Studley suffered what he describes as "waking paralysis." "I couldn't breathe, like there was a heavy weight on my chest," he told me. "Couldn't speak, couldn't shout. Psychological literature says I had a 'neurological short circuit' because there is no vocabulary for what happens when you are attacked by angry spirits. It wasn't a nightmare; I was awake."

Angry spirits—that's what Studley attributes it to. All but one of his Tibetan support crew abandoned the trip. They *knew*. The spirits of place that protect this region weren't benign.

Even though Studley had obtained the blessings of civic leaders before organizing the trip, he had not made an effort to appease the xenophobic and proud spirits. A silly oversight by a man who earned his PhD by living with Tibetan nomads and observing their relationship with nature.

Still shaken by the "waking paralysis," Studley and his friends visited a nearby temple where the necessary offerings were made and the appropriate blessings sought. The trip continued without incident. The following year, in similar blizzard conditions, he returned with 700 yaks to replenish the farmers' depleted herds. This time the humanitarian aid convoy reached safely.

~

John Studley is a proponent of giving nature spirits the legal rights of people so they can gain protection from destruction or damage in courts.

At first glance this sounds ridiculous, but such legal protection has been granted in a number of countries. For me it's an intriguing, and potentially useful, new tool in the fight to protect nature.

It's based on the Animistic concept of recognizing that natural objects (mostly living things like plants and animals, but also features like rivers, mountains, and stones) have spirits. Studley uses the terms "numen" or the plural "numina," which is Latin for "divine presence." Etymologically, the word means "a nod of the head," which could be expressed as a form of either the spirit's consciousness or an exhibition of its power.

Courts have granted juristic personhood to nature spirits worldwide.[107, 108]

- In their national constitutions, Ecuador and Bolivia have recognized Mother Earth as a "legal person." (In at least two cases in Ecuador involving pollution of rivers, the courts have stated that the rights of nature prevail over other constitutional rights.)

- Indian courts have granted "legal person" rights to the Ganges and Yamuna river systems.

- In 2014 New Zealand became the first nation on Earth to give up formal ownership of a national park when it declared that the area, Te Urewera, has "all the rights, powers, duties, and liabilities of a legal person."

- And in 2017, after some 170 years of litigation, a New

Zealand court recognized the status of the numina that inhabit each of the more than 240 rapids on the Whanganui River.

- In 2010 the city of Pittsburgh, Pennsylvania, became the first city in the United States to declare nature a "legal person" during a case to ban fracking within the city limits.

- The U.S. state of Hawaii heard a case in which a Native Hawaiian shaman testified that the numina that occupy the Mauna Kea volcano on the Big Island would be furious if a new telescope was constructed on its slopes. The court initially ruled in favor of the Native Hawaiian petitioners but reversed the decision after an appeal, deciding that the construction and management of the telescope could proceed as long as the development adhered to strict cultural and environmental safeguards.

I propose that we have a need/fear relationship with nature.

On the positive side, we come from nature; we are part of nature. This connection is deep, ancient, and very Jungian in its impact on our collective unconscious. Our very earliest ancestors, well before the development of agriculture and writing, before the wheel and fire, when people fought animals over carrion, found shelter in the forests and opportunity in the plains. They understood, at some level, the cycles of rain and drought. Our ancestors came from nature; nature was part of them. This may explain why today the presence of green scenery slows our blood pressure and relieves stress. It might explain why people working in bleak, anonymous offices nurture houseplants to reduce urban tension, and why people recover faster when their hospital window has a view of a park (curiously, even having a photograph of nature in the hospital room speeds healing compared to a barren wall).

A "need" relationship with nature is in our genes, in our cultural unconscious. The terms "nature" and "nurture" are linked.[109]

Throughout history, people have built on this fascination with non-human life and attributed form to nature spirits in the form of gnomes, nymphs, and sylphs; mermaids, dryads, and fairies; devas, whisps, and pixies. They are numerous. They thrive in undisturbed groves, unpolluted rivers. Like ghosts,[110] some people like to classify them into a spirit-taxonomy—spirits that are associated with water, earth, air, and fire, hence the often used term "elementals." These spirits invariably advocate that we must cherish the Earth and stop messing things up with our Western ways. As one medium says, "They are the workers of Lady Gaia—here to help support and heal Earth." Most people who speak with nature spirits say that they communicate in energy, in feeling, but not in words. Françoise explains that spirits of trees send her a subtle, persistent, tree-huggy message: "Recognize that we exist, and that we are precious."

And, again as with ghosts, there are people who claim they can describe the forms these elementals take. Some Earth spirits, for instance, take the form of whoever they interact with—the spirits might appear as short and stocky or lean and jittery. Other elementals are ethereal and visually metaphorical—a blur of color, a sudden burst of heat, balls of light, or the feeling of a delicate piece of silk brushing against your cheek. Even seemingly innocent and innocuous events like a beautiful cloud formation can indicate the presence of a nature spirit.

༜

Many people will argue that I am wrong to make a binary "we and them" distinction between people and trees. Trees and people are interlinked; we're all in this together. In *Overstory*, Richard Powers recounts the story of Ovid, who tells the story: "Two immortals came to Earth in disguise to cleanse the sickened world. No one would let them in but one old couple, Baucis and Philemon. And their reward for opening their door to strangers was to live on after death as trees—an oak and a linden—huge and gracious and intertwined. What we care for, we will grow to resemble. And what we resemble will hold us, when we are us no longer."

Powers's book is a fascinating ode to the intimacy between people and nature, and the inherent goodness, intelligence, and social engineering one finds in forests. "When you cut down a tree," he writes, "what you make from it should be at least as miraculous as what you cut down . . . Trees communicate . . . sense the presence of other nearby life . . . save water." Most intriguing, his fictional characters declare that if enough trees are linked together, the forest *grows aware*. "We scientists are taught never to look for ourselves in other species . . . but believe me, trees want something from us, just as we've always wanted things from them. This isn't mystical. The 'environment' is alive—a fluid, changing web of purposeful lives dependent on each other. Flowers shape bees as much as bees shape flowers, berries may compete to be eaten more than animals compete for the berries, a thorn acacia makes sugary protein treats to feed and enslave the ants who guard it."

So, there's the big issue. Science, yes science, can show that plants and critters perform what, to us, are almost miraculous feats in order to survive and flourish. But is this intriguing list of behaviors strictly due to evolution by natural selection, as I have grown up believing? Is there, as Wallace proposed for humans, a Superior Intelligence at work? And, by extension, do forest eco-systems have a form of consciousness?

༄

More intriguingly, some people claim to engage in detailed dialogues with nature spirits, and this fascinates me because such conversations are often lengthy, lucid, deeply philosophical, and illustrate a distinct New Age type of pompous and moralistic conservation consciousness. The result is as if a tree spirit is speaking with the eloquence of Deepak Chopra or Bertrand Russell. Imagine Plato (or Al Gore) reincarnated as an aggrieved mottled oak awash in pareidolia that scolds clueless *Homo sapiens* (with the exception of the interlocuter, who is generally one of the wise people who *understands*) for their careless treatment of nature. It's a morality play in a sylvan glen, an intensive chloro-political discourse.

Consider the books by Verena Stael von Holstein, who has the gift of speaking with nature spirits, and Wolfgang Weirach, who has the gift of transcribing and publishing such conversations. Their books (inspirational to some) feature dialogue in which nature spirits use complex, grammatically correct sentences and offer profound ideas about the often confrontational human–nature relationship. The opinions of the nature spirits as written in their books are as eloquent and well written as the conversations one might have with highly articulate, protest-marching, tree-hugging human beings. Call me old-fashioned, but I find it hard to understand how nature spirits are able to speak with greater eloquence than the majority of human spirits. I wish it were so, alas. Von Holstein and Weirach are either the most gifted people in the world or shameless frauds.

Some short excerpts from much longer exchanges they have published:[111]

Crown, the Tree Shepherd:
   "Hello, human."

Wolfgang Weirach:
   "Did you give yourself the name Crown?"

Crown:

"My name is really much longer, and more multidimensional."

WW:

"What tasks do you have?"

Crown:

"I am responsible for coordinating the migration of trees."

"There are roughly 12,000 tree shepherds on Earth."

WW:

"What is it like for you when trees from foreign parts are planted here in this region?"

Crown:

"It is difficult for us. You [humans] don't know what you're doing. You have to act globally, but do you also have to do it with the trees?"

"At present, the bees are having problems. They have too few nectar sources. I motivate the lime trees all over Europe to form lots of shoots, because lime trees are a source of nectar for bees at the height of summer."

"The birds understand a lot about these interrelationships and are easy to motivate."

WW:

"What happens etherically to the Earth when a large forest is cleared?"

Crown:

"Death and despair arise, a form of life disappears."

And observations from another nature spirit, *The Brown One*:

> "You're making your bodies sick even without genetic engineering."
>
> "A cloned animal has no soul."
>
> "When a human makes friends with an animal, and the animal with him—spiritual spaces are created."
>
> "Caged animals live like humans forced to live the whole of their lives isolated in a prison cell, being constantly given disgusting food. These animals are greatly in need of comfort. I sing children's songs to them—as you would put it in human words—so that these animals simply feel some warmth."

And another dialogue with nature spirits, recounted by holistic trainer and internet blogger Paul Chek:

> Once while hiking in the hills, I had a tug on my own spirit. I was attracted to some of the brush and sage plants.
>
> I stopped, touched them and asked if they wanted to talk to me. They said, "Yes."
>
> Then they asked, "Where are the rest of the people like you?"
>
> I said, "Who do you mean?"
>
> They said, "The people that use [sic] to live here and travel here."
>
> I said, "Do you mean the native Indians that once lived here?"

They said they use [sic] to talk to us and they were concerned about our needs, not just theirs.

They then said, "People walking these trails don't hear us, they don't see us, and many don't even care about us. We are concerned because the people here keep killing our home. We notice you are different. We've seen you here many times. We've heard your music when you play your rattles and your instruments as you hike. Where are the people like you? We want to talk to you."

A quick internet search will reveal dozens of similar exchanges.

Such unexpected eloquence reminds me of Chief Seathl (commonly referred to as Seattle).

During the 1980s Chief Seathl became a poster boy for the importance of respecting traditional cultures and the natural environments native people inhabited. Chief Seathl was a 19th-century leader of the North American Suwamish tribe who is reputed to have made an eloquent plea that 'the white man should leave the red man alone, since "the Indian alone knows how to live as part of nature." Cynics claim that Chief Seathl's speeches—"We know that the white man does not understand our ways . . . His appetite will devour the earth and leave behind only a desert . . .. If all the beasts were gone, men would die from great loneliness of spirit, for whatever happens to the beasts also happens to man. All things are connected, whatever befalls the earth befalls the sons of the earth."—were ghostwritten by the white missionaries who accompanied Chief Seathl on his lecture tour.

The point isn't to diminish Chief Seathl's conservation wisdom but to illustrate that publishing something as truth does not always equate with truth.

The Conversation *with* Spirits

Part I – The "Elvis" of Burmese *Nat* Shamans

For me the most productive location for contacting nature spirits is in Myanmar (formerly known as Burma). Mysticism permeates the heavy air, providing an added layer of intrigue to this multi-layered country.

Officially, some 88% of the country practice Theravada Buddhism. But bare statistics are misleading. Many Burmese, particularly in rural areas, have a syncretic attitude toward prayer. Yes, Lord Buddha will help you live a life of calm, understanding, and good actions in preparation for a better next life. But intertwined with the familiar saffron-robed clergy of Buddhism are the *nats*. Let's call them minor gods, or saints. These energies, which inhabit puppet-sized effigies, can influence the vagaries of daily life—earning money, finding love, and protecting from danger.

The intermediaries are called *nat kadaws*, or *nat* shamans.

I am introduced to one of the most famous *nat kadaws* in Myanmar's largest city, Yangon (formerly Rangoon). U Win

Hlaing is tall, middle-aged, with curly, thinning hair and wearing gold-rimmed glasses. He is calm, a touch formal, but welcoming. His large house in a Yangon suburb is a vast shrine of *nat* statues, many with offerings of coconuts, bananas, and bottles of whiskey. Since his clientele is upper class, the alcohol isn't homemade village rotgut, but genuine Johnnie Walker. U Win Hlaing's shrine room is bigger than a studio apartment; as in other *nat* shrines, the space is overflowing with gaudily painted wooden puppets. It reminds me of a creepy collection of an obsessive hoarder of dolls, or, in my darker moments, of a family gathering of cousins of Chucky, the evil doll from the *Child's Play* horror movies.

Most of the famous *nat* shamans are gay, transvestite, or transgender. I can't vouch for U Win Hlaing's orientation, but as we converse, I note his eye makeup, hairstyle, and swagger. I later go to his website and watch him in action on videos (bless the people who invented YouTube) and see a flamboyant, theatrical, cross-dressing performer in trance. He wears extreme mascara and has a preference for pastel chiffon and feathered turbans.

In his "civilian" aspect, U Win Hlaing is a generous teacher who patiently explains the different types of nature *nats*.

There are countless *nats*, he explains.

> "There's Koe Myo Shin, *a* nat *who protects towns and cities;* U Shin Ayi, *a spirt of the sea; and* Hpa Htyi *and* Ah Moe, *brother and sister* nats *who protect forests.*"

The list is endless, it seems, extending far beyond the 37 primary *nats*.

"What happens if you don't respect the *nats*?" I ask.

> "People come to me when they have angered the nats, and I try to make amends through a ceremony."

U Win Hlaing tells the story of one man who cut a large tree and was punished by the local *nat* and became mute. Another client of his, a Burmese geologist, wanted to do ultrasound research to study the archeology of an old temple. The spirit said don't do it, but he did. And because of his sin, lightning burned down his house.

> "Nats are like our ancestors, and we must respect them just as we respect our elders."

U Win Hlaing is the Elvis of Myanmar's *nat kadaws*, and has a large following throughout the country. His acolytes gather at *nat* festivals, called *nat pwe*. I attended the largest of these events, held annually outside Mandalay. They are garish, loud, stunning spectacles held in specially constructed compounds. Each *nat kadaw* rents a tent, like a wandering Bible-thumping preacher might have done in early America, where his fans will encourage him to enter a trance and bestow blessings. These believers join in the fun, partaking of palm wine and dancing ecstatically to the hypnotic beat of a percussion orchestra called *hsaing waing*. It's a Burmese equivalent of a frenzied evangelical shouting-in-tongues gathering in the southern United States, a bacchanal with a *nat kadaw* like U Win Hlaing performing as Dionysus.

U Win Hlaing is eager to tell me about his international travel, and he brings out two scrapbooks with photos and magazine stories that document his recent trip to Italy. I hadn't realized there was a demand for a *nat kadaw* to practice in Italy; truly, this is a brave new world we live in.

I ask U Win Hlaing if he can go into a trance and let me speak with a *nat*.

"Ah, you just missed a ceremony," he explains, but he quickly offers to put together a special event for me.

The story of my life. *You should have been here yesterday.* "How much?"

"We need to hire an orchestra, make offerings."

"How much?" I repeat. I feel a bit silly. It's like asking a priest how much he might charge for a wedding. But I sense that U Win Hlaing is no stranger to business dealings.

"A few hundred dollars, with a small band. About a thousand with a full-scale orchestra."

I'm reminded of the mediums in Pontianak and Ternate who quoted high prices for an intervention, offers that I declined.

But I'm wondering. Perhaps the result you get from a ceremony is in direct proportion to the amount you pay for a ceremony? I wonder if the size of the orchestra has an impact on which *nats* might appear and how well U Win Hlaing might do his job. I've seen such performances at the spectacular *nat pwe* held outside Mandalay each year. My fear is that my "special" ceremony will result in a lot of activity, with dozens of freeloading hangers-on moaning and waving their arms, pleading for help while a bunch of guys smash xylophones and cymbals and drums as U Win Hlaing goes into a trance and does his *nat kadaw* thing, and all I will see will be a gaily dressed person of fluid gender whirling about, rolling his eyes in a self-induced trance-stupor, and I won't be able to have a sensible tête-à-tête with a *nat*. Yes, I realize how ridiculous it is to seek a logical, intimate, one-on-one discourse with a spirit.

I decline politely and choose to head into the villages to try my luck with less famous shamans.

My first stop is the parched outskirts of Bagan, a World Heritage site of 5,000 temples and stupas. Closer to the earth. Closer to the *nats*, I suppose. One of my better decisions.

Part II – Watch What You Say in Myanmar's Sacred Forests

This holy grove of Zee-O Thit-Hla, some ten kilometers outside the historic site of Bagan, is so important that Daw Aung San Suu Kyi stopped there on her first nationwide "thank you" tour after being released from house arrest. She wrote: "This village bears the poetic name 'Old Plum, Beautiful Wood, Retainer of the Gods' . . . It is almost a haiku, certainly a more poetic description than the banal common translation 'beautiful old forest.'"

This is a place of *nats* and forest spirits, of taboos and punishments, a lesson I learned when I met Myint Naing.

Myint Naing has one of the easier jobs in the Myanmar forestry department. Since 1999 his task has been to protect the Zee-O Thit-Hla sacred forest, which has been a government forest reserve since 1988. Although it is home to some fifty species of trees, including dozens of large, commercially valuable trees, no one has cut a tree during that period. Is it the fear of a three-year prison sentence that has kept this green holy grove intact while its surroundings lie barren and baking? Or is its environmental integrity due to something mystical, something far beyond government control?

The sacred forest might have government protection, but I sense that its real power, and hence the reason it survives, lies in the protection of *nats*.[112]

During my first visit to Zee-O Thit-Hla some twenty years earlier, I became aware of the *nats'* importance.

Throughout Asia one hears stories of things that go bump in the night. A jealous wife puts a black-magic curse on her husband's mistress that makes the woman go mad. A man coughs blood, and when doctors X-ray his lungs they find dozens of metal pins, put there by a sorcerer. A farmer spends the night in the forest and when dawn comes, villagers find that he has entranced a man-eating tiger into a cage.

Trouble is, it's awfully hard to actually meet some of these magic-imbued people—these surreal episodes always seem to take place in Brigadoon-like localities: *In a distant village, over the next hill.*

When I ask what trouble could befall someone who violates the sanctity of this sacred forest, I expect the usual generalizations: *You'll fall sick* or *Bad things will happen.* So I listen with skepticism when I hear that a farmer's house had burned down after he and a companion cursed and acted disrespectfully in this holy grove. I figure it for just another Asian legend. Such stories are common but irritatingly hard to analyze—one would welcome a team of Mythbusters to put some scientific empiricism to reports about men who sell their children's souls, enabling them to turn into were-pigs to get rich. Soldiers whose sacred amulets have enabled them to survive being shot. People who eat glass. Even a car repair technique in Indonesia that relies on incantations and prayers instead of mallets and soldering irons.

My amateurish attempts at busting these myths usually

result in a stalemate due to too many degrees of separation—the person I'm talking with heard it from his sister-in-law who heard it from someone in the pub, that kind of thing. So, when I was told that people in Zee-O were punished for intruding on the sacred forest, I was skeptical.

"No, they're real," the village elder insists.

※

And so I meet U Aye San and his father-in-law U Aung Khin.

U Aye San, one of the men who allegedly broke the taboos concerning this sacred grove, is a middle-aged man who appears perfectly, well, normal.

> *"My father-in-law, U Aung Khin, was acting eccentric the morning that we entered the sacred forest,"* U Aye San says. *"Yes, we were disrespectful, but we didn't know were breaking any taboos."*

"Tell me what happened."

> *"A few hours after we returned to the village, I heard a commotion,"* U Aye San explains. *"U Aung Khin's house was burning. He was inside and got burned. But it was very odd. The cooking fire had been extinguished. The fire apparently started spontaneously, among the dried toddy palm leaves in the roof."*

I am introduced to the unfortunate, taboo-defying father-in-law. U Aung Khin is 84 ("my secret of long life is rice and toddy") and half deaf. Our translator shouts into his good ear but to no avail. My analytical left brain says he is old, infirm, and suffering from dementia. My right brain, the side of my cerebral cortex that allows for emotional, spiritual, and intuitive explanations, tells me that this sad, skinny old man sitting on the dirt outside a hut is being punished by spirits more powerful than he had ever imagined.

An open-air tin-roofed shed some thirty meters into the forest contains puppet-sized statues of the Zee-O Thit-Hla forest's guardian *nat* spirits, omnipresent demi-deities that in Myanmar control important events in people's lives. Small statues of the resident *nats* welcome visitors—U Hla Tin Aung and Daw Pun Nya Yin, *nat* brother and sister. They wear red robes, their hands are painted golden, and they extend their palms in greeting.

The air is cool inside the forest, a welcome relief from the arid, cactus-dotted landscapes outside the perimeter. I stroll amidst mature trees so large I can't put my arms around them, including several fine ficus trees, which are seldom found in the arid zone. Is Zee-O Thit-Hla a relict forest, the last example of a richer flora that existed, some experts speculate, prior to the 11th- to 13th-century construction of the great temples of Bagan (formerly Pagan), just ten kilometers away?

On departure, I ask Myint Naing, the Zee-O Thit-Hla forest guard, which is a stronger deterrent to villagers—the *nats* or the government. "The *nats*," he says without hesitation. "Definitely the *nats*."

I return to Zee-O-Thit-Hla to speak with these nature spirits.

My guide, Zaw Myo Win is young and enthusiastic. Some of the people remember me and bring out faded photographs of the first visit my wife and I made when we were honored to attend a wedding ceremony in progress.

Perhaps ten people are waiting for me and Zaw Myo Win at the small shrine housing the two *nats*. I note that the construction has been upgraded, thanks to a corporate sponsor—a sign reads, "Five, Brother Co—Ltd." Even local businesses appreciate the value of being nice to the *nats*.

The primary medium is U Maung Nyo, 46, a quick-to-smile middle-aged man with luxuriant black hair and a wide face, wearing a blue shirt and light blue *longyi*, the typical Burmese sarong worn by men.

With this warmth and the presence of village dignitaries I feel like I'm on a diplomatic mission, making contact with a wary, rarely visited potentate. I start formally: "Thank you for allowing me to come here to this important place."

"Why is this forest important to you?" the medium asks.

He speaks normally and he has yet to enter a trance. I sense he is deciding whether I am worth the effort.

"I first came here twenty or thirty years ago and was impressed by how the forest is protected by the *nats*. I've studied sacred forests like this one throughout Asia, and Zee-O Thit-Hla has exceptional energy. I'd like, with your permission, to speak with the guardian *nats*."

U Maung Nyo nods, then bows. He sprinkles water on the coconut and banana offerings, then mumbles a mantra.

Like other Asian mediums he quickly enters trance. His chanting becomes louder and he starts shaking. He waves his arms, clenches his fists with extended thumbs, rubs his hands together.

"I'd like to know why these two particular *nats* are here. How did they choose to stay in this forest?"

This, apparently, is a question that had never been asked. And it results in an astounding answer that surprises everyone present.

> "Daw Pann Mya Yin [the sister *nat*], *says she has always been here.*"

Then this conversation gets spooky. I ask a follow-up question. "And what about your brother?"

And U Hla Tin Aung, the brother *nat*, replies. During this exchange I shift my gaze between the medium and the marionette-like statue—the *nat* puppet is kind of cute, a touch effeminate. He rides a white horse, wears a pith helmet (very British, that), and has exaggerated eyelashes and red lips.

> Through the medium he says, *"I'm a newcomer."*

"Meaning what?"

> *"I used to live in a forest in Dann,"* he says, naming a locality near to Bagan. *"It was a good forest. But then the forest was cut. The British cut it. I had no place to stay, so I came here to be with my sister."*

And just like that I realize I have hit geopolitical-*nat*-jackpot. The *nat* U Hla Tin Aung has scolded the British for destroying nature, and has told the startled mediums that he is a relatively recent immigrant.

Things are happening quickly. I want to ask whether the *nat* punished the British offenders. But he's off on a riff.

> "My job is to protect the forest. If someone cuts a tree they get punished—maybe they become blind or ill, or their family starves."

This resonates with the story of the two men I met years earlier who desecrated the forest and whose house burned down as a result.

"Are you friends with other *nats*?"

I laugh to myself. I feel like I am channeling Verena Staël von Holstein and trying to engage in a lucid conservation discussion with a nature spirit about deep ecology and conservation.

> "No. I don't communicate with other nats."

I happily continue to speak to this lonely *nat* as if I'm chatting with a golf buddy. "Are you aware of other forests being cut in other parts of the world?"

> "Certainly. It's terrible."

"Do you have a message for other countries?"

> "Don't cut any more forests. What's happening is really sad, terrible, like what happened to my previous forest."

I get conservation platitudes coming from a lonely, angry, forest spirit in a dusty village in central Myanmar. Like his brethren spirits elsewhere, the brother *nat* U Hla Tin Aung speaks clearly and offers a basic and sharp conservation message. *Don't cut the trees. Or else.*

U Maung Nyo slowly comes out of his trance. He doesn't remember what happened and has to be debriefed. This isn't easy since for part of the time the *nat* was speaking in what was described as "an unknown Indian language."

The group of spectators has by now grown to some thirty people, all curious to hear what the *nats* have to say, all wondering why a foreigner with a notebook is so interested in this 40-acre (16-hectare) forest.

I'm reluctant to leave and ask the mediums for more information about the dynamics of conservation-by-*nat*.

Folks seem happy to tell their stories.

> "When an ox cart drives through the Zee-O Thit-Hla forest," one man says. "A forest department officer came to carry away petrified wood. He got sick. Even doctors in Singapore couldn't help him."

Remarkably, they know the name and backstory of this man.

> "The seeds of a giant Shorea tree, the holiest of the sacred trees in the forest, fly outside the forest's boundary. But the external seeds never germinate; only the seeds that fall near the tree produce offspring."

They take me to the courtyard of the local monastery, where I enjoy the shade of a huge tamarind tree, said to be a thousand years old. It is so expansive that six concrete pillars have been erected to support the tree's heavy, low branches that grow almost horizontally. Near the tree hangs a poster showing Daw Aung San Suu Kyi standing in the same spot. A sacred tree has given a politician a spiritual edge.

Part III – In One Myanmar Village, It's All About the Fish

"They use dolphins to catch fish."

I am intrigued. My Burmese friend Harry tells me about a fishing community that enlists the help of the rare freshwater Irawaddy dolphins to ensure a good catch.

I go to Hsithe Village, hoping against hope that someone there might be able to talk to a dolphin. That doesn't happen, but I meet an 84-year-old shaman who channels the nature *nat* that inhabits this stretch of the river.

The fishermen of Hsithe, a two-hour drive and a half-hour boat ride north of Mandalay, go about their business as they have for generations. Certainly, there are some technological changes—they now have small outboard engines on their canoes and monofilament fishing nets. A few fishermen have simple cellphones. No different to countless other villages in Myanmar. But what sets this village apart is that during the dry season, when the Ayerwaddy (Irawaddy) river is low and mid-river sandbanks impede the passage of larger vessels, the fisherman slap the water to alert the dolphins, who then act as aquatic sheep dogs. As fisherman U Tun Myat explains, the dolphins round up fish and push them toward the boat. The fisherman throws his circular net. The confused fish that escape the net are quickly gobbled up by the dolphins, the equivalent of giving a sheep dog a puppy treat. Win-win.

When I visit the village in early December, the dry season has just started and the dolphins aren't around. But I still go out fishing in the late afternoon with U Tun Myat and Ko Tin Naung. I love the sight of a fisherman gathering up the circular nylon net and sailing it out into the water. It lands in a perfect circle. The weights on the edges quickly sink to the bottom of the shallow, muddy river. After a few moments he hauls it up and, with a bit of luck, he gathers some fish. At first the catch is meager, a handful of small fish. Then, toward dusk, our luck starts to change and we land a few arm-long fish. I am served some of this fish for dinner. It is bony and, like most river fish, rather bland and muddy. But this is how U Tun Myat and Ko Tin Naung make their living. They are satisfied with the day's catch.

Over dinner I ask about their relationship with the dolphins. I'm hoping for them to tell me that they have clear conversations with the dolphins, that the dolphins complain about the large passenger boats that cruise these waters, their anger at how fishermen in other villagers use electroshock to stun large numbers of fish, giving the dolphins a jolt along the way. About how sometimes they must swim long distances to find food, and the importance for the fisherman to observe periods of no-fishing to give the river a chance to regrow.

"Nothing like that," U Tun Myat says. *"We don't speak with them. They know when we're around, and if they feel like it, they come fishing with us."*

"What about the local *nat*. Is that important to your fishing?

"Yes, that would be Boe Thone Tar," he says.

He is the ever-present local *nat* who protects this stretch of the river. Villagers make regular offerings of bananas, coconut, and local whiskey to this *nat* to ensure a good catch.

"And you speak with Boe Thone Tar yourself?"

"*Not directly,*" he says.

The fishermen rely on a *nat kadaw* in the village named Daw Tin May.

Hsithe is a moderately wealthy village, as Burmese villages go. Many of the houses are of sturdy construction, some with electricity. There is no drivable path to the main north–south road, but some villagers have motorcycles to provide easy access to a market and health center. I arrive by boat, a much more pleasant alternative.

I want to speak with the *nat* Boe Thone Tar, and after dinner, the taste of river fish still lingering, seek out Daw Tin May. Her house is one of the poorer dwellings in the village, with palm leaf walls and open rafters. Her few possessions fit into a couple of cabinets, with some clothes hanging on nails. As a medium she helps other people in the village earn a modest living, but the trickle-down economy hasn't helped her much.

I visit her around eight in the evening. She doesn't seem startled that a foreigner asks if she can channel Boe Thone Tar.

"*Now?*"

"Yes, if it's not too much trouble."

"*We need to make an offering. Some rice wine.*"

I have not brought any rice wine. My guide, Aung Toe Khaing, who is a director of the award-winning eco-tourism project that has brought increased revenue and visibility to Hsithe, arranges to borrow some of the neighbor's rice wine, which we will replace later. I'm advised to give her a donation when I leave.

Daw Tin May puts on a shawl, murmurs a mantra, goes into a trance almost immediately. She pounds her ears. She speaks broken Burmese in a loud voice.

Her family members explain that the *nat* Boe Thone Tar is hard of hearing, so she has to speak loudly.

Most startling, after a few moments, Daw Tin May begins to take off her shirt.

Her friends dissuade the 84-year-old woman from undressing. They explain that Boe Thone Tar is always naked, therefore, since Tin May is channeling his spirit, she too has to be naked.

Daw Tin May is crying. Squatting. Hitting her head with closed hands. Shaking her arms.

She speaks rapidly. It makes no sense. I don't get a chance to ask questions. The channeling of the nature spirit ends after about five minutes.

Daw Tin May returns to consciousness.

"Do you remember what happened?" I ask.

"No."

I ask my guide and friend Aung Toe Khaing to clarify. "Did you catch what she said?"

Aung Toe Khaing earnestly chats with the other ten people in the room. After a few minutes of heated discussion, he tells me something unexpected. Boe Thone Tar, speaking through Daw Tin May, said that it's okay to throw rubbish into the river, because the rubbish will turn into fish.

I'm bewildered by this astonishing comment. I thought nature spirits were conservationists, and that they would abhor the idea of throwing garbage into the river.

I thank Daw Tin May, leave an offering of around ten dollars, and leave confused.

As we walk back to the comfortable guest house built as part of the eco-tourism project I ask Aung Toe Khaing if he can clarify her comment. "I can't figure it out. Throw rubbish into the river? That doesn't make sense."

And Aung Toe Khaing offers me another way to look at a seemingly impossible statement. As Sultan Hamengku Buwono IX Hamengkubuwono told me, Aung Toe Khaing suggests I might be looking at the statement through a Western cultural prism. "I think Boe Thone Tar is referring to metaphorical rubbish," my friend says. "A good Buddhist divests himself of the 'rubbish' of pride, greed, ego, and anger. The *nat* wants the fishermen to denounce these bad habits and act as good Buddhists. Metaphorically he wants them to throw their 'wrong thoughts' into the river. Then he will reward them with a good catch and safe voyage."

And that explanation makes perfect sense. I kick myself for being so literal that I missed the allegorical point. Burmese *nats* work in consultation with Lord Buddha. Burmese believe that Lord Buddha handles the big things—salvation, reincarnation, spiritual harmony, righteous behavior. The multitude of *nats* help with the mundane challenges of daily life—curing an illness, doing well on school exams, snaring a good job, finding a spouse, winning the lottery. And in the case of Hsithe village, a *nat* like Boe Thone Tar helps fishermen catch lots of fish.

Part IV – Angry Nature Spirits Cause a Monk to Commit Suicide

Throughout Asia, people tell stories about how irreverent people who destroy nature are punished. For the most part it's virtually impossible to find evidence of such cause and effect. However, Venerable Thon Da, abbot of the Buddhist monastery in Hsithe village, north of Mandalay, Myanmar, tells a disturbing story that he is convinced proves that nature spirits are not to be trifled with.

Thon Da, 59, is afflicted with vitiligo, a skin disease that occurs when the cells that produce melanin die or stop functioning, resulting in a loss of pigmentation. His body is covered with formless white blotches, a series of Rorschach patterns. A white band stretches from ear to ear, and around his mouth, giving him the appearance of wearing a mask.

"When I was twenty, the chief monk asked me to cut a branch of a banyan tree. I don't recall the reason," he says.

"But banyan trees are sacred all over Asia," I tell him. "Surely you knew that."[113]

"Yes, but when the chief monk asks a young monk to do something, he has no choice."

I let Thon Da talk.

> "The odd thing was that I was unable to cut the branch. I used my machete but it bounced off the wood. I hacked away but only succeeded in breaking the metal blade, not cutting the tree limb."

"Even though you didn't cut the tree limb, you were punished by the *nats*?

> "Absolutely. I started bleeding from my mouth. I had pain in my stomach and was operated on in the hospital—they found blood in my stomach."

I urge him to continue.

> "Eventually I recovered from the bleeding. But slowly, over a period of months, I got this skin disease."

One of several possible triggers of vitiligo, according to the Mayo Clinic, is stress. Do we believe that the trauma of trying, and failing, to cut a branch of a sacred tree, was the cause of Than Do's illness? Or was it even more serious, a *direct* punishment from a *nat*?

> "You know, before Buddha there were nats. They have to be respected."[114]

I shook my head. What kind of abbot would ask a young monk to cut a sacred tree? What choice did the young monk have?

> "One farmer cut branches of an old tree, and when he returned home found his cow had died."

"Let's get back to the abbot. Did anything happen to him?"

> "The worst was what happened to the head abbot."

I urge him to continue and sit quietly.

Thon Da takes a while before finishing his story.

> "My abbot was upset that I couldn't cut the branch, so he decided to do it himself. He cut the tree with a saw."

"And then?"

Thon Da didn't mince his words.

> "He became crazy. After four months he couldn't take it anymore, and he hung himself."

Remorse? Fear of retribution? What force is so strong that it causes a seemingly healthy and righteous person to lose his mind and kill himself?

I look at Thon Da, wearing a simple monk's maroon robe. We are sitting in his room at the monastery. His accommodation is comfortable by Burmese village standards, but hardly luxurious. I ask about the TV and large speakers, half wondering whether he enjoys watching afternoon soap operas and hosting karaoke parties. Turns out I was doing him a disservice.

> "No," he laughs. "People from the village come and we watch religious videos."

"So, you use modern technology to teach the dharma?"

> "Yes, but people here are traditional; they believe in Lord Buddha and the nats."

He takes me outside to an enclosure where statues of sister *nats* Saw Nan Mon and Saw Kalar protect the adjacent Buddhist temple. The shrine is well maintained. I see the offerings of bananas, coconuts, and small banknotes placed in front of the *nat* images. I place a few banknotes in front of the statues, just in case.

EPILOGUE

WHAT IF?
Do I believe in spirits?
More important, do you?

So, what should I make of all this?

I've come to a few conclusions, based on dozens of conversations with mediums, shamans, and purported spirits in some 20 countries.

People believe in spirits. Increasingly, and in great numbers.

My granddaughter is eight. I wonder what she will do when she grows up.

Assuming she has the aptitude (she hasn't shown it yet), one career that is likely to increase in popularity is that of medium.

There's a big market—by a large margin, people believe in an afterlife, and the number is increasing.

In the United States (the country for which data are most readily available), 82% of people polled believe in life after death.

Where do these spirits reside? A 2016 poll found that 65% of Americans believe that people go to heaven, hell, or purgatory after death, 7% believe they go to another dimension, 6% believe they are reborn on earth, and 2% believe they become ghosts.[115]

More to the point of this book (and for consideration when my granddaughter chooses a career), regardless of whether people believe that folks who have passed are in heaven, in another dimension, or turned into a ghost, about one-fifth of Americans believe that *the deceased can communicate with those who are still alive.*[116]

A belief in spirits serves our sense of self.

This goes back to the fundamental questions: *Who are we? Why are we here? Do I have a value beyond my physical body?* Most people have egos that need to be stroked; what better boost than to believe "I'm gonna live forever!"

History by *Hantu* is unlikely to become a useful research tool.

Living people exaggerate, lie, filter about their lives constantly.[117] Why should we expect better behavior from spirits? For instance, let's grab a large measure of salt and believe that the mediums I consulted had genuine contact with Ali's spirit. Why should I accept what he said? Like Ali when he was alive, his spirit no doubt has distinctive thought processes. And he has cultural tendencies that color the spirit personality and voice. Why should we expect that Ali's spirit will be either accurate or truthful? Add the problem that spirits tend to speak in abstruse phrases that require interpretation. Lastly, each medium I visited put her own cultural spin on Ali's spirit's comments.

Not all mediums and psychics are created equal.

I believe that some mediums, shamans, and healers have psychic powers.[118]

And I believe that some mediums have enhanced telepathic and intuitive abilities.

However, many mediums are skilled entertainers. Just as gifted illusionists like David Copperfield, Cyril Takayama, and Harry Houdini[119] astound their audiences with stunts that make us gasp and murmur, "I don't believe it. How did he do that?", talented mediums and psychics (and let's not forget Filipino faith healers) employ a variety of techniques to practice their craft.

Psychics try to ensure "hits" and aha moments. They might offer the few facts they already know, or suggest generalities ("Someone close to you had a serious illness" or "You are a considerate person but there are times when you wish you were more selfish") and observe the clients' reactions—eye movements, facial expressions—and take their cue from those signals. They might make a high-percentage "yes" statement ("cancer, someone close to you"). They might disgorge a torrent of stream-of-consciousness impressions, like throwing out chum to attract fish—"face powder," "whirlwind romance," "old car," "sea, the beach, sand, and waves." They can easily shift away from their errors midstream: "Were you recently married? No? Do you know anybody going through a divorce? No? Well, one of your friends is going to divorce in the future and she'll need you to be a buffer." The sitter is receptive to these tricks because she *wants* to believe.

However, sometimes a medium surprises me. On numerous occasions I have been in a workshop and a medium, either the workshop leader or one of the participants, has approached me, cold turkey, and made a startling comment: "You've had two eye operations. You see much more clearly now." While it's unclear whether he's referring to literal sight or metaphorical insight, he's right. A few months earlier I had double cataract surgeries. I'm surprised by these insights, but also a bit perturbed. Even though we're in a workshop to develop psychic powers, these seers have no right to intrude on my thoughts like this.

～

Mediums express some cross-cultural similarities.

I found cross-cultural consistencies in how mediums contact spirits, their message content, and how they present information:

- The universe is good and loving.
- Spirits are well intentioned, rarely malevolent or mischievous.[120]
- Spirits decide whether they want to contact the living.
- Spirits rarely speak in coherent, complete sentences. They are generally cryptic, fond of throwing out tantalizing fragments of information that have to be deciphered and interpreted. Interpreting such pronouncements reminds me of scholars who try to determine the meaning of the Rosetta Stone, the Dead Sea Scrolls, or the visions of Fátima.
- Spirits can be frustratingly vague and obtuse. They seem fond of symbols and metaphors, and challenge the sitter to figure out the meaning—one example was when June-Elleni, channeling Wallace, came up with the image of "whales." "Whales" in reference to the animal didn't make sense, but the homonym "Wales," did, since that is where Wallace was born. Sometimes these flashes of insight resemble truncated telegrams in which important letters, even words, are missing. A quiz show hosted by mischievous short-attention-

spanned spirits. It's as if the spirits themselves have been channeling the Riddler in Batman, or having their thoughts translated multiple times and passed from person to person, like the party game Chinese whispers, until they barely resemble the original.
- Mediums work with a spiritual guide that functions as adviser, guardian, and gatekeeper.
- The medium uses one or more of the six methods of psychic contact: clairaudience (hearing), claircognizance (intrinsic knowledge), clairgustance (taste), clairolfactance (smell), clairsentience (feeling, intuition), clairvoyance (seeing).
- Some mediums enter a trance, others maintain consciousness.
- Spirits cannot communicate in a vacuum. They require feedback. Positive feedback, please.
- Spirits are gentle creatures. They respond best to soft, non-threatening language.
- Mediums rarely have a coherent concept of what happens when a person dies. Put another way, they find it difficult to explain where spirit-energy resides.

Are psychics born or made?

The psychic community makes a distinction between psychics, who are able to intuit and predict events, and mediums, who can communicate with spirits. Yet they can both be considered sub-specialties of psychic ability.

Are there certain biological, behavioral, or medical characteristics that make an individual more likely to have psychic skills?

One intriguing, perhaps overly complicated profile, was offered by researcher David Ritchey, who suggests Anomalously Sensitive Persons (ASPs) have a number of these characteristics:

- Female
- Left-handed
- Hypopigmented
- Career in the arts (acting, music, painting), investigative (science, computer, legal), or social (teaching, religion)
- Born as one of a set of twins or triplets
- Non-heterosexual orientation
- Physically mistreated as a child
- Overly responsive to colors
- Bothered by fluorescent lights
- And a multitude of medical and psychological problems, including:

  Food allergies
  Low blood pressure
  Low body temperature
  Autoimmune disorders
  Unusual health problems (Epstein-Barr, chronic fatigue syndrome)
  Sleep disorders
  Developmental learning disorders (dyslexia, Tourette's disorder)[121]

I find this interesting. Ritchey describes a left-handed, pale woman with a non-standard sexual orientation having a twin sibling. She has learning disabilities and debilitating chronic physical and psychological disorders. One gets an impression of a loner, perhaps an outcast, in need of regular medical care. Hardly the picture of vim and vigor I encountered in the many mediums and shamans I met.

One of Ritchey's many characteristics appears on other lists: left-handedness. The logic (if indeed logic plays a role) is that the 10% of people who are left-handed have a more dominant right brain, the hemisphere that influences emotion, creativity, and intuition. They might have a higher tolerance for ambiguity, which makes them more open to "outside-the-box" ideas and situations.[122]

Contact is not a sure thing.

Mediums stress the importance of *intention*—all parties have to be in sync. In this book I've described conversations in which the spirit is sitting by the phone, waiting for me to call—Wallace, *Pontianak*, the Mermaid Queen. Yet sometimes the spirit is elusive—Ali, for example, doesn't seem very keen to have a long chat. And most surprisingly, I find it difficult to connect with my father, whom I thought would have been the most accessible. Brigitte tried, and failed, as did Terri and Pauline at the Spiritualist Association of Great Britain. He could at least have said, "Sorry, son, this is my poker night. Call back later."

So I wonder. If I call and no one answers, what is the spirit doing? Shuffleboard? Heading off to the early-bird special at the Happy Dales Heavenly Old Folks Bar and Grill?

People who don't want to believe in spirits claim there is no scientific evidence.

Most people with a Western education prefer to have clear explanations to account for so-called mysteries. Our overactive left brains (logic, facts, statistics, engineering, documentation, details, analysis) often are more important to us than our less trusted right brains (emotion, story, questions, creativity).

So, it's natural that many people discount spiritualism (and similarly discount spiritualism's cousins—astrology, pendulums, angels, psychic ability, religious miracles, telepathy, even the existence of Atlantans and Arcturians in our midst) because *there's no proof*. I'm sympathetic to this view. Don't get me started about folks who believe in Atlantis.[123]

Yet scientists (and Spiritualists) regularly try to find "proof" of contact.

Some Spiritualists are content to accept psychic phenomena without overanalyzing the event. *Accept it, or not.*

Such vagueness bothers many scientists. They, and perhaps most people, agree with Francis Bacon that "knowledge is power." Steve Taylor, author of *Spiritual Science: Why Science Needs Spirituality to Make Sense of the World,* says: "To be able to explain the world brings a satisfying feeling of control—to feel that nature is 'under our thumb,' that it is in thrall to us. To admit that there are phenomena that we can't fully understand or explain, and that the world is stranger than we can conceive, weakens power and control."

Many scientists denigrate research into so-called "anomalous phenomena," which includes speaking with spirits and other psychic abilities, as "pseudoscience," "junk science," or "woo." They accuse researchers of fraud, explain away anomalous phenomena as hallucination or wishful thinking, argue that speaking with spirits is a form of mental illness, assert that anomalous phenomena violate known laws of physics, and insist that extraordinary claims require extraordinary evidence.

Yet scientists have shown that mediums (as well as people

who meditate and enter trance states) undergo physiological changes in brain activity when they communicate with spirits.

Nevertheless, there is zero scientific evidence that spirits exist, or that we are able to contact them.

So something is going on, but we can't define it or measure it.

To oversimplify, science and scientists don't leave much room for metaphor. Science values an on-off, yes-no, sunshine-moonlight explanation. (I accept that this binary model is challenged by disciplines such as quantum mechanics.) Except, and it's a big *except*, scientists are people, and people have that troubling desire to seek the in-between. Life is full of shades and shadows, the way the colors of a rainbow merge and it is impossible to delineate exactly where the indigo ends and the violet begins.

Some Spiritualists insist that Spiritualism deserves to be accorded scientific certification. They accept that the dominant left-brained paradigm of materialism is not a coherent theory for understanding anomalous phenomena that, according to the materialist point of view, should not exist.

These people invoke three arguments.

First is the concept that absence of proof is not proof of absence. This is the same argument used by people who believe in Atlantis and the yeti.

Second is the idea that science doesn't yet have the tools to properly examine psychic phenomena—before Hans Geiger invented his famous counter, we had no way of measuring radioactivity. Even today chemists see mysterious empty spaces in the periodic table and guess that certain new elements will be discovered to match those holes where elements *should* be found.

Third, Spiritualists accuse Western science of a whole range of prejudices that prevent learned researchers from studying (and therefore proving) the existence of psychic phenomenon, such as life after death.

Will left-brain technologically savvy researchers someday find empirical evidence that there is life after death?

I doubt it.

But Nikola Tesla, the noted engineer best known for his contributions to the design of the modern alternating current (AC) electricity supply system, disagreed. He said, "The day science begins to study non-physical phenomena, it will make more progress in one decade than in all the previous centuries of its existence."

∽

It probably doesn't matter if there is scientific evidence.

Every day we are confronted by the mysteries of the world, including the possible existence of spirits. Can we explain these things using logic and science? Absolutely not, at least not yet.

Are spirits real? Perhaps, but unlikely. Is there proof? No. And I doubt there ever will be.

Both believers and skeptics have tried vainly to "prove" the existence of spirits.[124] Some phenomena are explainable as the work of clever charlatans or illusionists. And some phenomena are inexplicable using the techniques of scientific analysis we have at our disposal.

And I think this search for "proof" doesn't matter, because in this case logic is antithetical to belief.

I suggest that it is *not necessary to have a scientific underpinning for everything*. Certainly, we rely on our brains to make sense of what we experience through our five senses. But what if there is a sixth (or seventh, or eighth) sense that deals with concepts like telepathy, intention, or clairvoyance? How can we dissect and analyze emotions—anger, love, longing, bereavement? We can see the physical symptoms of such emotions—changes in blood pressure, electrocortical activity, pulse, respiration, and lack of concentration plus digestive or sleep disturbances. But the existence of emotions resides in the working environment of poets, philosophers, healers, and dreamers.

Novelist Peter Pullman, writing about a 2018 Oxford, UK, exhibition about witchcraft wrote: "Rationalism doesn't make the magical universe go away. Reason is the wrong tool. Trying to understand superstition rationally is like trying to pick up something made of wood by using a magnet. Reason is a good servant but a bad master, and its powers are limited; no work of art was ever reasoned into existence."

Again, as Sultan Hamengku Buwono IX told me, "You either accept it or you don't." Or as Hamlet pointed out, "There are more things . . . than are dreamt of in your philosophy."[125, 126]

I recall a conversation with Manolo, a faith healer in the Philippines. He was wildly successful, treating thousands of suffering people each year at his modest rural clinic north of Manila. He didn't charge a fee, and he told patients who asked that they should only give a donation if their heart said they should. He lived in a modest village house, but the rumor mill said that he owned a penthouse and a Mercedes in Manila. People went to him to be cured of cancer and heart disease. And then a TV crew came to document his success and found that he was a skilled illusionist, and the malignant tumors he allegedly pulled from patients' bodies were bits of chicken guts. Many people were outraged. "Fake! Cheat!" they cried. But the steady stream of patients never abated. I asked him about this seeming conundrum. "Yes, I use some tricks," he said over rice wine one night. "But it doesn't matter. You see, even though people know it's a trick they still recover. Most of them get better. They *want* to believe. Their cancer disappears."

Perhaps this spirit business is similar to our view of medicine. For many people, the only effective medical treatment of illness comes from allopathic pharmaceuticals, prescribed by a medical doctor (a modern shaman, actually, but that's another issue), that are manufactured by giant companies, have undergone double-blind clinical trials, have been approved by governmental health agencies, and cost a bundle. But other people swear by homeopathic remedies that seem to work in mysterious ways and which have no official endorsements by medical authorities. Left brain or right brain? Your call.

Perhaps Einstein said it best: "There are only two ways to live your life. One is as though nothing is a miracle. The other is as though everything is a miracle."

People who do believe in spirits can be gullible.

People believe what they choose to believe. "Denier" has become an all-too familiar term to describe people who, in spite of massive scientific evidence, do not believe that man is responsible for climate change, or that there is such a process as evolution, or that the Holocaust occurred.

Some people are "blinded by love" and marry poorly. Others keep their faith in tyrants, despots, prophets, and cult leaders regardless of their leaders' distasteful actions. Many people choose one media outlet over another because they "trust" it.

So, it's not surprising that many people believe in spirits without scientific evidence to support that view. They *choose* to believe.

Jill Neimark, writing in *Psychology Today*, says that "The tendency for people to agree with what they've been told at [psychic and spiritual] readings has been dubbed the Barnum effect, in honor of P.T. Barnum's line 'There's a sucker born every minute.' A legendary test of the Barnum effect was offered in Paris in the 1970s by Michel Gauqelin, who placed an ad offering free personal horoscopes. Later, 94% of the recipients rated their horoscope accurate. Each person had received the same horoscope, that of one of France's most notorious mass murderers."

Officials at Trump University recognized the anti-intellectual power of passions over logic when they instructed their salespeople to emphasize a person's ambitions rather than the realities: "Don't ask people what they *think* about something you've said. Instead, always ask them how they *feel* about it. People buy emotionally and justify it logically."

Belief in spirits can be a valuable method of dealing with grief.

Most psychics offer a spiritual version of the Beatles song "She Loves You." Regardless of how cruel, standoffish, arrogant, or selfish a relative was in life, once he or she dies, and once contact is made through an appropriate medium, the loved one becomes a genial bundle of joy. "He's sorry for abusing you," a medium might relate. "Now that he's passed he wants you to know he loves you and protects you." Crying often ensues.

Mediums have a term for this: "Proof of survival." It's a bit like when someone is kidnapped by a terrorist group and demands ransom. Before the ransom is paid, the negotiator is likely to demand "proof of life," generally in the form of a photo of the person kidnapped holding that day's newspaper.

In most Western cultures traditional grief counseling focuses on the client's acceptance of separation and integration of loss, an Elizabeth Kubler-Ross view of dealing with death. "Your mother's gone, departed. Yes, grieve, but then get on with your life." A medium, however will offer an alternate scenario that promotes an ongoing relationship between the living and the deceased. *Your loved one is still around. No need to think of her death as a definitive break. She is watching over you.* Such a "continuing bonds paradigm" can have a positive impact on dealing with the death of a loved one.[127]

The fluffy terms "passed away" or "crossed over" have the "just maybe, I hope—I hope" optimistic ambiguity of the mother of a 15th-century sailor setting off to sail around the world. But the harsh term "death" emits the irreversible finality of a tympani roll followed by the clash of the cymbals, the end times "whoosh-thump" of a guillotine.

I saw one example of "I hope" in my family. My Aunt Sarah and her husband Dave made a pact that whoever died first would try to contact the other. Dave "passed" first, and Sarah noted many inexplicable signs that Dave was saying hello. She would return to their apartment after a day's work and find that all the pictures on the wall were skewed. They had a small picture-framing business, so that form of signal was particularly appropriate. She would wake up and find that paintings had been taken off their hooks and placed carefully on the floor, leaning against the wall. She regularly found coins in full view in the hallway minted in the year that Dave had died. At first, she was pleased to have this regular "conversation" with her husband. But after a while these contacts became exhausting, and she realized that the bond had to be severed. She said to Dave's spirit, "Okay, Dave, good to hear from you. I'm sure you're sending your love. But I'm fine. It's okay for you to leave and go to wherever it is that is your next destination." And that was the end of the skewed paintings and found coins.

Be afraid.

Countless friends, when I explain my quest to speak with spirits, have told me to "be careful."
    Of what?
    The answers differ.
    Of being sucked into the netherworld.
    Of a curse.

Of the medium taking control of your soul.
Of the medium taking control of your wallet.
Of the medium taking control of your destiny.
Of getting mugged in some dark alley in a distant country.
Some people say to me, "You're very brave."
Others think, "You're very stupid."

And the game goes on.

I continue to seek mediums to speak with Wallace, Ali, and other characters who interest me. Once in a while I'll go off on a tangent and have an encounter with a female vampire ghost (who hates men), or the Mermaid Queen (who loves men).

Will this journey result in either a scientific or psychic breakthrough?

Unlikely.

Can you contact me when I go to the "other side?"

Don't bet on it. Best to stick with email while I'm alive. Don't delay.

Emails are more likely to get through.

ENDNOTES

THE THREE TENETS OF SPIRITUALISM

1 One observer declared that the soul, generally considered ethereal, *has* physical weight. In 1907, a Massachusetts physician named Duncan MacDougall attempted to measure the mass lost by a human just after the moment of death. One of his six subjects lost 21.3 grams – about the weight of a small mouse – giving rise to the much-discussed concept that the soul has a physical presence that departs the body on death. Wikipedia elegantly calls MacDougall's scientific method "an example of selective reporting."

PROLOGUE:
THE BIG QUESTION

2 In downtown Geneva recently, I noticed a man who wore a T-shirt that said "I don't need Google, my wife knows everything." Indeed. So I went next door to my gadget-loving neighbors and asked their voice-powered Google Assistant, "Hey Google. Is there life after death?" And Google Assistant replied, in a neutral, female voice, "Sorry, I don't understand." So either Google Assistant can't comprehend the question, or (the conspiracy theorist at work) Google Assistant actually *does* know but has been programmed to obfuscate and not give away the answer. I then tried "Hey Google. What happens when you die?" Google took this one personally and replied, "For me it's a server reboot."

3 Or, as C.S. Lewis put it: "Humans are amphibians—half spirit and half animal. As spirits they belong to the eternal world, but as animals they inhabit time."

4 A useful word here might be "grok," the only Martian word used in common English. Coined by Robert A. Heinlein, it roughly means to understand something profoundly and intuitively.

5 Walt Disney memorably captured this concept when Jiminy Cricket sang "When You Wish Upon a Star."

[6] Certainly, immortality comes genetically by having children. It might come if we are famous. We might leave artistic legacies. It might be as ephemeral as Elie Weisel suggests: "The only thing we can be remembered for is our good name, our honor, our respect." We might have a new species named after us—Olaf Rudbeck gave Carl Linnaeus (who created the system of binominal taxonomy) his first job. In thanks, Linnaeus saw to it that Rudbeck became immortalized as a flower, *Rudbeckia hirta*, the American black-eyed Susan. Linnaeus wrote to his professor: "So long as the earth shall survive, and as each spring shall see it covered with flowers, the Rudbeckia will preserve your glorious name." And not to be outdone, Hugh Hefner, of *Playboy* fame, paid a bundle to have an endangered subspecies of marsh rabbit named after him: *Sylvilagus palustris hefneri*.

MOSES SENDS ME ON A PEACEKEEPING MISSION

[7] Terzani, who died in 2004, was a noted journalist. He was one of very few reporters to witness, in the mid-1970s, both the fall of Saigon to the hands of the Viet Cong and the fall of Phnom Penh at the hands of the Khmer Rouge. In 1991 he covered the breakup of the Soviet Union.

[8] In Great Britain, an act of Parliament prohibiting witchcraft was put into effect in 1735; it lasted until 1951.

[9] James Vlahos had a novel approach to speaking with his dead father John by creating what he termed a "Dadbot," a chatbot that would speak in his father's style, vocalizing his father's voice and thoughts. While John was being treated for what turned out to be incurable lung cancer, James recorded hours and hours of conversations with his father. When transcribed, the 91,970 words filled "203 single-spaced pages with 12-point Palatino type." It included countless details of his father's life—how to say "instrumentality" in Portuguese, him singing "Me and My Shadow," his boyhood crush on a little girl down the street named Margot, and how his mother told him his pet rabbit, Papa Demoskopoulos, had run away but had actually been kidnaped by his aunt and cooked for supper. The resulting chatbot performed the function of a séance with his father, no doubt providing more and better information than any medium would be able to relate.

[10] Bereavement counseling, in the Western model, typically involves accepting that a loved one has died and isn't coming back, and therapists help people to come to grips with this final and irreversible separation. However after-death communication (ADC) with loved ones seeks the

opposite mind-set. The deceased individual is *not* gone forever and the living and the deceased can therefore maintain an ongoing relationship.

[11] I see this same woman, always immaculately dressed in a vaguely 1950s style, at subsequent gatherings at SAGB. To me she appears to be a psychic groupie, and attending such readings seems to be the focal point of her social life. She has a bit of an aloof Stepford Wife demeanor. Several times I try to engage her in conversation, but she isn't interested in such trivial pursuits.

[12] Yan Mokoginta died a year after our séance. We never traveled to the Holy Land; there is still no peace in the Middle East.

"Beings of a Like Mental Nature to Ourselves"

[13] Sochaczewski, Paul Spencer (2017).

[14] I challenge you to go into your backyard and look for ants. You might find a red one, a black one, maybe a large one with a sharp bite. Sure, Wallace was in the tropics, where there are more species. But two hundred *new* types of ants? Identified and classified without good reference books or fellow experts to consult? Remarkable.

[15] By doing so, Wallace also let Darwin take on much of the heavy lifting to promote the theory to a skeptical British audience.

[16] In one memorable passage in *The Malay Archipelago*, he writes emotionally about being a surrogate father to an orangutan baby he had orphaned by killing her mother. He cared for the infant ape like a child. When it died of poor nutrition, he switched back into scientist/collector mode and boiled the bones to obtain a commercially valuable skeleton that he sold to a UK museum.

[17] G.K. Chesterton said Wallace was "[one of the two, the other was Walt Whitman] most important and significant figures of the nineteenth century . . . for he has been the leader of a revolution and the leader of a counter revolution [materialistic evolution studies, and humanistic social and spiritualistic studies]."

[18] One obituary said: "Science has lost its 'grand old man' . . ..the greatest of all modern scientists." Another: "By the death of Alfred Russel Wallace this country loses not only a great scientist, but the last of the men who made the early part of the Victorian era so memorable. His interests were as wide as human life, his modesty as remarkable as his genius, and his enthusiasm for humanity as sensitive as his vision was wide."

[19] Wallace, Alfred Russel (1869).

[20] Wallace found Spiritualism so fascinating (and important) that he wrote this book three years before he completed his classic *The Malay Archipelago*, which took him six years to write after his return to England.

[21] Charles H. Smith, a history professor at Western Kentucky University who maintains a respected website devoted to Wallace's writings and life, notes with an even tone that "Wallace's association with spiritualism has generally been regarded as his greatest intellectual inconsistency . . . a little probing, however, reveals that there is considerably more intellectual content to spiritualism than a simple belief in disembodied spirits." Even Carl Jung noted that Wallace's interest in mesmerism, phrenology, and spirit manifestations merited praise for 'having thrown the whole of [Wallace's] authority on to the side of non-material facts, regardless of . . . the cheap derision of [his] contemporaries; even at a time when the intellect of the educated classes was spellbound by the new dogma of materialism, [Wallace] drew public attention to phenomena of an irrational nature, contrary to accepted convictions."

[22] Wallace, Alfred Russel (1874).

[23] Ibid.

[24] Ibid.

[25] Wallace, Alfred Russel (1896).

[26] Wallace, Alfred Russel (1896).

[27] Wallace's preferred medium was a celebrated, physically immense charlatan who called herself Mrs. Guppy. Molly Whittington-Egan (2015) said Mrs. Guppy wove a "bogus family history" to improve her modest social standing and was "an opportunist of the actress type with natural dramatic ability." For Wallace, Mrs. Guppy "was the enchantress," and Wallace was "blind to her legerdemain and gross conjury." In addition to table-rapping and psychic writing, Mrs. Guppy was noted for her apports (objects that appeared mysteriously in the séance room), which included live starfish, lobsters, butterflies, doves, ducks prepared for the oven, and, "enough fruit and flowers to keep Covent Garden in business by herself."

[28] Wallace, Alfred Russel (1893).

[29] Wallace's "scientific explanation" of Spiritualism can be tainted by the likelihood that Wallace *wanted* to see fairies and ghosts. We know that Wallace had invited his brother Herbert to visit him in Brazil, only to take responsibility when his brother died of yellow fever. He was a sensitive man. As Molly Whittington-Egan writes: "For some sensitive people, personal loss

led to the dark consolation of the séance room. The prospect of a barren land and empty skies receded and death lost its sting."

30 Letter to Mr. Romanes addressing "common fallacies of beginners in coming to hasty conclusions from a few isolated facts." Wallace, Alfred Russel (1905).

31 Wallace, Alfred Russel (1901).

32 Arthur Conan Doyle mentions Alfred Russel Wallace in *The Lost World*, and modeled the character Stapleton in the Sherlock Holmes story "The Hound of the Baskervilles" after Wallace. Conan Doyle, a strong believer of Spiritualism, claimed that "an invisible and friendly presence" often provided him with wise advice; he apparently felt that this "presence" was the ghost of Wallace. He wrote: "How I wished that I had the brain of a Russel Wallace and could read more clearly the illuminated page of Nature . . . His biography was a favourite book of mine long before I understood the full significance of Spiritualism, which was to him an evolution of the spirit on parallel lines to that evolution of the body which he did so much to establish."

33 It was a mutual admiration society. Wallace similarly admired Conan Doyle, even making a point of visiting Reichenbach Falls in Switzerland, the site where Sherlock Holmes fought to the death with Professor Moriarty in "The Final Problem."

34 Arthur Conan Doyle was a splendid storyteller, but, like so many writers he was sloppy when it came to accuracy. In *The History of Spiritualism* Conan Doyle twice referred to Wallace as "Dr. Wallace." Wallace left school at the age of 13 and never went to university, let alone earned a graduate degree, but he did receive two honorary doctorate degrees, from Oxford University (Doctorate of Civil Law) and Trinity College, University of Dublin (Doctor of Laws). He declined honorary degrees from Cambridge University and the University of Wales. Even today, with accurate references readily available, a frustratingly large number of writers identify Wallace as either "Dr." or "Sir" or "Professor." He was none of the above. And misspellings of his name are rife, the most common fault being writing "Russell" instead of the correct "Russel."

35 In *Confessions of a Ghost-Hunter*, Harry Price, who became famous for exposing fraudulent spiritualist mediums, revealed Hudson's methods. "When the plate slide was inserted, this action brought the paper positive of the 'ghost' up against the sensitive plate. When the shutter bulb was pressed, this image and the picture of the sitter were captured on the plate. Thus, a single exposure on this plate carried both images."

36 Wallace, Alfred Russel (1905).

37 Wallace, Alfred Russel (1866).

38 Ibid.

39 See Sochaczewski, Paul Spencer (2017) for a detailed discussion of this issue.

40 Certainly, they had other disagreements: Darwin argued that competition between members of the same species led to adaptation, while Wallace asserted that environmental pressures led populations of various locations to diverge.

41 Wallace, Alfred Russel (1905).

42 Ibid.

43 As illustrated by a letter to his sister in which Wallace wrote: "In my early youth I heard, as 99-hundredths of the world do, only the evidence on one side, & became impressed with a veneration for religion which has left some traces even to this day. I have since heard & read much on both sides, & pondered much upon the matter in all its bearings. I spent, as you know, a year and a half in a clergyman's family [from 1844 to1845 he lived in the house of the headmaster of Collegiate School in Leicester, Rev. Abraham Hill] & heard almost every Sunday the very best, most earnest & most impressive preacher it has ever been my fortune to meet with, but it produced no effect whatever on my mind. I have since wandered among men of many races & many religions. I have studied man & nature in all its aspects & I have sought after truth. In my solitude I have pondered much on the incomprehensible subjects of *space, eternity, life & death!* I think I have fairly heard & fairly weighed the evidence on both sides, I remain an *utter disbeliever* in almost all that you consider the most sacred truths."

44 When Wallace went off on these kinds of spiritual musings, he sounded suspiciously New Agey—recall what James Redfield, the author of the wildly successful (and poorly written) *The Celestine Prophecy*, wrote: "I [saw] in one flash the entire story of evolution," Redfield writes of an epiphany that followed a narrow escape from nasty Peruvian soldiers. "[I saw] the story of matter coming into being and then evolving, as if under some guiding plan, toward ever higher vibrations, creating the exact conditions, finally, for humans to emerge . . . for each of us, as individuals, to emerge." Many mediums and psychics I have met espouse similar beliefs and give credence to tomes such as the *Akashic Records*, the *Knowledge Book*, the *Sacred Book of Thoth*, and the works of Erich von Däniken.

45 Ibid.

46 In 1951 the British Parliament introduced the Fraudulent Mediums Act that prohibited a person from claiming to be a psychic, medium, or other

spiritualist while attempting to deceive and to make money from the deception (other than solely for the purpose of entertainment). It was in turn repealed in 2008 by new Consumer Protection Regulations following an EU directive targeting unfair sales and marketing practices. For this reason, many UK mediums will promote their efforts as "for entertainment only," which they probably feel is self-demeaning and untrue.

[47] Like virtually all of my friends, I have no idea what will happen to my library when I die. Each of us has a large library of books related to our individual interests. Unfortunately, our interests are of little interest to others. And paper books are becoming like fossils—curiosities of a bygone era.

[48] Lovely word. According to the *Oxford English Dictionary*, it first appeared in English slang usage in the 18th century, created as an arbitrary invention suggested by flabby (adj) or flap (n) and aghast (adj).

[49] After the channeling, Rita says she hates bees and can't understand this reference. I tell her that Wallace collected plants as well as critters. More to the point, he married Annie Mitten, whose father was a noted botanist, and Wallace and his father-in-law spent many happy weeks plant-hunting in England and Switzerland. And one of the highlights of Wallace's extensive visit to the United States in 1886–1887 was when he explored the Rocky Mountains with botanist Alice Eastwood, writing: "We found a valley not visited by botanists, a perfect garden of flowers, in the woods, pastures, high meadows and rock slopes—flowers everywhere by millions." But there are other possible explanations. Wallace's preferred medium, Mrs. Guppy, was noted for her ability to make large quantities of fresh flowers appear; since Rita was channeling Wallace, perhaps he was thinking along that line of inquiry. Or he could simply have been remembering playing in his rose garden with his children. Or none of the above.

[50] A comic theatrical device later borrowed by Gilbert and Sullivan in *Pirates of Penzance*.

[51] Six foot one inch (185 cm) when in his twenties.

[52] On reflection, my analysis is ridiculous—surely spirits are pure energy and not subject to corporeal aches and pains.

[53] Of course, this kind of notification can also work to a medium's advantage. If she fails to make a connection, then she can claim it's not due to her inability to connect, but rather the spirit isn't available right now, or is having a bad hair day.

THE SEARCH FOR ALI

[54] I am not the first to consider a form of History by *Hantu*. French author Victor Hugo had conversations with Mozart, Dante, Plato, Galileo, and Moses. Jesus visited Hugo three times, during which he suggested a new religion with Hugo as its prophet. Hugo also channeled Shakespeare, producing a play featuring Heaven, Hell, Paradise, Louis XV, and a peasant maiden named Nihila. In one long soliloquy Paradise tells Hell: "How happy mankind is! No more evil! . . . Mankind is an immense flower whose roots are bathed in light and who has as many petals as the mouth of God has kisses."

In another oft-cited case, in the 1920s the Rev. John Lamond spent his holidays at the village house in Domremy, France, where Joan of Arc grew up. As recounted by Lamond's friend Graham Moffat, Lamond spent hours meditating beside the famous "fairy tree" where Joan saw her visions and heard the voices of her guides. Moffat wrote: "By this means, though he himself was devoid of psychic gifts, [Lamond] hoped to get in touch with the still living spirit of the 'Maid of Orleans.'" Back in London Lamond had numerous "interviews" with Joan through the trance mediumship of a psychic named Mrs. Mason, learning "much interesting information that was entirely unknown to [Joan's] biographers." The result of this spirit-enhanced research: A biography—*Joan of Arc and England*, and a play about her life. "While it must be admitted that G.B.S. [George Bernard Shaw] has given us a drama more skilfully constructed and more intensely dramatic, Dr. Lamond's work depicts the real Joan," noted Moffat, a playwright himself who believed that his dead father and brother helped in writing his plays. "When we consider that it was written by a Scottish parson whose knowledge of theatrical technique cannot have been very profound, [Lamond's] play is an astonishing fine piece of work. Here is no credulous village girl deceived by church bells into thinking that she hears voices; no victim of hallucinations; but a clairvoyant and clairaudient maid directly inspired from the spirit world and raised by Heaven-given power to be the saintly heroine of France . . . divinely inspired, her campaign against the English invaders of her country was designed and carried out with the aid of her spirit guides."

[55] Wallace, Alfred Russel (1905).

[56] Ibid.

[57] Cranbrook, Earl of, and Adrian Marshall (2014).

[58] Wallace, Alfred Russel (1869a).

⁵⁹ It might more accurately have been named "Ali's Standard-wing/*Semioptera alii.*"

⁶⁰ Wallace, Alfred Russel (1869a).

⁶¹ Ibid.

⁶² Ibid.

⁶³ Ibid.

⁶⁴ Ibid.

⁶⁵ Ibid.

⁶⁶ Ibid.

⁶⁷ Ibid.

⁶⁸ Ibid.

⁶⁹ Wallace, Alfred Russel (1905).

⁷⁰ Wallace, Alfred Russel (1867).

⁷¹ Wallace never indicated Ali's patronym.

⁷² McLaughlin, Tom, and Suriani binti Sahari (In press).

⁷³ *Panglima* refers to a commander or general. Compare this with the observation of the medium Ms. Iis in Ternate (see following section) in which she said that Ali was royalty from Ternate and was sent as part of a group of noblemen to Sarawak by the sultan of Ternate.

⁷⁴ van Whye, John, and Gerrell M.Drawhorn (2015).

⁷⁵ I have problems with Cranbrook and Marshall's conclusion that the "Banyak quot bitchara orang Arru" quote indicates Ali was not from Sarawak. First, the incident occurred after Ali had been with Wallace for two years; plenty of time for him to have become accustomed to speaking "standard" Malay. Second, Wallace was recalling a relatively unimportant conversation and there is no reason to think that Wallace would have either remembered it accurately (can you remember verbatim a mundane conversation you had just yesterday?). Third, Wallace provided the essential meaning of Ali's statement, using the basic Malay that would be recognizable to any reader familiar with the region. Writers "approximate" all the time. I don't place too much credence that this particular piece of evidence answers the questions about Ali's origin.

⁷⁶ A small number of historians have in recent years expended considerable

energy dissecting this phrase, considering it a Rosetta Stone–like looking glass into Ali's origins. It could mean that the Aru people speak loudly and aggressively. Or it could mean that they are hard bargainers. For a detailed analysis of the linguistics behind this phrase, and a discussion of the various forms of Malay used in the archipelago during the time of Wallace's visit, see: Drawhorn, J. (2016).

77 What I find interesting is that people seem to answer questions like this in one of two ways. Some people have an ingrained opinion and then seek evidence to support their views (for instance, people who espouse creationism and use Biblical references and circular logic as their proof). Other people might step back, examine data and come to a conclusion based on statistics, logical arguments, and replicable experiments (for example, people who believe in climate change because the science is, in their minds, sufficiently convincing). Often it is a combination of what we want to be true, united (or justified) with a dose of hard evidence. The balance between the two options varies depending on our personalities, education level, and social environment. Consider how we judge a politician running for elected office. Do we believe the countless stories circulating about her? What news stories do we believe? What rumors do we believe? Is there any unassailable "truth?" For example, do we believe, in our hearts, that President Barack Obama was born in Kenya in spite of hard evidence he was born in Hawaii? Do we believe that U.S. astronauts really landed on the moon, or are we convinced the 1969 moon landing was a hoax produced in a top-secret government TV studio in Nevada? What is the tipping point that causes our support (or disapproval) to flip? So it is with the search for Ali's retirement home.

78 I asked McLaughlin to explain the contradiction of Ali having a Sarawak wife, since Wallace twice mentions that Ali married in Ternate—see below. McLaughlin suggested that I was looking at the situation with an overly Western perspective in which monogamy is the norm, and noted that polygamy was permitted both by Islamic Shariah law as well as by *adat*, the traditional culture and value system to which Ali would have adhered. Also, according to McLaughlin, Ali had made a promise to look after the children of his brother Panglima Osman (Seman), and familial responsibility in Sarawak overcame the obligation of his marriage in Ternate. For me, there is no "proof" that Ali had such a familial loyalty.

79 McLaughlin, Tom, and Suriani binti Sahari (in press).

80 Boyle, Frederick (1865).

81 Drawhorn, J. (2016).

82 Boyle, Frederick (1865).

83 Drawhorn writes: "I do think that Ali Kasut is 'most likely' Wallace's Ali.

Just too many convergences. The fact that Ali Kasut (and Wallace's Ali) were in Singapore at the same time. That Ali Kasut (unusually) wore Western clothing (and that Wallace's Ali purchased a set of Western clothing . . . and not at Wallace's behest, who thought that he looked better in his traditional attire). That Ali Kasut spoke some English. That Ali Kasut was experienced in outfitting the needs of Europeans on expeditions. That Ali Kasut was 'well-travelled' and was familiar with Sarawak and Borneo (they hired him as a guide). That would suggest that he was not a Singapore Malay . . . most of the trade at that time was undertaken by Sarawak Malays. Ali Kasut seemed familiar with the Brooke administrators. Like Wallace's Ali, Ali Kasut seemed quite responsible and organized."

"The counterpoints to this are that Frederick Boyle does not mention Ali being Wallace's assistant. But then again, Boyle doesn't mention Wallace at all. From our perspective that might seem odd, but remember that Wallace was not widely known outside of the actual biological community and was just beginning to establish his fame as 'more than a collector' back in London at the time of Boyle's journey. Ali, himself, might not have name-dropped [which I find difficult to imagine since Wallace implies Ali fancied himself a bit of a raconteur]. And no other writer from the era mentions anything about Ali or his return.

"So, while I lean to the general accuracy of Boyle's account, it also likely contains some literary license and exaggerations. I also think that Ali Kasut is most likely Wallace's Ali. Nothing in his account clearly eliminates this, and much within it supports that view." Drawhorn, J. (2018) Personal correspondence.

[84] Wallace, Alfred Russel. (1869a).

[85] Wallace, Alfred Russel (1859).

[86] Wallace, Alfred Russel (1905).

[87] Ali had advantages that would have made him a desired husband. Besides having some cash and a reputation of having traveled widely with a European, Ali likely was acquainted with a Dutchman named van Duivenboden, whom Wallace dubbed the "King of Ternate "in recognition of the man's wealth and influence. Duivenboden became a friend to Wallace and assisted him in finding a house, among other favors. Duivenboden (correct name: Maarten Dirk van Renesse van Duivenbode) no doubt knew of the young man's reliability and experience. We know that van Duivenboden also collected and sold bird of paradise skins, as did other well-placed Ternate-based merchants such as Samuel Corneille Jean Wilhelm van Musschenbroek. We have no proof, but it is likely that if Ali remained in Ternate, he would have found regular employment working for these men, since Ali had extensive

experience organizing collecting expeditions to New Guinea and throughout Maluku, shooting birds, and preparing the skins for sale in Europe.

88 Barbour, Thomas (1912).

89 Barbour, Thomas (1921).

90 Some critics take issue with this quote, arguing that Ali might have more naturally addressed Barbour in Dutch or Malay. From my point of view there are several valid explanations. Undoubtedly, Ali would have learned a bit of English while with Wallace, and he was dredging out his limited English vocabulary to impress foreign visitors who obviously were interested in biology, particularly after having heard them speak English among themselves. Perhaps Ali *did* address Barbour in Dutch or Malay, and Barbour simply gave readers the English translation. And as for Ali referring to himself as Ali Wallace, well that makes sense, since Malays don't use family names but refer to themselves as the son or daughter of so-and-so. Why wouldn't Ali consider himself Wallace's son, or at least an adopted or honorary son? (And the common honorific throughout Indonesia given to an older man is *bapak*, or "father.") Perhaps the encounter was not even as theatrical as Barbour claims; he might have dramatized it for the sake of his narrative. But it might well have occurred as reported since we know Ali was a bit of a showman, as evidenced by Wallace's recollection of Ali's pleasure in telling exaggerated stories that enhanced his standing in the community. And it is unlikely anyone except Ali would have had a serious discussion with a foreign collector about an obscure lizard. For me there is no reason to doubt Barbour's sincerity and accuracy in reporting meeting Ali.

91 Barbour, Thomas (1943).

92 It would have been nice if Wallace had also written a note to Ali.

93 I think it is important that Wallace expressed no surprise that Ali was living in Ternate, so his letter to Barbour is one more piece of evidence that Ali "retired" to Ternate.

94 Wallace, Alfred Russel (1867).

95 Trying to make a windfall profit from a gullible foreigner seems to be a regular practice among some of the mediums I visited. See similar attempts to get rich quick from the medium in Pontianak (chapter "Are You Strong Enough to Go Through with This?"), and the *nat* medium in Yangon (chapter "The Trees Speak").

96 Sultan of Ternate Mudaffar Syah of Ternate, Ofa Firman's father, reigned from 1975–2015.

"Are You Strong Enough to Go Through with This?"

[97] See Epilogue for polling information on the belief in ghosts, miracles, and afterlife.

[98] Ahok's penchant for making politically incorrect statements had serious consequences. While campaigning for re-election in 2016, Ahok, a Christian of Chinese ancestry, was accused by Islamic fundamentalists of insulting the Q'uran. He lost the election. Then, following a contentious trial, he was convicted of blasphemy and inciting violence and sentenced to two years in prison.

[99] Linnaeus's solution was what we call binominal nomenclature, a formal system of naming species of living things in which the first part of the name identifies the genus to which the species belongs and the second part identifies the species within the genus, for instance *Solanum lycopersicum* for the common tomato, or *Homo sapiens* for human beings.

[100] Glen Goei, an ethnic Chinese, had difficulty getting funding for the project because he insisted that his film be shot in the Malay language, rather than the more commercially viable English, and wouldn't feature any Chinese actors. Goei, however, stuck by his artistic principles, noting he wanted to be faithful to the original spirit of the *pontianak* films produced in Singapore and Malaysia in the mid-20th century. "These movies were in Malay and were watched by many Singaporeans, regardless of their race or the language they spoke," Goei said, adding that he wanted his film to be seen "as a cultural product" and not merely an "economic commodity."

[101] Julia Perez (Jupe), who succumbed to her cancer in 2017, was one of Indonesia's most hardworking actresses; her career blossomed partly because of her outspoken approach to life and performing.

In August 2012 Jupe carried out a promise that when she reached one million Twitter followers, she would perform a pole dance at a busy traffic intersection in downtown Jakarta. This performance, plus the fact that she wore skimpy clothing, plus the fact that it was the Muslim fasting month, did not endear her to the more conservative of Jakarta's tastemakers.

Moralistic officials and religious leaders abhorred her sexy persona and denounce her suggestive singing and dancing (she is probably responsible for the creation of the Indonesian word *bomseks*, from the English "sex bomb"). Righteous men and women have banned her from performing in many cities. Jupe defended herself by declaring, and I'm paraphrasing: The men who criticize me are the ones who take bribes, who cheat on their wives, who use taxpayer money to fill their own bank accounts. Who is committing the sin? Me, who entertains people, or these hypocritical men, who steal from the people?

Jupe wrote a book in which she describes the secret of her success: The Five Bs: beauty, brains, behave, bitchy, and boobs. This is not the place to elaborate on her life strategy, but no doubt a PhD awaits someone who can put a post-modern Indonesian spin on her philosophy.

[102] The Indonesian film industry is in the doldrums, and according to film journalist Bobby Batara, it's due to poor governance. There are about 120 Indonesian films made each year, Bobby says, of which about 20 are horror films. "The government regulation of 2009 specifies that there should be two Indonesian films distributed nationally for each foreign film, but the handful of cinema owners who control the market ignore that ruling. Indonesian filmmakers have to beg, bribe, and coerce to get their films shown."

AN INVITATION TO MEET THE MERMAID QUEEN

---

[103] Few things are straightforward in Javanese cosmology. Muhammad Sholikhin, who has analyzed the Mermaid Queen's role in Javanese society, says that she is accorded different titles, and varying levels of importance, in different parts of central Java. She might be: Nyai Roro Kidul—foreign minister, Nyai Riyo Kidul—interior minister, or Nayi Loro Kidul—armed forces general.

[104] Jordaan, Roy (1996).

[105] Geertz, Clifford (1960).

THE TREES SPEAK

---

[106] For more on this theme, see Sochaczewski, Paul (2018d): "We vs Them"

[107] Such protection is not limited to natural sites. Even inanimate, man-made objects can be legally protected provided they are "proven" to be inhabited by spirits. During the British Raj, colonial judges in India granted juristic

personhood status to some deities and their abodes (idols and temples), as long as the deities were consecrated and enspirited during a religious ceremony.

[108] For a fictional account of how environmentalists might argue such a legal case to protect the Borneo rainforest, see *Exceptional Encounters: Enhanced Reality Tales from Southeast Asia*. Sochaczewski, Paul Spencer (2018b).

[109] For more on this theme, see Sochaczewski, Paul Spencer (2018a) "Need/Fear Relationship with Nature."

[110] For more on ghost taxonomy, see chapter "Are You Strong Enough to Go Through with This?"

[111] Staël von Holstein, Verena, and Wolfgang Weirauch (2012).

[112] For more about the Zee-O-Thit Hla forest see Sochaczewski, Paul (2015). For more on sacred forests in general, see "The God Who Flew Off with a Mountain." Sochaczewski, Paul Spencer (2010).

[113] The banyan tree, sometimes called the "strangler fig," is respected throughout the Southeast Asia region where Theravada Buddhism is practiced. Cutting a banyan, and indeed damaging any large tree, is tantamount to assaulting a monk. One of the more successful conservation efforts in Thailand, I recall, was when villagers asked monks to bless large trees in a community forest. To enforce the spiritual importance of the trees, the monks encircled them with golden robes of sanctity, making the trees virtual monks. The scheme worked for years, until outside commercial interests overpowered the inviolability of sacred trees recognized by virtuous rural folks.

[114] Just as ancient promoters of Hinduism incorporated Animistic beliefs in a powerful elephant spirit, resulting in the hugely popular and influential elephant-headed god Ganesha, early kings of Burma realized that it was better to consolidate their new religion by formalizing *nat* worship rather than discarding such spirit beliefs. The result: In the 11th-century, King Anawrahta established the Theravada school of Buddhism as Burma's primary religion. When his attempts to eliminate *nat* worship, considered a form of occultism not accepted by Buddhist scriptures, proved fruitless, he decided to adopt it instead, creating an official pantheon of 37 spirits to be worshiped as subordinates of the Buddha. Intriguingly, most of these major *nats* are spirits of exceptional persons who died gruesome deaths, or localized variants of Hindu deities. For example, the *nat* king, Deva Indra Sakka, is derived from Indra, the head of the Vedic Hindu pantheon, who is similar in stature and power to European gods such as Zeus, Jupiter, Thor, and Odin. Subsequently countless minor *nats* were maintained by local villages, to protect for example an important section of a river or specific

hill. Dramatic geographical features—a mountain ridge, or a waterfall—are particularly favorable spots in which *nats* find residence. Where the land is featureless, such as in a paddy field, villagers can easily attract a guardian *nat* by building a *nat* shrine.

EPILOGUE:
WHAT IF?

[115] I find the whole idea of heaven (and hell) intriguing. What might heaven look like? A country club (guaranteed to hit the ball long and straight) built on clouds where, to gain entry, you have to first get approved by Saint Peter? An Islamic oasis with 72 virgins, just for you? (See "72 Virgins" on Wikipedia for an interesting summary of this concept). A peaceful forest glen filled with gamboling nymphs and Dionysus pouring endless quantities of fine Burgundy to accompany slabs of foie gras produced without harm to the duck? (See Garrison Keillor's delightful story "The Mid-Life Crisis of Dionysus.") Maybe heaven is an ideal alternate reality world where I am a world-class big wave surfer and share funny rainforest tales with thoughtful (but short attention-spanned) orangutans? A serious hierarchal heaven, perhaps like Dante's "Nine Spheres of Paradise?" Or perhaps something out of 2001: *A Space Odyssey* that is so strange and miraculous that we can't even begin to imagine it?

[116] Such statistics seem to be robust, with similar results from a number of studies in the United States and United Kingdom. I have not listed all of the sources, but two (of many) meta-analyses are Greeley, Andrew M, and Michael Hout (1999) and Roper Center for Public Opinion Research (2018).

[117] Written memoirs are notoriously inaccurate. I had a Romanian aunt, Anisoara Stan, who left an autobiography—a cookbook filled with personal anecdotes, letters, and private documents. She positioned herself as a minor royal, a protégé of Romania's Queen Marie (Queen Victoria's granddaughter). She implied Queen Marie had sent her to the United States to be an ambassador-at-large charged with improving Romania's standing in the United States in the period between World War I and World War II. That's the story my family believed.

But I learned a more nuanced version of the story when I met a local historian in Cluj, Transylvania, Anisoara's home town, who dissected her book, incident by incident, claim by claim. "Here she's exaggerating," my friend said. "Here she's lying. Here she's pretending to be someone else." All for good reason, perhaps Anisoara had an agenda, in her case to ingratiate herself with the new Romanian nationalist policies to which her nouveau bourgeois family aspired. Anisoara lied. We all lie. See: Sochaczewski, Paul Spencer (2018c).

[118] There is an increasing body of research that shows that mediums in trance undergo physiological changes, similar perhaps to the altered states of Tibetan monks in deep meditation. In one of many studies, Arthur Delorme (2013) wrote: "As with meditation, receiving information about unknown people who are deceased involves calming mental chatter and becoming receptive to subtle feelings and sensations." His group collected psychometric and brain electrophysiology data (including electrocortical activity, galvanic skin conductance, respiration, heart rate, and blood flow) from six mediums and concluded "that the impression of communicating with the deceased may be a distinct mental state distinct from ordinary thinking or imagination."

[119] Besides being a master magician, Houdini was a vocal critic of charlatan mediums.

[120] This seems to be a Western interpretation; the nature spirits John Studley encountered in China, and the protective *nat* spirits of Myanmar, are not hesitant to aggressively protect their turf and punish wrongdoers.

[121] David Ritchey (2003) estimates more than five million Americans are "Anomalously Sensitive Persons (ASPs)." Such people exhibit uncommonly high levels of sensitivities, not only in the emotional realm, but also in the physiological, cognitive, altered states of consciousness, and transpersonal ("metaphysical") realms.

[122] The downside is that in some religions and cultures, left-handed people are considered immoral, evil, or even witches. Is this a reflection of the fact that they are merely in the minority, or a recognition that they have special, perhaps ungodly, powers?

[123] Stuart Kaufmann, a physicist at the Santa Fe Institute, says: "Paradise has been lost, not to sin but to science." He notes ways science has shattered our sense of importance. First came Copernicus, who proved that we are not the center of the universe; then came Newton, who proved that gravity, not God, made the arrow arc toward its target; and the final blow was struck by Darwin, who said that we are merely "the result of a chain of accidental mutations."

[124] See the chapter "Beings of a Like Mental Nature to Ourselves" to read how the noted scientist Alfred Russel Wallace strove to "prove" the existence of spirits.

[125] A *60 Minutes/Vanity Fair* poll asked, "Can science provide an answer to whether there is an afterlife?" Sixty-seven percent of respondents said "no."

[126] In a related question, almost eight out of ten people polled in Great Britain agreed with the statement that "there are things in life that we simply cannot explain through science or any other means." It seems that a strong majority of people (at least in the United States and Great Britain), believe that science cannot explain all the mysteries of the world.

[127] Beischel, Julie, Chad Mosher, and Mark Bocuzzi (2015).

References

Barbour, Thomas (1912). "A Contribution to the Zoogeography of the East Indian Islands." *Memoirs of the Museum of Comparative Zoology at Harvard College*, vol XLIV. no 1.

Barbour, Thomas (1921). "Aquatic skincs and arboreal monitors." *Copeia*, 97 (31 Aug.): 42–4.

Barbour, Thomas (1943). *Naturalist at Large*. Boston: Little, Brown.

Barušs, Imants, and Julia Mossbridge (2017). *Transcendent Mind: Rethinking the Science of Consciousness*. American Psychological Association. Washington, D.C.

Beischel, Julie; Chad Mosher, and Mark Bocuzzi (2015). "The possible effects on bereavement of assisted after-death communication during readings with psychic mediums: A continuing bonds perspective." *OMEGA—Journal of Death and Dying*. The Windbridge Institute for Applied Research in Human Potential. Tucson.

Boyle, Frederick (1865). *Adventures Amongst the Dyaks of Borneo*. London: Hurst & Blackett.

Carpenter, J.C. (2004). "First Sight: Part one, A model of psi and the mind." *Journal of Parapsychology*, 68: 217–54.

Carpenter, J.C. (2005). "First Sight: Part two, Elaborations of a model of psi and the mind." *Journal of Parapsychology*, 69, 63–112.

Chek, Paul. Internet blog. https://www.paulcheksblog.com/relax-and-see-the-nature-spirits/

Conan Doyle, Arthur (1926). *The History of Spiritualism*. Surrey: The Spiritual Truth Press.

Cranbrook, Earl of, and Adrian Marshall (2014). "Alfred Russell Wallace's assistants, and other helpers, in the Malay Archipelago 1854–62." *Sarawak Museum Journal*, 73 (ns 94): 73–122.

Delorme, Arnaud, Julie Beischel, Leena Michel, Mark Boccuzzi, Dean Radin, and Paul Mills (2013). "Electrocortical activity associated with subjective communication with the deceased." *Frontiers in Psychology*. November 20. Volume 4, article 834.

Drawhorn, Jerry (2016). "The Alienation of Ali: Was Wallace's Assistant from Sarawak or Ternate?" *Sarawak Museum Journal* LXXVI: 97 (ns): 165–200.

Drawhorn, Jerry (2018). Personal correspondence.

Geertz, Clifford (1960). *The Religion of Java*. Chicago: University of Chicago Press.

Greeley, Andrew M., and Michael Hout (1999). "Americans' increasing belief in life after death: Religious competition and acculturation." *American Sociological Review*. 64(6), 813–35.

Jordaan, Roy, editor (1996). *In Praise of Prambanan: Dutch essays on the Loro Jonggrang temple complex*. Leiden: KITLV Press.

Lim, Danny (2008). *The Malaysian Book of the Undead*. Kuala Lumpur: Matahari Books.

McLaughlin, Tom and Suriani binti Sahari (In press). "Ali of the 'Malay Archipelago': His Life and Times."

Moffat, Graham (1950). *Towards Eternal Day: The Psychic Memoirs of a Playwright*. London: Rider & Co., excerpted in: Price, Leslie (2016). "Joan of Arc and Dr. Lamond." *Psypioneer*. Vol. 12, No. 3, May–June.

Newcott, Bill (2007). "Is There Life After Death?" *AARP The Magazine*, September.

Price, Harry (1936). *Confessions of a Ghost-Hunter*. London: Putnam & Co.

Ritchey, David. (2003). *The H.I.S.S. of the A.S.P.: Understanding the Anomalously Sensitive Person*. Headline Books. Terra Alta, West Virginia. The lengthy H.I.S.S. questionnaire can be viewed on Ritchey's website: http://www.davidritchey-author.com/hoa-are-you-an-asp.htm

Roper Center for Public Opinion Research (2018). "Paradise Polled: Americans and the Afterlife." Roper Center, Cornell University.

Sholikhin, Muhammad (2009). *Kanjeng Ratu Kidul: Dalam Perspektif Islam Jawa*. Yogyakarta: Penerbit Narasi.

Sochaczewski, Paul Spencer (2010). "The god who flew off with a mountain." http://www.sochaczewski.com/2010/06/25/the-god-who-flew-off-with-a-mountain/

Sochaczewski, Paul Spencer (2015). *Curious Encounters of the Human Kind—Myanmar (Burma)*. Geneva: Explorer's Eye Press.

Sochaczewski, Paul Spencer (2017). *An Inordinate Fondness for Beetles.* Second edition. Geneva: Explorer's Eye Press.

Sochaczewski, Paul Spencer (2018a). "Need/Fear Relationship with Nature." http://www.sochaczewski.com/2017/04/05/needfear-relationship-with-nature/

Sochaczewski, Paul Spencer (2018b). *Exceptional Encounters: Enhanced Reality Tales from Southeast Asia.* Geneva: Explorer's Eye Press.

Sochaczewski, Paul Spencer (2018c). "Uncle Joe and Aunt Anisoara." http://www.sochaczewski.com/2017/04/05/uncle-joe-and-aunt-anisoara/

Sochaczewski, Paul Spencer (2018d). "We vs Them." http://www.sochaczewski.com/2017/04/05/we-vs-them/

Staël von Holstein, Verena, and Wolfgang Weirauch (2012). *Thoughts That Shine Like Stars: Further Conversations with the Nature Spirits.* Everswinkel: The Mill Press.

Taylor, Steve (2018). *Spiritual Science: Why Science Needs Spirituality to Make Sense of the World.* London: Watkins Publishing.

Van Wyhe, John, and Gerrell M. Drawhorn (2015). "'I am Ali Wallace': The Malay Assistant of Alfred Russel Wallace." *Journal of the Malaysian Branch of the Royal Asiatic Society.* 88:1:3–31.

Wallace, Alfred Russel (1859). Letter to Samuel Stevens, from Awaiya, Ceram. Nov. 26.

Wallace, Alfred Russel (1866). *The Scientific Aspect of the Supernatural: Indicating the Desirableness of an Experimental Enquiry by Men of Science Into the Alleged Powers of Clairvoyants and Mediums.* London: F. Farrah.

Wallace, Alfred Russel (1867). "On the Races of Man in the Malay Archipelago." Lecture.

Wallace, Alfred Russel (1869a). *The Malay Archipelago: The Land of the Orang-Utan, and the Bird of Paradise, a Narrative of Travel, with Studies of Man and Nature.* 2 vols. London: Macmillan & Co.

Wallace, Alfred Russel (1869b). "Charles Lyell on Geological Climates and the Origin of Species." *Quarterly Review* 126: 359–94 (April 1869: no. 252).

Wallace, Alfred Russel (1870). "The Limits of Natural Selection as Applied to Man." In *Contributions to the Theory of Natural Selection: A Series of Essays*. London and New York: Macmillan.

Wallace, Alfred Russel (1871). *Contributions to the Theory of Natural Selection: A Series of Essays*, 2nd edition. London and New York: Macmillan & Co.

Wallace, Alfred Russel (1874). "A Defence of Modern Spiritualism," Pt. 2. *Fortnightly Review* 15, No. 90 (1874): 801.

Wallace, Alfred Russel (1893). "Notes on the Growth of Opinion as to Obscure Psychical Phenomena During the Last Fifty Years." *Religio-Philosophical Journal*, n.s., 4, No. 15: 440–41.

Wallace, Alfred Russel (1896). *Miracles and Modern Spiritualism*. London: George Redway.

Wallace, Alfred Russel (1901). *Miracles and Modern Spiritualism* (Revised edition 1901). London: Nichols & Company.

Wallace, Alfred Russel (1905). *My Life: A Record of Events and Opinions*. 2 vols. London: Chapman & Hall.

Wallace, Alfred Russel, and James Marchant (1916). *Letters and Reminiscences*. London: Cassell and Company.

Whittington-Egan, Molly (2015). *Mrs Guppy Takes a Flight: A Scandal of Victorian Spiritualism*. Castle Douglas: Neil Wilson Publishing.

Praise for
PAUL'S OTHER BOOKS

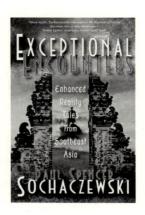

EXCEPTIONAL ENCOUNTERS:
ENHANCED REALITY TALES FROM SOUTHEAST ASIA

Explorer's Eye Press. Geneva. 2018.
ISBN: 978-2-940573-29-5

Exceptional Encounters takes the seeds of true stories and applies the classic fiction writer's aerobic exercise by asking: *What if?* These enhanced-reality fabulations draw the reader into tales of just over-the-rainbow Asian kindness, greed, passion, and dreams.

"A touch of George Orwell for our challenging times."
—Robin Hanbury-Tenison,
founder of Survival International

"At turns outrageous, thoughtful, and darkly satirical. Pushes the frontier of personal travel literature into a new dimension."
—Simon Lyster, chairman World Land Trust

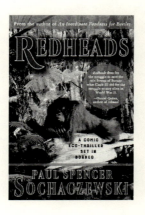

Redheads:
A comic eco-thriller set in Borneo

Explorer's Eye Press. Geneva. 2016.
ISBN: 978-2-940573-18-9

In the middle of a Borneo rainforest, a band of near-naked Penan tribesmen, encouraged by a similarly clothes-challenged renegade Swiss shepherd, blockade a logging truck. Nearby, a researcher studying orangutans is threatened with being thrown out of her study site unless she can reach a delicate compromise with the powerful minister of the environment.

Will the threatened homeland of people and orangutans survive?

"*Redheads* does for the struggle to save the rain forests of Borneo what *Catch*-22 did for the struggle to stay alive in World War II."

—Daniel Quinn, author of *Ishmael*

AN INORDINATE FONDNESS FOR BEETLES:
CAMPFIRE CONVERSATIONS WITH ALFRED RUSSEL WALLACE ON PEOPLE AND NATURE BASED ON COMMON TRAVEL IN THE MALAY ARCHIPELAGO, THE LAND OF THE ORANGUTAN, AND THE BIRD OF PARADISE

Explorer's Eye Press. Geneva. 2017.
ISBN: 978-2-940573-25-7

An Inordinate Fondness for Beetles follows the Victorian-era explorations of Alfred Russel Wallace through Southeast Asia.

Sochaczewski examines themes about which Wallace cared deeply and interprets them through his own filter with layers of humor, history, social commentary, and sometimes outrageous personal tales.

"The rhythm and magic of a verbal fugue. A new category of nonfiction—part personal travelogue, part incisive biography, part unexpected traveler's tales."
—Dato Sri Gathorne, author of *Mammals of Borneo*

SHARE YOUR JOURNEY:
MASTERING PERSONAL WRITING

Explorer's Eye Press. Geneva. 2016.
ISBN: 978-2-940573-15-8

Share Your Journey is an easy-to-use handbook for people who want to write their personal stories but aren't sure how to start and how to make them interesting. It's based on the writing workshops Sochaczewski has run in more than twenty countries. The book's Ten Writing Tips will give you the techniques professional authors use to write memoirs and travel stories that connect with readers and editors.

"This is a lifetime's wisdom, offered by a pro. Put *Share Your Journey* next to *The Elements of Style* by Strunk and White—they'll be the only two writing books you'll need."
— Thomas Bass, author of *The Spy Who Loved Us*

CURIOUS ENCOUNTERS OF THE HUMAN KIND:
TRUE ASIAN TALES OF FOLLY, GREED, AMBITION, AND DREAMS

Explorer's Eye Press. Geneva. 2016.

A five-volume series—Myanmar (Burma), Indonesia, Himalaya, Borneo, and Southeast Asia—containing true stories based on Sochaczewski's fifty years of living and exploring in curious corners of Asia. This is Asia as you've probably never imagined, full of memorable people, startling happenings, and unexpected moments of humanity and introspection, giddiness and solemnity, avarice and ambition.

"The spirit of Kipling in contemporary Asian journalism. This collection is essential reading for anyone who wishes to pass beyond even the unbeaten track, right to the heart of Asia."
—John Burdett, author of *Bangkok Asset*

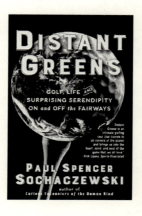

DISTANT GREENS:
GOLF, LIFE, AND SURPRISING SERENDIPITY ON AND OFF THE FAIRWAYS

Explorer's Eye Press. Geneva. 2016.
ISBN: 978-2-940573-21-9

Distant Greens travels to the highest golf course in the world, where breathless Tibetan precepts come face to face with the Indian military. To a golf course in the Amazon rainforest, near the source of rubber, that revolutionized the game. To the Middle Kingdom, to examine claims that it was the Chinese who invented golf.

It also shows how golf can be a force for nature conservation and delves into the soul of the sport.

"An intimate golfing tour that travels to all corners of the planet and brings us into the heart, mind, and soul of the game that we all love."

—Rick Lipsey, *Sports Illustrated*

SOUL OF THE TIGER:
SEARCHING FOR NATURE'S ANSWERS IN SOUTHEAST ASIA

Jeffrey A. McNeely and Paul Spencer Sochaczewski
University of Hawai'i Press. Honolulu. 1995.
ISBN 0-82481-669-2

A classic in the literature of modern conservation. One recent reviewer noted: "Age has not diminished the value of this book; it remains a classic in the genres of both conservation and travel literature." *Soul of the Tiger* identifies the four "eco-cultural revolutions" that have dramatically changed the face of Southeast Asia, and suggests a fifth revolution, which could lead to a new sustainable relationship between people and nature.

"One revealing, insightful, and stimulating account after another, focusing on the relationship between our own and other species. Importantly, it reveals why traditional human–wildlife relations should be encouraged in a world that seeks to balance economic growth and environmental preservation."
—John Noble Wilford in *The New York Times*

ECO-BLUFF YOUR WAY TO GREENISM:
THE GUIDE TO INSTANT ENVIRONMENTAL CREDIBILITY

Paul Sochaczewski (in this book writing as Paul Wachtel) and Jeffrey A. McNeely

Bonus Books. Chicago. 1991.
ISBN 0-929387-22-8

The guide to attain quick and painless eco-credibility, with essential advice on such things as how to deal with people who prefer elephants to human beings, how to establish your street-cred by explaining the public relations coup of Chief Seattle, and how to stir up a party by roaring like an eco-guerilla.

"What a book! Covers insights into potentially disastrous global issues in a bright and enjoyable way. Takes no prisoners and opens our eyes to a new and more effective vision of the pathway to environmental sanity."
—Noel Vietmeyer, US National Academy of Sciences

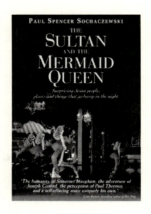

THE SULTAN AND THE MERMAID QUEEN:
SURPRISING ASIAN PEOPLE, PLACES, AND THINGS THAT GO BUMP IN THE NIGHT

Editions Didier Millet. Singapore. 2008.
ISBN 978-981-4217-74-3

Why do Javanese sultans owe their power to the Mermaid Queen? Why are isolated Indian villagers angry at the Monkey God Hanuman for not returning their sacred mountain? Why was the ninety-year-old "last elephant hunter" of Vietnam offered a lucrative product endorsement for a virility tonic? This collection of seventy essays and articles describe seldom-written-about, unnerving, off-the-radar Asian people, places, and events. The true stories reflect Sochaczewski's unique voice as one of the leading travel writers of his generation.

"The humanity of Somerset Maugham, the adventure of Joseph Conrad, the perception of Paul Theroux, and a self-effacing voice uniquely his own."
—Gary Braver, author of *Skin Deep*

About the Author

Paul Spencer Sochaczewski doesn't believe in spirits, ghosts, or psychic phenomena.

Nevertheless, he is convinced that there are some happenings that cannot easily be explained by our Western, Cartesian, science-oriented set of beliefs.

Let's call him an Agnostic Spiritualist.

By all accounts he enjoys a good life. He might grumble about his golf swing and being overlooked by the Pulitzer Prize committee, but no one pays much attention to such petty irritations. He applauds people who respect language, who do not abuse their cellphones in public, and who teach their children not to stand on seats on buses and trains. He would like to do nasty things to businesspeople who destroy rainforests to create oil palm plantations.

He's not sure to whom (or to what) he owes his good fortune. Perhaps the answer will become clear one day. Or maybe he'll find out in the next life. Try to contact him.

But for the moment, write to Paul at:

www.sochaczewski.com

Made in United States
North Haven, CT
13 January 2023